British Social
Attitudes
the
1984
report

British Social
Attitudes
the
1984
report

Edited by
Roger Jowell & Colin Airey

Gower

SOCIAL AND COMMUNITY PLANNING RESEARCH

© Social and Community Planning Research 1984

Published by
Gower Publishing Company Limited,
Gower House,
Croft Road,
Aldershot,
Hants GU11 3HR,
England

Gower Publishing Company,
Old Post Road,
Brookfield,
Vermont 05036,
U.S.A.

Typesetting by Origination Set-Up, Pimlico, London SW1V 4DG
Printed and bound in Great Britain
by Billings & Sons Limited, Worcester.

British Library Cataloguing in Publication Data

British social attitudes: report.–1984
    1. Public opinion – Great Britain – Periodicals
    2. Great Britain – Social Conditions – 1945 – Periodicals.
    941.085 '8' 05 HN400.P8

ISBN 0-566-00735-5
    0-566-00737-1 (pbk)

Contents

Foreword

by **SIR CLAUS MOSER**, KCB, CBE, FBA

Vice-Chairman of N. M. Rothschild & Sons Ltd.
Warden-Elect, Wadham College, Oxford

In the late 1960s I was involved in the setting up of *Social Trends,* a publication of the Government Statistical Service. Happily that has now become an established annual source of facts about the social condition of Britain. What has been missing is something similar to throw light on changes in social attitudes, and I am delighted to welcome this new series with precisely that in mind.

Thanks to the generosity of the Nuffield Foundation and the ESRC, the first year has produced a solid data base, which will be enhanced during the next three years (at least) by further data designed to throw light on changes in attitudes and values. Funding for these years has been guaranteed by most generous support, principally from the Monument Trust, with additional help from the Department of Employment, the Nuffield Foundation, Marks & Spencer plc, Shell UK Ltd, the University of Pittsburgh.

What makes the series so important is precisely that it is a series. It is from the monitoring and understanding of *trends* in attitudes that one can learn most about what is happening in a society, and this new series promises to be much more enlightening than findings from isolated and unrelated surveys. Now we can look forward to a sustained look at trends by an institute in which we have good cause to have confidence.

The editors faced a difficult task in deciding what type of book to produce. In the event, they have chosen to put their emphasis on timeliness, even if this means some loss of detailed analysis. I am sure they are right. The main point of the survey after all is to provide a publicly available dataset which *others* can utilise. So this book and each successive volume will introduce the data, relate the main findings, and encourage interested academics, civil servants, journalists and others to dig deeper into whatever aspects of this survey they particularly want to pursue. That is why a selection of microfiche tables is contained in the hardback edition, why questionnaires containing all marginal totals are contained as appendices in both editions, and why the data will be lodged in the ESRC Data Archive as soon as each volume is published.

Britain is an increasingly well documented society and even social statistics, long the Cinderella of the statistical world, have gained increasing attention. This new SCPR series will fill the gap in our knowledge of how we think and feel as a nation, rather than who we are or what we do. It is greatly to be welcomed.

1 Introducing the survey

*Roger Jowell**

This book is no more than a guided tour through a large and complicated dataset. It is not a comprehensive account of our survey, only a first look at some of its principal findings. We are content to leave more detailed applications of the results to other interested researchers.

The aim of the planned series of surveys is to produce an annual, publicly available data resource on British social attitudes in the expectation that it will encourage others to ask more penetrating questions of the data and to undertake more powerful analyses than we are able to do ourselves each year. Our main task is, we believe, to supply and summarise the results from each round of fieldwork in a systematic and manageable form. A selection of the material will appear in each annual report while the whole dataset will be lodged simultaneously in the Economic and Social Research Council's Data Archive at the University of Essex.

Our belief that others will actually make use of the data is based partly on the experience of a similar series carried out by the National Opinion Research Centre in Chicago. Over 650 reports and publications have flowed from these surveys during the last ten years or so, the great majority of them by academics and others *outside* the study team (see Davis, 1982). As a result, a great deal more is known about the direction and extent of change in American social attitudes than any number of *ad hoc* social surveys would have been likely to reveal.

It was the paucity of such data in Britain that prompted us to launch the series. There are admittedly a large number of polls and surveys that provide regular attitudinal data on one topic or another. The problem faced by the analyst of social change, however, is that most of these sources of material are

---

*Co-director of SCPR; Visiting Professor at The City University

derived from different questions in different contexts using different sampling methods. There are now several excellent annual sources referring to Britain's changing social conditions and behaviour patterns (Social Trends and the General Household Survey, for example), but no equivalent, freely available source for charting the nation's attitudes, values and beliefs. This series is designed to fill that gap, or at least to reduce its size.

The planned series

Funding has now been obtained to enable the survey to run annually for at least four years. At every round (fieldwork takes place each spring), we will attempt to interview a national probability sample of around 1,700 adults – see Technical Appendix for details of methods. Some questions will be repeated every year, others less frequently, but all questions have been designed for re-inclusion at some future round. We will depart from this plan only where we feel that a question has not worked or that circumstances have rendered a topic redundant. The principal object of the series is to measure attitudinal movements during the 1980s.

As directors of the project, Colin Airey and I have been greatly helped by the formation of a working advisory group comprising the other four contributors to this book – Nick Bosanquet, Harvey Goldstein, Antony Harrison and Ken Young. They participated both in questionnaire design and in the analysis of results. The composition of this group will vary somewhat from year to year according to the topics we wish to investigate.

The first year's questionnaire was divided into sections roughly corresponding to the five remaining chapters. All respondents were also invited to answer a self-completion supplement covering a variety of topics, and 94% did so. The second fieldwork round will include some of the same topics (around half of the questions will be identical) but will introduce new topics too. Further members of the working group have already been recruited for this purpose.

In addition to selecting a fresh cross-sectional sample in the second round, we have been awarded separate funds from the ESRC to return to about half of our first year's respondents with a slightly adapted questionnaire. We had asked and received permission from respondents to recontact them during our first interview. The existence of these two sets of responses will enable us to examine and compare individual as well as aggregate changes in attitude. If the 'panel' component turns out to be successful and useful, we will seek further funds to continue and enhance it in future years. For the moment it remains an experimental extension of the cross-sectional series.

Another extension, also funded separately – this time by the Nuffield Foundation – consists of a series of meetings between the four national teams who are currently involved with similar studies – National Opinion Research Centre (USA), Zentrum fur Umfragen Methoden und Analysen (West Germany), the Australian National University, and ourselves. Our plan is to design questionnaire supplements with equivalent questions which each national survey will carry at every fieldwork round. Systematic cross-national comparisons should begin to emerge in the 1986 report.

The funding for the first round came jointly from the Nuffield Foundation, who gave us our initial impetus with a development grant, and the ESRC who, by supplementing that grant, enabled us to extend the first round into a benchmark study. Generous core funding for the next three years has been provided by The Monument Trust. This large and long term commitment has enabled us to introduce questions and topics rationally over a number of years, a great advantage in a monitoring study which would otherwise have suffered the usual fate of having to improvise from year to year. These core funds will be supplemented by contributions from several organisations: the Department of Employment, whose interest in our employment-related questions has led them to provide funds to ensure adequate coverage of these topics over the next three years; Marks & Spencer plc and Shell UK Ltd., who have provided support to help ensure the continuation of the series for at least three years. In addition, the University of Pittsburgh and the Nuffield Foundation have jointly funded Michael Johnston (a professor at Pittsburgh) to work with us in the development of questions on attitudes towards private and public morality.

Deficiencies in social reporting

Public attitudes are as much a part of social reality as are behaviour patterns, social conditions or demographic characteristics, but their measurement has never been accorded the same priority. Official censuses, for instance, have apparently been undertaken on and off for thousands of years and routinely so for over 150 years. Yet even now, in an extraordinarily well-documented age, we have to rely largely on snippets of information to inform ourselves about how people think and what they believe.

A number of factors may have contributed to such a patchy coverage of research on social attitudes, the most important of which is probably that nobody has felt responsible for initiating it. British governments have generally accepted the need to find out about the public's behaviour patterns and social conditions so that their policies can take account of them. Curiously, however, they have been much less concerned to ensure that their policies take account of public attitudes. Or, if they have been concerned, they have derived their information mainly from sources other than their own. True, the Office of Population Censuses and Surveys frequently asks attitudinal questions, but an attitudinal equivalent of their General Household Survey would almost certainly be unthinkable, and perhaps properly so. A government-initiated study of social attitudes might run the risk of delving into areas that are not seen to be the government's domain. Questions on such topics as sexual morality (unless they were specifically linked to policy issues of fertility and family planning, as in Dunnell's study to which we refer in Chapter 6) would possibly be regarded as too sensitive or intrusive to be asked by state agency. Similarly, questions on constitutional issues – the role of the monarchy, the future of the House of Lords, electoral reform, extra-parliamentary action – would all be less than tactful or too controversial for a government department to initiate.

Other questions that could and perhaps should be initiated by government do not get asked largely because HM Treasury rarely if ever commissions or funds social research itself. The Treasury's failure to cause research to be done on attitudes to public expenditure, for instance, or taxation, remains a mystery. These issues are core concerns for any government, yet public attitudes towards them are either imputed — 'everyone wants lower taxes' — or ignored. Our data suggest that people's attitudes to taxation and public expenditure are much more complicated than that slogan implies (see Chapters 3 and 4); MORI has recently produced similar findings (Lansley and Gosschalk, 1984). But where is the Treasury's own accumulated evidence on these and related questions?

Newspapers and broadcasters frequently initiate opinion research, but their deadlines and budgets for these projects are usually too tight to allow lengthy consideration to be given to either the questions they ask or the answers they receive. The media's use of opinion polls tends to be topic-specific and peremptory. As Teer and Spence (1973) pointed out from their perspective as pollsters, a question that may be of potentially great interest to a researcher is usually of transitory interest to a news journalist, who is understandably more concerned with impact, timing and influence than with niceties of design or impressive execution. So the fascinating material that has been produced over the years by polling organisations such as Gallup, NOP, MORI and others remains a frustratingly incomplete patchwork. Webb and Wybrow's recent Gallup Report (1981) draws some of the threads together, but much of the Gallup material obstinately resists attempts to be organised *post hoc* into a coherent time series. Opinion pollsters in Britain have, perhaps, been more strongly influenced than have their American counterparts by their clients, the media, and less so by their own research instincts. Which is one reason that we have jealously guarded the independence of this project; our funders are invited to *support* the project, not to determine the questions we ask.

So neither government departments nor the media were ever likely to initiate a sustained research programme on social attitudes in Britain. British industry was not ready to do so either, though we are delighted to have secured the support of two major firms for this project. As is so often the case, the only avenue for large-scale support for studies of this kind was through the foundations and the ESRC. But they are, to a large extent, responsive to applications and ideas from the academic community, who tend to have specialist interests. So whereas a number of excellent attitudinal studies have been funded over the years on, say, relative deprivation, poverty or the welfare state, their focuses have been fairly narrow and they have been updated only irregularly if at all. The British Election Studies, which appear after each general election, stand out as the single academic example of solid time series data on public attitudes in Britain. And even that series only narrowly escaped being discontinued during 1983.

A simpler possible explanation for the non-appearance so far of a regular, publicly available series on social attitudes in Britain is that the demand for one is too small. That could turn out to be the verdict on our series, but we doubt it. We might not have succeeded in selecting the best indicators of change or in asking questions that others would have chosen, but we are convinced that the regular appearance of a wide range of data on social attitudes will stimulate important analytical work that would not have been possible otherwise. The American experience strongly supports this view (see Smith's Annotated Bibliography, 1980).

But it is not just to the academic community that systematic data on social attitudes ought to appeal. Democratic societies require data about themselves and their collective characteristics to enable them to become better analysts of their own condition. Without such data they are at risk of adopting sterotypes about themselves (or about subgroups in the population). If attitudes are not measured they will be imputed; self-selected messages will be mistaken for facts; aberrant data from one source or another will be grasped as evidence of change in the public's position on an issue. Yet on many social issues, we do not yet even have a starting point from which to measure change.

Elections may be a good way of selecting governments, but they are a rather poor method of measuring public attitudes to specific issues. The party system ensures that even those people who wish to vote on the basis of policy preferences —rather than habit or predisposition — can in the end choose only a package of policies with one or other party label. That such a choice is often interpreted as a mandate for *particular* policies is simply an anomaly of the electoral system.

It is tempting, for instance, but risky to conclude that the British electorate has in recent years moved sharply to the right in its political attitudes. Its voting behaviour clearly indicates a movement to the right, as does the American electorate's voting behaviour. Yet US survey data argue persuasively that the last twenty-five years have witnessed a dramatic increase in social liberalism in the United States (Davis, 1980; Smith, 1982). They also show that this movement, which has been more or less equally apparent in all parts of the social structure, may recently have reached a plateau, but it has *not* reversed its direction. Only a long term, well-planned process of data collection could have charted such trends and detected the inconsistencies within them. Indeed, the exceptions to a general movement, both in respect of issues (such as American attitudes to divorce) and in resepct of subgroups, are often more illuminating than the trend line itself.

One problem with such data is that they are often regarded with deep suspicion. Many people who seem to have unquestioning faith in behavioural data retreat into agnosticism when faced with attitudinal data from similar samples. They argue either that attitudes are too ephemeral to matter – that they depend more on mood and circumstances than on conviction – or at any rate that attitudes are too elusive to be captured by social surveys which, they claim, produce spurious answers to barely comprehensible questions.

Can social attitudes be measured?

It is undeniable that survey questions often obtain responses even when they are badly worded, unclear, ambiguous or virtually meaningless. The existence of replies is by no means an asssurance of validity. It is also well established that attitudinal questions are particularly subject to variations in wording or context (see, for instance, Schuman and Presser, 1981). Moreover, no amount of effort can ensure unbiased question wording, the quest for which Marsh (1982, p.145) describes correctly as "philosophically naive". Both in the selection of topics for inclusion and in the choice of questions to be asked, the researcher is required to make numerous value judgements. Impartiality remains an essential but imperfectly attainable goal of research. Measurement fallibility is also common to all research.

The relationship between objective and subjective 'facts' is complicated and the distinction between them is often blurred. An excellent discussion of these complications is contained in Turner and Martin (1981), but a few points are worth emphasising here.

First, even apparently objective survey measurements frequently contain a (sometimes large) subjective element. Whether a person is classified as 'unemployed', for instance, depends largely on how that person defines his or her own position; the answer could turn as much on his or her state of mind as on actual circumstances. A survey can ask supplementary questions to achieve greater uniformity of definition, such as whether the person is seeking work, registered at a benefit office, and so on. But in the end, the decision as to whether or not he or she is classified as 'economically active' relies to a considerable extent on subjective criteria. The same holds true for a large number of behavioural questions (leisure activities, use of a car, readership), and for many factual questions too (ethnic group, experience of crime, housing conditions).

That being so, it is perhaps more surprising that behavioural and factual measures are often accepted and quoted so uncritically than that attitudinal measures are not. Scepticism is, we believe, the most appropriate vantage point from which to view all survey data, initially at least. Belief in them should develop or not according to their methods rather than their subject. For this reason, the methods and questionnaires we used and the data themselves are fully exposed to anyone who wishes to use the results. We urge every user to examine the responses we obtained in the light of the questions we asked and to make his or her own evaluations. It must be appreciated, however, that the principal aim of the study was not to measure social attitudes in 1983, but to measure *changes* in them during the 1980s. So our selection of topics and questions was not always as it would have been if we had wanted to produce a single reading.

Despite piloting, a few of our questions do not seem to have worked very well, and we mention this when referring to the results. Other questions, which appear to have worked, may in the end turn out to have been particularly subject to wording or order effects, and this may become apparent only from the panel experiment or from future rounds of fieldwork. In all cases, however, we tried to ensure that our questions were comprehensible to potential respondents and that they dealt with subjects with which most people had at least a passing acquaintance. This process inevitably involves some loss of nuance. Subjects such as race prejudice or economic policy are patently too large to embody in a few precoded questions and answers. They are also too important to omit. Aspects of them had to be selected for treatment and, even then, for very cursory treatment.

Similarly, we did not want to push people into simulating attitudes they did not hold. So we encouraged interviewers to accept 'don't know', neutral or 'other' answers as legitimate responses. In the event, some questions generated a fairly high proportion of non-committal answers and we have not attempted to redistribute them as if they were an aberration; they appear as an integral part of the dataset. Nonetheless, some respondents will still undoubtedly have failed to say 'don't know' or 'don't care', when that would have been the apposite response, in order to avoid conveying an impression of ignorance or apathy. Surveys cannot altogether counteract these sorts of evasive measures on the part of respondents, but there is no reason to assume that they introduce systematic biases in one direction or another (see Schuman and Presser, 1979).

But such evasions are only part of the problem. Anyone attempting to measure social attitudes also has to contend with the fact that attitudes are structured in a variety of ways and exist on a number of levels. Leaving aside for the moment the distinction between attitudes, beliefs and opinions, on which a considerable body of psychological literature exists, surveys are restricted to measuring *expressed* attitudes. On a subject like race prejudice, for instance, the expressed attitude might be a function of several underlying factors, such as personality variables (xenophobia or authoritarianism), or circumstantial variables (fear of competition), or behavioural variables (custom or habit), or any combination of these factors and many others. Moreover, people may display apparently contradictory attitudes: hostility to ethnic minorities may be expressed on one dimension but not on another related dimension. That would be surprising only if one starts from the hypothesis that attitudes are *supposed* to be consistent, that people ought to conform to tidy descriptions such as racist, radical, reactionary, romantic. We hope that no such illusion exists and that subsequent attempts to explore the data for clusters of attitudes will point out that convenient labels like these often conceal the degree of inconsistency that exists among apparently like-minded people or groups — a subject I will briefly return to.

So we make no claim that our survey has somehow managed to avoid the many inherent problems of survey measurements in general and of attitude measurements in particular. In case it needs emphasising, we ought to point out too that no finding we report is intended to be a precise statement about British public attitudes. Every finding is an approximation, part of a body of evidence which needs to be examined in the context of other evidence. The fact that on most subjects we have asked several questions that explore different components of people's attitudes will make it easier for the analyst to draw conclusions about the robustness or consistency of attitudes. Similarly, our inclusion of a wide variety of demographic variables will assist the examination of subgroup variations in attitude. Over the years, it may even be possible to cumulate some annual answers of small minority groups in order to study their attitudes with more confidence.

In general, the longer our series continues the more confidence we will have in particular results, not because the questions on which they are based will become less subject to criticism, but merely because many questions will remain the same. We will then be measuring responses to much the same stimuli on separate occasions, so that any question-wording effects will, on the whole, be present at each measure equally. Changes in distributions will thus be likely to reflect some underlying change.

For the moment we are seeking benchmark measures which, by their very nature, are unverifiable in any scientific sense of the word. Behavioural measures are, in principle, more verifiable than attitudes, but are only exceptionally subjected to independent verification. Nevertheless, as Turner and Martin (1981, p.19) point out, "in so far as one wants to know what people think and believe about their world and themselves, there is no substitute for asking them directly".

The Clapham omnibus fallacy

Lord Bowen's nineteenth century creation, 'the man in the Clapham omnibus', who was supposed to encapsulate the nation's attitudes, has nowadays merely given way to the even more ubiquitous 'man in the street'. We do not suppose that anyone really believes in these unlikely people (they are, of course, both male but, surprisingly, only the first is a Londoner), yet they are too frequently quoted and, when quoted, apparently too influential to be ignored. Moreover, many people claim to have an intimate knowledge of what these 'average' people think about almost every conceivable issue. It is this view of and approach to public opinion that we hope our survey will help to undermine.

The term 'public opinion' is itself misleading. Our data demonstrate that on nearly all social issues there are actually several publics and many opinions. Differences within the population are sometimes small but there are always differences. Even on the handful of social issues where near unanimity appears to exist, shades of opinion are usually revealed by closer analysis. The relentless search for consensus impedes the exploration of diversity. By far the most interesting and revealing findings in the chapters that follow refer to subgroup differences rather than to the total distributions.

Moreover, the population's attitudes steadfastly resist being divided neatly or consistently according to age, sex, class, region or any other single variable. They divide very differently on different issues. Whereas a person's age seems to be the most powerful discriminator on some issues, sex, employment status, social class or party political differences explain much of the variation on others, and so on. The differences we find are often large and intriguing, casting serious doubt on the view that a common British attitudinal culture is somehow waiting to be discovered. The idea that the public can usefully be classified into two categories – for and against – on most social issues is shown to be unhelpful. Various groups display different attitudes with different degrees of force.

The exploration of the dataset has only just started in that we have so far carried out only the barest primary analyses. Our aim has been to release the data as quickly as possible for others to apply within their fields. Our only practical option for this book was to describe the data within various subject headings – politics, economics, social policy, education, social morality. A potentially more interesting approach for others would be to examine the data *across* headings, to answer such questions as whether people who take a radical position on economic issues also tend to take a radical position on social issues; whether people who express race prejudice are likely to display other aspects of an 'authoritarian personality'; to establish how attitudes to a *range* of issues vary with age, sex, social class, region, party identification, and so on; to discover, in short, how attitudes group or cluster within different sorts of people. The possibilities are almost endless and will become richer with each successive fieldwork round.

In future years, particularly if the survey continues to include a panel element, we should be able to go further with the analysis. The data will begin to suggest which attitude changes depend on cohort replacement (people growing older and carrying their attitudes with them), and which depend on conversion (changes of heart or mind among the same groups). In other words, although the survey will never produce direct evidence of attitude causation, it is likely over time to give useful clues as to the processes at work. For now we are stuck with the important but more prosaic task of making sense of the initial readings.

As a first stage we have confined ourselves largely to two-way and three-way analyses of the data, with all their intrinsic hazards. The sophisticated reader will be aware that when we describe a difference in attitudes between, say, younger people and older people, the age factor (though valid) does not necessarily *explain* that difference. Other factors that are associated with age may, in the event, turn out to be better predictors of the attitude than age itself turns out to be. For instance, young people tend to remain in full-time education longer nowadays than they used to. So age and school-leaving age are interrelated, and further analysis is required to sort out the relationship, using more powerful analytical techniques than those we have employed so far. In this report we attempt onlt to reveal and describe the differences we found. Explanations of these differences (albeit tentative ones) will emerge later from multivariate analyses and much lengthier consideration of the dataset.

We have calculated a substantial number of sampling errors on the data, and these calculations will be lodged with the archived datatape. A few examples of error ranges are also included in the Technical Appendix. From the calculations we have made we are confident that complex sampling errors for most variables − given the design of the survey − are not much larger than those for a simple random sample. Each contributor has tried to avoid overinterpreting differences in the findings, but we have not subjected every difference or pattern reported to tests of statistical significance. We will have the opportunity in future years to test whether or not these patterns are reproduced.

We must apologise to the reader who has turned to this book for a definitive analysis of the British social condition. That analysis, if it ever takes place, is very unlikely to be based solely on our data. Insights are, we believe, already available from the dataset, as we hope the following chapters will confirm. But we will have to wait, as the impatient reader will, for secondary analyses and more carefully considered commentaries to illuminate and enrich our findings. That task will, we trust, be performed by the social science community to whom this dataset is dedicated. Our task now is to return to the production of their next round of raw material.

Acknowledgements

Many colleagues advised us on aspects of the questionnaire. They are mentioned at the end of the appropriate chapters and we are extremely grateful to them. They should not get the blame for the questions we ended up with, only the credit for helping to improve our earlier drafts.

James Cornford, Pat Thomas, and Raymond Illsley have been valued advisers on the whole survey. It was their encouragement that led us to pursue the initial idea of the project and we owe a great deal to their support and vision. Similarly, Hugh de Quetteville's help and enthusiasm was a major factor in the successful transformation of an *ad hoc* survey into a four year series. His advice has been, and continues to be, much appreciated.

As for our colleagues within SCPR, who cannot be singled out because all have been involved in one way or another, we are deeply indebted to them for their help, guidance, criticism and, most of all, for their indulgence. Our other co-workers, the interviewers and coders, have once again proved themselves to be the cornerstone of a survey's success. We continue to depend heavily on their skills and endurance.

But our most heartfelt vote of thanks must surely go to 1,761 anonymous, voluntary respondents, without whom it can truly be said this survey would have been highly improbable.

References

DAVIS, J. A., 'Conservative Weather in a Liberalising Climate: Change in Selected NORC General Social Survey Items, 1972-1978', *Social Forces 58,* June 1980.

DAVIS, J. A. 'Have We Learned Anything from the General Social Survey?'. *Social Indicator's Newsletter, No. 17,* August 1982.

LANSLEY, S. and GOSSCHALK, B., 'Tax Cuts Welcome, But Not At Any Price', *The Guardian,* 8 February 1984.

MARSH, C., *The Survey Method: The Contribution of Surveys to Sociological Explanation,* George Allen & Unwin, London (1982).

SCHUMAN, H. and PRESSER, S., 'The Assessment of "No Opinion" in Attitude Surveys', in K. Schuessler ed. *Sociological Methodology,* Josey Bass, San Francisco (1979).

SCHUMAN, H. and PRESSER, S., *Questions and Answers in Attitude Surveys: Experiments on Question Form, Wording and Content,* Academic Press, New York (1981).

SMITH, T., *Annotated Bibliography of Papers Using the General Social Surveys,* NORC, Chicago (1980).

SMITH, T., 'General Liberalism and Social Change in Post World War II America: a Summary of Trends', *Social Indicators Research 10,* March 1982.

TEER, F. and SPENCE, J. D., *Political Opinion Polls,* Hutchinson University Library, London (1973).

TURNER, C. F. and MARTIN, E. (eds.), *Surveys of Subjective Phenomena: a Summary Report,* National Academy Press, Washington D.C. (1981).

WEBB, N. and WYBROW, R., *The Gallup Report,* Sphere, London (1981).

2 Political attitudes

*Ken Young**

This part of the report is concerned with attitudes to politics and government, with the working of the political system and with Britain's place in the world. It is not concerned with domestic policy issues. The principal findings suggest that the changes in the British political system identified by other recent commentators will exercise a powerful influence on the fortunes of the political parties. In particular, the polarisation of party support on class lines continues to decline. Nonetheless, attachment to party in general remains quite strong with little support for tactical voting and with greater significance being attached to the party labels of candidates than to their personal qualities.

Foremost among the other changes in popular orientations to politics are indications of a decline in political passivity in the face of unwelcome government actions. Compared with the evidence of two decades ago, today's electors are more active; in particular, the propensity to combine with others in political dissent appears to have increased, as has the propensity to register an individual protest. Even so, passivity is still more characteristic than protest.

Of related interest is the apparent sympathy of younger people towards civil disobedience and their propensity to advance the claims of conscience against those of law. Although we know little as yet of the circumstances which might prompt political disobedience, it is worth noting that a sizeable majority of young women and a majority of young men believe that the presence of US nuclear missiles on British soil makes Britain less, rather than more, safe. There are strong pointers here for exploration in future years.

The issue of US missiles, which elicited a very different pattern of response from that in respect of the British nuclear deterrent, is one of several questions

*Senior Fellow, Policy Studies Institute.

(others including the future of Ireland and the presence of British troops there) where there was a striking degree of partisan polarisation within the sample. It is not surprising that Government supporters should identify more strongly with the policies of government than did the rest of the sample, but it is interesting that this difference should be more marked in relation to 'high politics' – the great issues of defence, national integrity and international alliances – than in relation to domestic social policy issues.

Overall, substantial proportions of the sample inhabit the broad middle ground between the policy positions of the major parties, which are themselves supported by fairly small minorities, particularly on the left. Moreover, there is considerable general support for and satisfaction with British institutions. But this is not to say that the future holds no terrors. It is noteworthy that many people have pessimistic expectations of the next few years, especially in relation to political terrorism and urban disorder.

Party identification and partisanship

Patterns of identification

Unlike the periodic British Election Studies (BES) this survey was not primarily concerned with electoral choice. However, the fieldwork was carried out in the months preceding the general election of June 1983, when there was con- siderable speculation as to the possibility of an imminent election; accord- ingly, the responses to the question on party identification have a particular interest and call for the exploration of trends in that variable in other election years. Although the BES and other studies take voting as their primary interest, data are also available from the BES on party identification just following each election.

Party identification has been commonly viewed as an attachment to a particular party which serves to simplify the confusion of political life and to make it more manageable for the individual elector (Budge et al., 1976). The individual elector places himself or herself as more or less 'close' to one or other political party. Our survey obtained a broad measure of such placement from fairly searching questions about party support. Respondents were asked up to three questions: first, *do you think of yourself as a supporter of any one political party?* If this question failed to elicit a choice, we asked *do you think of yourself as a little closer to one political party than the others?* and if this second question still failed to elicit a choice, we asked finally: *If there were a general election tomorrow, which political party do you think you would be most likely to support?* These questions gave us a four-way measure of party identification: partisans, sympathisers, residual identifiers and (in the case of those who indicated no voting preference) the non-aligned. The first three groups combined are referred to as 'identifiers'.

For those not familiar with the BES party identification questions, it must be pointed out that our questions were different. We were not interviewing, as in the case of the BES, immediately after a general election (so we had no measure of how people claim to have voted), and we were seeking a rather more searching measure of support (or resistance) to parties as an analysis variable for future rounds of our series. Nonetheless, some comparisons are possible as the following paragraphs suggest.

Table 2.1 at the back of this chapter gives the distribution of answers to this question: overall, at the time of our fieldwork, 38% of the sample identified with the Conservatives, 33% with Labour, and 15% with the Liberal/SDP Alliance.

The actual electoral fortunes of the various parties are of course largely dependent on the strength of the commitment obtained from their notional identifiers: those professing the weaker forms of identification may be thought of as less close to their favoured party and more likely to switch their support on polling day. It is well established that much of the identification with the Liberal party, and, by extension, with the Liberal/SDP Alliance is 'soft' in this sense (Himmelweit et al., 1981), and among our sample 69% of Alliance identification could be so described. More important, perhaps, in view of later events, was the proportion of Labour identifiers who could be classified as 'soft' — 48% as against 38% of Conservative identifiers.

Considerable attention is given in modern election studies to the relationship between party identification and occupation. Our survey, which used the Registrar General's Social Class classification, confirmed this relationship, but in a somewhat weaker form than hitherto. We also coded socio-economic groups, however, so that others can use those breakdowns if they wish to.

Party identification by social class

Social Class

	I/II	III non-manual	III manual	IV/V
	%	%	%	%
Conservative identifiers	54	43	34	24
Alliance identifiers	19	19	14	10
Labour identifiers	17	26	38	50
Non-aligned/others	11	11	12	15

Miller (1978) has argued that the analysis of class based politics in terms of occupational categories is fraught with difficulty. We avoided some of the pitfalls to which he refers by, for example, assigning social class on the basis of the respondent's occupation, not that of the respondent's head of household. (The cost of this is that a large minority of respondents were classified as 'looking after the home' (20%) or were otherwise unclassifiable into occupational groups.) Nonetheless Miller emphasises the important link between party identification and subjective or self-assigned social class. Indeed, the historic association of class and party plays an important part in locating the individual within the social structure; thus, departures from class bi-polarity in party identification are of considerable potential significance for the future of the British party system. So an important finding of our survey was that as many as 60% of those who consider themselves to be working class do not identify with the Labour party. (See Table 2.2 for details.)

Class polarisation of party support

Self-assigned social class

	Middle Class	Working Class	None
	%	%	%
Conservative identifiers	54	33	38
Alliance identifiers	17	14	7
Labour identifiers	18	39	26
Non-aligned/others	10	13	26

Any trend study which seeks to explore the changing basis of party choice must focus upon two key relationships: the declining extent to which the two major parties enjoy popular support, and the weakening association of class self-images with particular party identifications. This association has occupied a central place in British political analysis since Abrams and Rose (1960) posed the question 'must Labour lose?' Attempts to change the class image of the Labour party and thereby diminish what was considered to be an electoral liability were fiercely contested in the party's Gaitskell years. The debate subsided with the party's electoral successes under Harold Wilson, and in face of new evidence that indicated that, while the class allegiances and lifestyle of 'affluent workers' were more fluid, their identification with the Labour party remained.

More recent electoral events have revived interest in the association of class and party images. The experience of the 1970s provides powerful evidence of a process of partisan dealignment at work. First, the strength of attachment to party is weakening in the electorate as a whole; second, there has been a notable shift away from class based identification and (to a slightly smaller extent) class-based voting (Miller 1978; Sarlvik and Crewe 1983).

The strength of the association between social class and party identification can be expressed in terms of a level of 'class polarisation'. This measure is of particular value in exploring the changes in the relationship between class and party over time. It may be calculated on the basis of self-assigned class or occupational status and in ways which emphasise two-party or multi-party competition. Alford's (1964) version is the most widely used and compares the proportion of (in this case) Labour identifiers among manual workers with that of Labour identifiers, among non-manual workers. Class polarisation in this sense is expressed as a positive, but declining, value: it fell from 39% in 1964 to 38% in 1966, 31% in 1970, 32% in February and 27% in October 1974 to 23% in 1979 and 18% in our own 1983 survey. Miller (1978) takes a different approach, and measures half the difference between the Conservative lead over Labour among middle class and working class self identifiers. On his measure, class polarisation declined from 37% in 1966 to 32% in 1970; 30% in February and 27% in October 1974 to 29% in 1979 and 21% in our own survey. Our results therefore provide some further evidence of long-term structural change in the British political system, a trend which the 1983 Oxford/SCPR British General Election Study might be expected to confirm.*

The other important feature of the dealignment argument – that party identification is weakening because of the replacement of elderly partisans by cohorts of increasingly non-aligned new voters – is consistent with the findings of this survey. We found very low levels of party identification among new

(18-24 year old) voters. Indeed, partisans (those volunteering an immediate identification of themselves as 'supporters' of any party) comprised only 25% of this age group, scarcely more numerous than the 17% who had no voting preference. There is indeed a marked association of partisanship with increasing age, as will be seen from **Table 2.3**. Of particular interest is the sex difference in partisanship within this relationship: partisanship increases more rapidly at first for men than it does for women; and women between the ages of 25 and 44 have weaker party identification than do men of the same age.

The two-party share of total identification also varies with age. Identification with the Labour and Conservative parties is highest amongst the oldest voters: 76% of the over-65s identify with one or other of the two main parties. This figure falls to around 70% for most other age groups and is lowest, at 65%, among the 18 to 24 year olds. That these figures are far higher than those cited for example by Sarlvik and Crewe in their definitive exploration of recent trends in alignment is due to our rather persistent search for part identification; the dealignment thesis is indeed supported more strongly when partisans are considered separately from sympathisers and residual identifiers.

We also examined the relationship between level of education and party identification. Support for the Conservative party is higher amongst those staying on at school or receiving some further education, but falls again in the (small) group whose education ended at 19 or above. Support for the Labour party follows the converse pattern. But this familiar curvilinear relationship is less marked than hitherto, owing to the positive and linear association of education with support for the Alliance. Although the numbers in the higher educational groups are small, the direction of the relationship is apparent, and there was slightly more support for the Alliance than for Labour among the small group of students.

Partisanship and the party system

So far this discussion has been confined to the patterning of party identification. We also asked a series of questions designed to elicit the degree of support for the two-party system, as indicated by attitudes to coalition government, to the importance of party labels in electoral choice, and to the prospect of casting a 'tactical' vote in elections where one's most favoured candidate has no chance of success. The results were somewhat surprising and, given the dynamics of Britain's simple majority electoral system, somewhat inconsistent. A priority for later years of this series will be a further exploration of respondents' attitudes to the working of the electoral system itself. We asked:

---

*Although the broad trend is clear in each case, the figures are subject to measurement differences. In particular, the 'Alford' figures for 1979 and 1983 are based upon the occupation of the respondent, rather than (as in the case of the earlier years) that of the head of household. Recalculation of the 1979 figures on a head of household basis gives a score of 26% rather than 23%. We have not performed this calculation for 1983, but it might be expected to raise the level of class polarisation by a few percentage points.

Which do you think is generally better for Britain: to have a government formed by one political party, or for two or more parties to get together to form a government?

	Total	Conservative	Alliance	Labour	Non-aligned
	%	%	%	%	%
Government by one party preferred	47	58	34	43	36
Government by two or more preferred	49	39	61	54	52

The table shows a population that is evenly divided on coalition government. It is perhaps to be expected that a majority of the non-aligned should express a preference for coalition; it is, in present circumstances, not surprising that a large proportion of Alliance supporters (61%) should do likewise; but it is striking that, despite that party's traditional hostility to coalition, 54% of Labour supporters should prefer parties to 'get together' to form a government. This might reflect the apparent hopelessness of the Labour cause in the spring of 1983. Conservative supporters, as we have noted, generally express a higher level of partisan commitment; and only 39% of them favour a coalition government. We have already seen that men appear to be more partisan than women in most age groups, and this characteristic is also reflected, albeit slightly, in attitudes to coalition. In no age group does a majority of women favour single party government while among men this option is favoured most strongly (at 60%) in the (highly partisan) 35-54 age group.

The extent of the gulf between partisans and the non-aligned voter is thrown into sharp relief by the extent to which their voting behaviour is influenced by the relative attractions of the party imprimatur and the personal qualities of a candidate. The 'loyalist' voter will tend to vote for the candidate of his or her preferred party irrespective of the candidate's personal qualities; the 'independent' voter will tend to vote for a candidate irrespective of party affiliation; and the 'qualified loyalist' votes for the preferred party only if he or she is satisfied with its candidate. As is to be expected, major party partisans are predominantly loyal (73%) and the non-aligned voter has the lowest level of loyalty (20%). In the sample as a whole, the proportions who fell into each of the three categories were:

loyalists	58%
qualified loyalists	24%
independents	5%

Differences of party loyalty on this dimension did not vary much according to party identification, except that Alliance identifiers were more inclined than others to be qualified loyalists. Does this reflect the fact perhaps that for around half of the Alliance identifiers, their General Election candidates were at that time being chosen by members of a different party from their own? Or is a higher degree of discrimination to be expected among supporters of 'anti-party' parties?

Which of the four statements on this card comes closest to the way you vote in a general election?

	Total	Conservative	Alliance	Labour	Non-aligned
	%	%	%	%	%
I vote for a party regardless of the candidate	58	65	53	66	20
I vote for a party only if I approve of the candidate	24	26	32	20	17
I vote for a candidate regardless of his or her party	5	3	7	6	9
I do not generally vote at all	12	5	7	7	51

A further, and electorally more important, aspect of partisanship concerns the propensity to cast a 'tactical' vote in those elections where the preferred party's candidate is seen to have no chance of winning. Tactical voting has received a great deal of attention, particularly since the formation of the Alliance, with evidence being adduced of a more sophisticated and tactically discriminating electorate, at least in by-elections. We presented respondents with the choice of continuing to vote in these adverse circumstances for the preferred party, of voting for another party or candidate, or of abstaining. The responses signify quite different orientations to the act of voting: we might say that the 'symbolist' votes expressively for the party with which he or she identifies, regardless of the odds; the 'tactician' votes instrumentally, switching his or her vote towards the second preference; the 'abstainer' chooses in these circumstances not to vote. We asked:

Suppose in the next general election the party or candidate you prefer has no chance of winning in your constituency, do you think you would:

	Total	Conservative	Alliance	Labour	Non-aligned
	%	%	%	%	%
still vote for that party or candidate,	74	81	81	76	36
vote for another party or candidate	5	7	4	6	1
or not bother to vote at all?	3	4	1	4	2
Not likely to vote	16	7	11	11	59

The pattern which emerges from the data provides little support for the notion of a tactical electorate. 74% per cent of all respondents, and 87% of those who would expect to vote, claim to cast what appears to be an expressive or symbolic vote. Only 5% claim to vote in an instrumental or tactical fashion, and fewer than 4% of the would-be voters would abstain in these circumstances.

There may be some clues here to the failure of widespread tactical voting to manifest itself in the 1983 general election after expectations had been raised by by-elections of preceding years. But perhaps general elections and by-elections differ not just in the extent to which their outcomes matter but also in the emotional loading for the elector which arises from the collective act of choosing a government; how else might we account for such very high levels of symbolic action? As the summary table above shows, there appeared to be no party dimension on the symbolist-tactician-abstainer continuum; Alliance identifiers, despite their higher degree of candidate discrimination, were slightly *less* likely to vote tactically than those of the two major parties.

Political representation

Political life is, for all but the professionals, a life of relative passivity, and for most citizens political participation is an episodic activity. Yet, whatever the voter's level of political involvement – as party member, partisan, sympathiser, residual identifier or habitual abstainer – each enjoys representation in government, central and local. In a subsequent section we examine the degree to which respondents feel that, being represented, they can expect responsive government. In this section, we consider the ways in which our respondents view the representative linkages as such.

Representation may be understood both to mean 'acting for' and less directly, as 'resembling' in the sense of representatives having characteristics in common with the represented. Both aspects are centrally important to arguments about political representation, for they imply quite different mechanisms of selection and connection between the representatives and those whom they seek to represent. Correspondingly we asked two kinds of question, the first to elicit responses about the accountability of the MP – for whom should he act? – the second to elicit the qualities and qualifications which respondents ideally sought in those who represent them – the resemblance aspect of representation.

As **Table 2.4** shows, there is a remarkable cross-party consensus on the role of the Member of Parliament, though there are some differences of emphasis: Labour identifiers are somewhat less inclined to put first the MP's responsibility to represent the views of his constituents, yet those subscribing to this view are still the largest single group and a majority of Labour identifiers. Also, there is marginally greater support amongst Labour identifers for weight to be given to the views of the local party, unsurprisingly given the successes of the Campaign for Labour Party Democracy in recent years. Yet the broad picture remains: the primary role of the MP is to represent the views of his constituents, however derived. Here at least is an area where we might expect partisanship to be associated with a conception of the MP's role as delegate of the party. Yet the consensus largely holds: as the summary table below shows, there is an association between degrees of partisanship and views on the accountability of MPs, but it is a very weak one. Nor do striking patterns emerge if views on accountability are analysed by social class, terminal education age or region; nor, perhaps surprisingly, is there a relationship with trade union membership, past or present (see **Table 2.5**).

Accountability of MPs by degree of partisanship

	Partisans	Sypathisers and residual identifiers	Non-aligned
	%	%	%
MPs should most take into account:			
Views of party conference	20	13	8
Views of local party	9	8	7
Views of constituents	54	60	61
Views of fellow MPs	8	9	7
Own views	7	7	8
Other/don't know/ not answered	2	3	9

Given the strength and spread of this consensus across all social and political groupings, responses to the question on the personal qualities and qualifications of MPs are of particular interest; how like ourselves do we expect our representatives to be? On the whole, the answer given by the respondents is 'not much'. As **Table 2.6** shows, there is a strong cross-party consensus that MPs should, above all, be well educated and have local connections. Conservatives, as might be expected, put a stronger emphasis on business experience, while Labour supporters are somewhat more inclined than the others to emphasise trade union experience, but in neither case to any marked degree.

There is also a fairly strong expectation of loyalty to the party, particularly among Conservative partisans, which contrasts sharply with their lack of support for party accountability. Its converse, independence of mind, is less highly prized among Labour supporters than knowledge of the problems of the poor. Local roots are widely thought desirable for MPs. Overall the expectations of the supporters of the parties broadly reflect the principal images of the parties themselves. Analysis by social class rather than by party reveals little other than the expectation of business experience amongst the higher status respondents. Table 2.6 gives the distribution by party and by social class. The summary table overleaf shows only the total distributions for both MPs and councillors.

The arguments about the working of representative democracy are common to both national and local politics. Do voters look for similar qualities in MPs and local councillors or does 'representation' have a different quality at the town hall level? Here the distinction between modes of representation comes into its own: as the table overleaf shows, our respondents differentiate strongly between the qualities expected of an MP and those of a local councillor. For the latter, educational attainment drops into the background and local roots assume overwhelming importance. Given the distinctivness of popular characterisations of social space, to 'be local' is to be 'of the people' in that locality. In comparison with the many cited ideal qualities of an MP, localism was *the* quality cited as desirable for a councillor.

Thinking of MPs/local councillors which of the personal qualities on this card would you say are most important for an MP/a councillor to have? Any other qualities?

	For MPs	For Councillors
	%	%
To be well educated	50	31
To have been brought up in the area he/she represents	48	76
To be loyal to the party he/she represents	42	21
To be independent minded	37	29
To know what being poor means	27	17
To have business experience	22	19
To have trade union experience	14	8
None of these	1	1

Political efficacy and protest

Democratic politics is the politics of demands; yet the stable polity is one which achieves a fine balance between activism and acquiescence, between expectations of government and their satisfaction. So argued Almond and Verba in their pioneering study of The Civic Culture (1963). The intervening period has seen an apparent transformation in the level of citizen demands in Western industrial societies. By the mid-1970s the phenomenon of governmental 'overload', a term used originally to denote a worsening ratio of demands to governmental capacities in developing nations, was being anxiously cited in the West, and above all in Britain. The logic of overloaded government is clear: enhance the capacity to deliver, or depress popular expectations. The strategy of lowering expectations has been pursued in Britain for almost four years by the present administration: how far can it continue to count on popular acquiescence? To what extent are people inclined to protest – individually, collectively, unlawfully – against unwelcome government actions?

This section focuses on people's expectations of being able to wield effective political influence, the issue at the heart of the relationship between the individual and the state. It asks how far individuals feel able to protest against an unjust or harmful legislative proposal, what channels of action – personal or collective – they would choose and which of these they would expect to be most effective. As a supplement to this exploration of political action, it also considers what value respondents put on observance of the law and how far they will test it against the dictates of conscience.

Political efficacy and activism

Almond and Verba postulated that attempts to influence government are more likely to arise 'where an individual perceives that an activity of the government is threatening to him' (p.184). Almond and Verba placed their respondents in a hypothetical situation and sought to elicit the 'influence strategy' that would be chosen. We followed the same approach, attempting first to anchor the hypothetical situation in real experience by asking whether respondents had ever considered a law 'harmful or unjust' and what actions — if any — they had taken on that occasion. Thus we asked respondents first whether there had ever been an occasion when a law was being considered by Parliament which they thought was really unjust or harmful; we then invited respondents to recall whether they had taken one or more actions of those listed in the summary table below; we then asked which of these actions they would take if such a law 'was now being considered'. Finally, we asked respondents to assess the single action which, in their view, would be the most effective in influencing a government 'to change its mind'. This gave us both a patterning of preferred actions and, in sum, an overall measure of efficacy.

The table below sets out the pattern of actions, hypothetical responses, and judgement as to their relative effectiveness. It is striking that the great majority of respondents (69%) claim never to have considered a law unjust or harmful. Moreover, of those who had done so, a majority (nearly two thirds) had at the time taken advantage of none of the listed avenues of influence open to them. Consequently, the number of actual protesters is too small for further analysis although the broad pattern of protest corresponds with the pattern revealed by earlier studies: signing petitions is the most popular medium of protest (although only about one in ten of the respondents think it the most effective), followed by contact with the protester's MP (generally considered the most effective single channel). There are important disparities between actual and hypothetical protest actions, and between these choices and respondents' judgements of their effectiveness.

**Responses to the prospect of an unjust or harmful law:
actual, hypothetical and 'most effective' actions**

	Have taken	Would take	Considered most effective
	%	%	%
Personal action :			
Contact MP	3	46	34
Speak to influential person	1	10	4
Contact government department	1	7	5
Contact radio, TV or newspaper	1	14	23
Collective action :			
Sign petition	9	54	11
Raise issue in an organisation			
I belong to	2	9	2
Go on a protest or demonstration	2	8	5
Form a group of like-minded people	1	6	4
None of these :	19	14	9
Never considered a law unjust or harmful	69	x	x

The relatively high proportion of actual and hypothetical protesters who reject any of the offered avenues of influence or who choose avenues that they believe to be ineffective underlines the prevalence of acquiescence — and perhaps a sense of powerlessness — in the face of unwelcome developments. The 1979 British Election Study encountered similarly high levels of acquiescence with, once again, contacting MPs and petitioning as the most favoured forms of political expression. Almond and Verba took it as axiomatic that a civic culture rested upon a high degree of 'subjective political competence' although they too found that 'many respondents make it quite clear that they believe there is nothing they can do, either because they consider themselves too powerless or because they consider government activities are outside their sphere of competence' (p.185, n.4). The interest of The Civic Culture lay in its cross-national comparisons in these and other dimensions; the virtual replication of the competence question in our own study enables us to make a limited comparison over time.

The following table must, however, be read with great caution since the 1963 study (fieldwork for which was carried out during 1959-60) was based on unprompted responses; yet the patterns it seems to reveal are nonetheless remarkable. It provides some evidence of the very transformation in the level of citizen assertiveness that has been mentioned by recent commentators, most strikingly in respect of collective action, an area in which differences between UK and US responses merited particular comment by Almond and Verba. At the same time, the proportion of respondents rejecting all the alternative courses of action has apparently declined. Plausible explanations of the increased emphasis placed upon collective action abound. Perhaps the one with the greatest intuitive appeal is that which accords influence to the developments in public participation since the late 1960s. It is undeniable that the scope for, and the expectation of, assertive collective action in neighbourhood issues, health, housing and a wide range of other issues, has been transformed in recent years. Assertiveness at this level may well spill over into national concerns; how far the two levels of public decision are seen as interdependent, and how far this apparent activism is reflected in the responses to unwelcome local actions are issues which we shall explore in future years.

Political Efficacy in 1960 and 1983:
proportions choosing action and inaction

	1960	1983
	%	%
Faced with the prospect of an unjust or 'harmful law' respondent would:		
take personal action	47	77
take collective action	23	77
do nothing	32	14
don't know	6	1

The ratio of those choosing action to those choosing inaction is clearly important; and, given the opportunity of making multiple responses, there may be a surplus of chosen courses of action over inaction. This can be expressed in the form of a single index for both personal and collective action:

$$\frac{P - i}{n} \quad \text{or} \quad \frac{C - i}{n}$$

P is the number of 'personal' actions mentioned (contact MP, speak to influential person, contact government department, or take the matter up with the press, radio or television); C is the number of 'collective' actions (sign petition, raise the issue in an organisation of which the respondent is a member, form a group of like-minded people, go on a demonstration or protest); i is the number of persons choosing none of these eight courses of action; and n is the number in the group under consideration. This provides a single measure of the level of potential activism in a group as a whole in relation to the eight possible courses of protest actions we offered. Note that neither the Personal Action Index (PAI) nor the Collective Action Index (CAI) directly reflects the proportion of activists in a group, but rather the proportion of actions considered. As such, the indices permit sharp discrimination between more and less active populations, for respondents in a more active group will amplify their higher propensity to act by choosing more – up to four – possible courses. Thus the maximum value of both the PAI and the CAI for any population is 4: this will be attained where there are no 'passivists' and where every respondent chooses all four courses of action in concert.

Such high values are unlikely to be approached. As the following tables show, the value of PAI or CAI for most groups is close to zero (the point at which the number of active responses is equalled by the number of passivists) and can attain a negative value (where the number of passivists outweighs the number of active responses). If, for the purpose of illustration, we were to ignore the biases arising from the two different question forms in the 1960 and 1983 studies we would find the values of PAI and CAI for the two studies to differ markedly, from around zero for both in 1960 (with a slight negative value for CAI) to 0.63 for PAI and 0.64 for CAI in 1983. In what does this quality of acquiescence reside? Clearly, a sense of powerlessness or non-competence may reflect accurately the circumstances of an individual's life and his or her real resources for political influence; we might then expect it to be closely associated with social class. Equally, however, it is a measure of a subjective power; because education can be thought of as a process of (subjective) empowerment, we might expect an association between activism and education. The membership of certain occupational groups also provides access to influence; this is particularly true where unionisation provides both the opportunity and the perception of collective influence. All of these expected relationships are borne out by the data.

Only the briefest commentary on the table overleaf is called for. There is a particularly strong association of political efficacy with education; although the disparity in the size of the groups prompts cautious interpretation, the direction of the relationship is very clear and corresponds closely with the similar relationships which Almond and Verba found to hold for the US, UK, West Germany, Italy and Mexico in 1960. Note also the indications of a class and occupational association with the preference for collective over personal action, which holds for those in full-time employment and for Social Class III non-manual. A converse preference for personal over collective action is seen among the retired and the self-employed.

**Political efficacy scores by education,
occupational status and social class**

	PAI	CAI
Total	0.63	0.64
Age of completing full time education		
19 or over	1.03	1.03
17, 18	0.78	0.63
16 or under	0.56	0.59
Employment status		
full time employed	0.70	0.75
self-employed	0.64	0.54
retired	0.57	0.50
looking after home	0.53	0.51
seeking work	0.50	0.61
Social class		
I	0.81	0.84
II	0.82	0.75
III non-manual	0.74	0.90
III manual	0.58	0.53
IV	0.51	0.60
V	0.33	0.36

Trade union membership, whether past or present, is associated with fairly high scores for both collective and personal action. The relationships between party identification, partisanship and political efficacy are also particularly interesting. The data suggest strong associations between orientations to the political system and a sense of political efficacy (suggesting thereby that the construct has some validity); but note also the high collective action score for Alliance supporters, which lends some support to the view that attachment to the Alliance is itself an expression of protest against mainstream politics.

**Political efficacy scores by trade union membership,
party identification and partisanship**

	PAI	CAI
Total	0.63	0.64
Trade union membership		
current member	0.73	0.78
past member	0.67	0.69
never a member	0.51	0.49
Party identification		
Conservative	0.72	0.60
Alliance	0.74	0.89
Labour	0.60	0.67
Partisanship		
partisans (all parties)	0.76	0.70
non-aligned	0.36	0.36

None of these apparent relationships is particularly surprising; the more significant ones are all in the expected direction. More interesting are the unexpected associations of political efficacy with region, although the possibility of sampling error influencing regional results with these sample sizes is considerable. Taking the results at face value, the table below shows relatively little deviation from the overall pattern, but the exceptions are intriguing. The South West shows very high scores on both personal and collective action, whereas Scotland, and to a lesser extent Wales, displays unusually low scores on personal action. From **Table 2.7** it will be seen that the South West's high score is attributable in part to a high propensity to contact MPs and the media and in part to the very small proportion (5%) who would choose none of the offered courses of action. The low score for Scotland is based on the converse of these characteristics; as in Wales, only one-third of respondents would contact their MP; the Scottish score for contact with government departments and the media is low; both Scottish and Welsh respondents revealed an equally strong propensity not to act at all.

Political efficacy scores by region

Region	PAI	CAI
Yorkshire	0.58	0.55
North	0.60	0.46
North West	0.61	0.58
West Midlands	0.67	0.71
East Midlands	0.65	0.54
South East	0.66	0.69
GLC	0.73	0.72
South West	0.93	0.81
Scotland	0.32	0.58
Wales	0.45	0.57

The characteristics of the regional populations can account for these differences only in small part. If there is a genuine regional effect here we must look to the operation of political institutions and to regional political culture for its explanation. The South West is characterised by a rather independent style of politics with a strong grassroots tradition and highly active Members of Parliament with strong personal followings, a number of them (before the June 1983 election) being national figures. Yet the degree of decentralised government currently enjoyed by Scotland and Wales might be expected to find some reflection in enhanced accessibility; their MPs enjoy a closer relationship with the respective Secretaries of State. So too might we expect Cardiff and Edinburgh to seem more approachable than London. We are then led to suspect that the answer lies in the distinctiveness of regional (or national) political cultures and in the pervasiveness of the nationalist debate in Scottish and Welsh politics.

The striking deviations from the regional pattern are, in the case of Scotland and Wales, quite consistent with the regional patterns of dissatisfaction with government manifested in the Kilbrandon devolution study (1971); dissatisfaction then is associated with low efficacy scores now. But not in the South West. Here, a level of dissatisfaction almost unique among the English regions in 1971 (the North ran it a close second) is inversely associated with political efficacy today. It is to be hoped that the current University of Manchester/SCPR study of political participation might cast further light on these tentative findings.

Observance of the law

Although most law breaking is apolitical it remains an option in the extreme case where the normal channels of political influence are seen not to work: that is, beyond the limit of political efficacy where civil disobedience is the avenue of last resort. The 1979 BES results indicate that large majorities reject direct action: 70% 'certainly would not' participate in a banned protest march; only 4% were 'likely' to do so. This question of political law breaking has been fully explored only in one previous study, that by Marsh (1977). We did not seek to link observance of the law specifically to the issue of political efficacy, for example by asking respondents to identify circumstances in which law breaking was justifiable. Instead, we simply asked two questions: one designed to elicit views on the relative claims of law and conscience; and one to test how far respondents saw the law as a constraint on their own likely future actions.

Just as assertiveness in the political sphere appears to have increased markedly over the last two decades, so too has the perception that in certain (unspecified) circumstances, it may be justifiable to break the law. The most striking relationships were those between observance of the law and age and sex. The responses to both questions are shown below for men and women in several age groups. There is a strong generational influence: people in the older age groups are, in their own estimation, both less likely to break the law and more likely to agree that it should be obeyed 'without exception'. It is the newer, younger entrants to the electorate who dissent from the absolute claims of law and whose presence largely accounts for the apparent shift over time towards a more pragmatic view of the law. Men in all age groups are more likely to break the law than women, with men under the age of 35 being evenly divided as to whether they might break the law under certain circumstances.

Majorities of men and women under the age of 35 dissent from the proposition that the law should be obeyed 'without exception'. But, interestingly, women in the 35-54 age group retain a markedly greater readiness to invoke conscience against the claims of law in comparison with men of the same age.

In general, would you say that people should obey the law without exception, or are there exceptional occasions on which people should follow their consciences even if it means breaking the law?

	Total	Men			Women		
		18-34	35-54	55+	18-34	35-54	55+
	%	%	%	%	%	%	%
Obey law without exception	53	35	55	69	44	45	68
Follow conscience on occasions	46	63	44	31	56	54	30

Are there any circumstances in which you might break a law to which you were very strongly opposed?

	Total	Men			Women		
		18-34	35-54	55+	18-34	35-54	55+
	%	%	%	%	%	%	%
Yes	30	48	39	24	34	26	15
No	61	48	51	71	57	62	78
Don't know	8	4	9	5	10	12	7

Political tolerance

We have seen how far our respondents conceive the claims of law as transcending or as subordinate to those of conscience. But how far are they prepared to extend equal rights under the law to those who adhere to extreme political views? Other chapters of this book examine the tolerance extended to those who deviate from social, and particularly sexual, norms. Our concern here is with political tolerance, specifically as it is extended to freedom of speech and the right to hold educational posts, of two polarized groups: revolutionaries (or, as we described them in the question: *people who wish to overthrow the system of government in Britain by revolution)* and racists (or as we described them: *people who say that all blacks and Asians should be forced to leave Britain).* We asked, *there are some people whose views are considered extreme by the majority. Consider people who.........Do you think such people should be allowed i) to hold public meetings to express their views? ii) to teach in schools? iii) to teach in colleges or universities? iv) to publish books expressing their views?*

Political tolerance: attitudes to extremists

	Revolutionaries	Racists
	%	%
Should be allowed to :		
publish books	74	71
hold public meetings	57	56
teach in colleges	37	41
teach in schools	25	31
None of these	21	23
All of these	21	25

If the question form implied a broad equation between the respective claims of these two groups, it was one adopted readily enough by the respondents. Responses to the four questions were highly consistent as between revolutionaries and racists. As the table above shows, the crucial distinction for our respondents was between ordinary political rights, for which there was majority support for the civil liberties of both groups, and access to positions of educational influence, which the majority of the sample opposed — again for both groups. The same relativities between these four rights held throughout the sample: among all groups 'publishing books' was conceded the most tolerance, public meetings had rather less support, teaching in college or university had considerably less support and teaching in schools less still. This broad pattern of tolerance (or intolerance) was similarly extended to both extremist groups.

There was, however, a discernible difference in political tolerance according to party identification, social class and age of completing full time education (see **Tables** 2.8 and 2.9). In the case of party, this patterning was most apparent in the responses to civil rights for racists. Labour identifiers were less willing to accord to racists the right to hold public meetings and to publish books than were Conservative and Alliance identifiers, although the differences were not great and did not carry over into the right to hold educational posts. The inter-party differences were sharpened, however, when only the partisans of each party were considered. To some extent, the modest party dimension in tolerance of racists reflects the generally low levels of tolerance among working class electors and those who completed their education at an earlier age; blue collar workers generally distinguished less sharply between freedom of speech and occupational rights than did white collar workers.

Britain's institutions

We explored a number of aspects of opinion on major British institutions: the monarchy and the House of Lords in the interview, and other major governmental and non-governmental institutions within the self-completion questionnaire. The principal interest in these questions is not to be found in the distribution of opinion in any one year, but in the monitoring of change over time. The pattern of responses is also difficult to interpret because of the different salience of the institutions themselves; evaluations of, for example, the prisons as 'well run' (46%) are, for most respondents, not made on the basis of direct experience, whereas similar responses for the NHS (49%) generally are. The police (72%), banks (85%), the BBC (67%) and independent broadcasting (69%) are probably of high salience to most respondents and all receive highly positive evaluations. The civil service (40%) and manufacturing industry (40%) are of less salience to most, and, like the prisons, probably have a somewhat blurred image. However, the overwhelmingly unfavourable image of the nationalised industries (20%) and the trade unions (27%) is of some political significance given the historic association of the Labour Party with these institutions. The following table shows the total responses in order of positive evaluation.

Listed are some of Britain's institutions. From what you know or have heard about each one, can you say whether, on the whole, you think it is well run or not well run?

	Well run	Not well run
	%	%
Banks	85	5
The police	72	18
Independent TV and radio	69	20
The BBC	67	22
The press	49	40
The National Health Service	49	42
Prisons	46	41
Manufacturing industry	40	47
The civil service	40	48
Local government	33	56
The trade unions	27	62
Nationalised industries	20	69

We also asked for responses to three live policy issues concerning the state's role in local government and in British industry. The questions were: *do you think local councils ought to be controlled by central government more, less or about the same as now?* (with a similar question for *British industry*); and *on the whole, would you like to see more or less state ownership of industry, or about the same amount as now?* Once again, interpretation of the answers for only one year is difficult given our lack of knowledge about the salience of the issues to our respondents. For instance, the response 'about the same' could indicate a considered judgement that the boundary was drawn at the right point, or a disinclination to voice a particular viewpoint.

This aside, almost half the sample expressed support for change in the relationship between central and local government during this period of increasing politicisation and conflict in central local relations. But few of these respondents wish to see greater central control: Conservative identifiers themselves are, at 15%, barely more enthusiastic about more central government control than is the sample as a whole. There is fairly strong support for decentralisation of control among Alliance identifiers. These figures have to be judged in the light of the widespread view, reported in other surveys, that local government already has very little power in relation to the centre; these issues will be explored more fully in the future.

As the summary table overleaf shows, the inter-party differences emerge more sharply on control of British industry and state ownership. On these issues Alliance identifiers are closer to the Conservatives in opposing further central control and nationalisation while Labour identifiers are distinguished by their desire in particular not to see less state ownership; still, only about one in five would like to see more nationalisation. Nevertheless − and perhaps surprisingly − there was no increase in the party polarisation on these issues when only partisans are considered. Although identifiers of the different parties display conflicting positions on the issue of state control, these differences do not appear to be amplified by strong identification with the parties.

Central government control analysed by Party identification

	Total	Conservative	Alliance	Labour	Non-aligned
	%	%	%	%	%
Of Local government					
More	13	15	10	12	11
Same	45	52	41	44	35
Less	34	26	44	38	32
Of British industry					
More	11	8	10	17	8
Same	38	37	36	41	33
Less	43	50	47	33	39
State ownership of industry					
More	11	5	4	22	8
Same	33	23	34	46	33
Less	49	68	55	25	43

Attitudes to the monarchy are strongly in the direction of uncritical support among all social groups. The least supportive of the monarchy are the unemployed; yet even here just over half consider the monarchy to be 'very important' and only 15% consider it to be unimportant. 60% of men of all age groups, and 69% of women consider the monarchy to be 'very important'. Among women over 55 there is near unanimity about the importance of the monarchy. If the distinction between 'very' and 'quite' important is ignored, 96% of Conservative partisans, 88% of Alliance partisans, and 77% of Labour partisans regarded the continuation of the monarchy as important for Britain. This question clearly need not be repeated annually.

How about the Monarchy or the Royal Family in Britain. How important or unimportant do you think it is for Britain to continue to have a Monarchy?

	Total
	%
Very important	65
Quite important	21
Not very important	8
Not at all important	3
Should be abolished	3

More polarisation on partisan lines is to be found in the patterns of support for the House of Lords. Here, not surprisingly, Labour identifers are fairly critical of the institution, with a minority favouring no change. Alliance identifiers fall between the other two parties in their attitudes.

Do you think the House of Lords should remain as it is or is some change needed?
IF SO: Do you think the House of Lords should be replaced by a different body,
abolished and replaced by nothing or should there be some other kind of change?

	Total	Conservative	Alliance	Labour
	%	%	%	%
Remain as is	57	72	55	44
Change needed	34	22	39	48
Replaced by a different body	10	6	12	14
Abolished and replaced by nothing	8	3	6	15
Some other change	16	13	21	19

Expectations

The evaluation of Britain's institutions leads naturally to consideration of how far they might be relied upon to prevent and mitigate some catastrophic future change in the quality of life. Presented with a list of predictions about problems that Britain might face within the next ten years, respondents were asked to assess their likelihood. The predictions covered political terrorism, riots and civil disturbance, a world war involving Britain and Europe, a serious accident at a nuclear power station, police incapacity to protect personal safety on the streets. and the overthrow of Government by revolution.

Here is a list of predictions about problems Britain might face. For each one, please say how likely or unlikely you think it is to come true in Britain within the next ten years?

	Very likely	Quite likely	Not very likely	Not at all likely
	%	%	%	%
Acts of political terrorism in Britain will be common events	15	38	33	6
Riots and civil disturbance in our cities will be common events	15	41	31	5
There will be a world war involving Britain and Europe	6	17	45	23
There will be a serious accident at a British nuclear power station	10	32	40	9
The police in our cities will find it impossible to protect our personal safety on the streets	17	33	35	8
The government in Britain will be overthrown by revolution	2	5	31	54

Our sample was, then, relatively sanguine about the larger catastrophies, but notably pessimistic about the deterioration of aspects of life that might touch them more personally. Such was their position early in 1983. Some trend data are available for some of these predictions. The shifts over time, where these are measurable, are shown overleaf. From this it will be seen that expectation of world war, while still relatively low, has risen quite considerably since similar questions were asked in 1975 and 1980. Our present sample was somewhat more optimistic than its predecessors on the issues of nuclear accident and revolution, but very much more pessimistic about political terrorism and safety on the streets. In these respects, the perception of violence in domestic society is very much greater. On the other hand, in respect of rioting – the one area where there has *in fact* been an increase – there has been no major shift in expectations. Possibly the question form may have influenced responses here: the 1979 and 1980 studies specifically asked about *race* riots. It will be interesting to monitor answers to these same questions over the next few years.

Recent changes in expectations of the next ten years*

	1979	1980	1983
	%	%	%
Nuclear accident			
likely	51	48	42
unlikely	43	41	49
don't know/not answered	6	11	8
Race riots			
likely	52	62	56
unlikely	36	36	36
don't know/not answered	12	2	8
World War			
likely	15 ⎫	14	23
unlikely	71 ⎬ 1975	79	68
don't know/not answered	14 ⎭	7	9
Unsafe on streets			
likely	30	26	50
unlikely	59	70	42
don't know/not answered	11	3	8
Political terrorism			
likely	26	43	53
unlikely	65	50	39
don't know/not answered	2	6	8
Revolution			
likely	11	x	7
unlikely	77	x	84
don't know/not answered	2	x	2

Sources: Gallup (1975) BES (1979) New Society (1980)

Britain and the world

Most of the predictions to which we invited responses concerned domestic political events. But we did include a question on the likelihood of world war, and one on political terrorism, an issue in which domestic and international implications are inextricably interwoven. Indeed, it is particularly difficult to interpret a set of trend responses that indicate a rising expectation of political terrorism, for it is uncertain how far events in Northern Ireland are imagined in these terms. Accordingly, we begin our discussion of Britain and the world with the sample's views on that troubled province on the ground that its status as part of the UK cannot be taken for granted in a survey of people's opinions.

We asked respondents what they thought the long term policy for Northern Ireland should be: to remain part of the UK, or to reunify with the rest of Ireland. As many as 58% of the sample favoured reunification and, as the table below shows, there are rather modest differences between the supporters of the respective parties: little more than a third of Conservative identifiers favour the maintenance of the Union, as against around a quarter of Labour and Alliance identifiers. The Conservative Party is, of course, the Conservative and *Unionist* Party and this difference over the future of Ireland is rather more sharply reflected amongst Conservative partisans, the only group in the sample where there was not 50% or more in favour of reunification. There was no such strong association of views with strength of party identification for the other parties.

Do you think the long-term policy for Northern Ireland should be for it to remain part of the United Kingdom, or to reunify with the rest of Ireland?

	Total	Conservative	Alliance	Labour	Non-aligned
	%	%	%	%	%
Remain in UK	28	36	25	23	25
Reunification	58	50	61	65	55

We also asked whether government policy towards the province should include a complete withdrawal of British troops. Opinion on this issue is strongly polarised: 60% of the sample placed themselves at one or other of the extreme points of strongly supporting or strongly opposing withdrawal, with only a third choosing to qualify their position. There was also quite strong party polarisation on this issue. Among the third of the sample who opposed withdrawal were about a quarter of Labour identifiers and about half of the Conservatives. 58% of the sample supported withdrawal. Conservatives were the only group where there was not a majority in favour of withdrawal, yet even here, a quarter of that party's identifiers strongly supported it. Again, on this issue, Conservative partisans are quite distinct from the less committed identifiers of the party, who differ only marginally from Alliance identifiers. This intra-party cleavage does not apply to the Alliance or Labour Party. The following table shows the Conservative division alongside the answers of all Labour and Alliance identifiers.

Some people think that Government policy towards Northern Ireland should include a complete withdrawal of British troops. Would you personally support or oppose such a policy? Strongly or a little?

	Total	Conservative partisans	Other Conservatives	Alliance identifiers	Labour identifiers
	%	%	%	%	%
Support strongly	38	20	36	39	48
Support a little	21	18	20	20	22
Oppose a little	13	19	14	14	11
Oppose strongly	22	36	21	19	14

This pattern of a discernible cleavage among Conservative identifiers is also to be found in the responses to questions on defence policy. Here, however, the cleavage was repeated among Alliance identifiers, but not among Labour identifiers. There was strong support among our respondents for the proposition that possession of British nuclear defences made Britain a safer place in which to live, and little support for unilateral nuclear disarmament. On the question of the presence of US missiles in Britain, however, the balance of opinion was in the opposite direction, with 48% of the sample considering that Britain was made less safe by this presence, and only 38% considering it enhanced our safety. As the table below shows, Labour and Alliance identifiers are in broad accord on this issue, with less than a third in every group believing that US missiles make Britain safer. The apparent sharp difference between Conservative identifiers and the rest of the sample is largely accounted for by the very much stronger support for current defence policy among the large group of partisan Conservatives, who – once again – hold views in this issue which are distinctly out of accord with the Party's less attached identifiers. The reservations of Conservative sympathisers and residual identifiers place them closer to the opposing parties. It should, moreover, be borne in mind that our fieldwork preceded the arrival of cruise missiles by more than six months.

Do you think that the siting of American nuclear missiles in Britain makes Britain a . safer or a less safe place to live?

	Total	Conservative		Alliance		Labour	
		partisans	others	partisans	others	partisans	others
	%	%	%	%	%	%	%
Safer	38	60	39	24	32	32	29
Less safe	48	27	45	61	54	59	59

We also asked about the possession of British nuclear weapons: did they make this country a safer or a less safe place to live? And we asked whether British nuclear policy should be based on the retention or the renunciation of nuclear weapons. The results – in sharp contrast to those relating to American missiles – were as follows:

Do you think that having our own independent nuclear missiles makes Britain a safer or a less safe place to live?

	Total	Conservative		Alliance		Labour	
		partisans	others	partisans	others	partisans	others
	%	%	%	%	%	%	%
Safer	60	78	63	59	61	52	54
Less safe	28	12	24	32	29	40	38

Which, if either of these two statements comes closest to your own opinion on British nuclear policy: Britain should rid itself of nuclear weapons while persuading others to do the same; Britain should keep its nuclear weapons until we persuade others to reduce theirs?

	Total	Conservative partisans	others	Alliance partisans	others	Labour partisans	others
	%	%	%	%	%	%	%
Rid itself	19	6	12	21	22	33	25
Keep	77	93	83	78	74	64	72

Once again, we see noticeable party cleavages on the issue, widened further when we look separately at those with the strongest identification with their party. Even Labour partisans split two thirds in favour of the maintenance of nuclear weapons on British soil; Conservative partisans meanwhile attain near unanimity.

Even more interesting variations occur when we examine the answers by age and sex. There is in total a strong vein of hostility to the US nuclear presence co-existing with support for British nuclear weapons and a rejection of unilateralism. The greater hostility to nuclear weapons in general comes from the young, and this hostility decreases with age. Women are also generally more hostile towards nuclear weapons on British soil than are men. Whereas men in all age groups are more or less evenly divided on the US nuclear presence in Britain, young and middle-aged women are divided almost 2:1 against. It is interesting therefore that the Greenham Common protest should be a women's protest. Is this a result of women's much stronger opposition, or has Greenham influenced women's views more than men's?

Attitudes to nuclear weapons by age and sex:

	Men				Women			
	Total Men	18-34	35-54	55+	Total Women	18-34	35-54	55+
	%	%	%	%	%	%	%	%
US missiles								
make safer	45	41	46	47	33	28	33	38
make less safe	44	46	43	44	50	60	52	40
British missiles								
make safer	62	54	65	67	59	54	59	63
make less safe	29	36	26	27	28	34	29	22
British nuclear arms								
retain	79	72	82	82	76	69	77	82
renounce	19	24	16	16	20	26	20	14

An interesting sidelight on these findings is that the public on this issue can hardly be accused of being slavish followers of party political positions. On the contrary, the broad public position on nuclear weapons was distinctly different from any of the major party's positions. Caricaturing the differences between the parties at the time: the Conservatives wanted Trident and cruise, the Labour Party wanted neither, the Alliance was sympathetic to cruise but not Trident, while the public was sympathetic to Trident but not cruise. It will be interesting to monitor changes in opinion now that cruise missiles have actually arrived in Britain.

The breakdown of opinion on the one remaining defence issue – that of Britain's continuing membership of NATO – shows yet a different pattern.

Continued membership was overwhelmingly favoured by our sample, at 79% to 13%. This pattern of support was quite firm throughout the age ranges for both sexes. It does indeed seem that a sharp distinction is made between the need for the Atlantic Alliance and trust of the American nuclear presence within it. How far respondents see NATO as a *European* rather than as an Atlantic Alliance is not possible to determine on the basis of this limited evidence. This too is an issue for further exploration. Continued membership of NATO does, however, emerge to some degree as a partisan issue: 92% of Conservative partisans and 89% of Alliance partisans favour continuation, as against only 71% of Labour partisans. The strongest support for withdrawal (30%) was among Labour's residual identifiers.

Moving to non-military matters, the solid consensus in favour of NATO is not parallelled by any similar body of support for the European Community as such. A bare majority (53%) thought Britain should continue EEC membership; 42% favoured withdrawal. This pattern of opinion was fairly consistent when broken down by region. But there were fairly marked differences by type of occupation. Those working in agriculture were the most favourable to continued membership (76%) followed by those in finance (68%). Engineering (40%) and other manufacturing (45%) provide some indication of where EEC membership is thought to have adverse consequences; however, the numbers in these sectors are very small. Collapsing the SIC categories into a simple trichotomy of public sector/private non-manufacturing/private manufacturing served to confirm rather than eliminate the apparent relationship, support running from a public sector high of 60% through 56% for the non-manufacturing private sector to 45% for manufacturing.

The question of EEC membership raises one further issue of partisan division. Support for the EEC is strong among Conservatives (67% overall and 72% of partisans) and, to a lesser degree among Alliance identifiers (57% overall, and 59% among partisans). Labour supporters on the other hand favour withdrawal by a substantial majority of 58% to 37%, with no very sharp divisions of opinion between partisans and others.

Finally we asked respondents to the self-completion questionnaire to state the degree to which they admired a range of foreign countries and Britain. This is the first stage of a monitoring exercise that will seek to elicit changing views of Britain's place in the world, its relative influence and standard of living. The findings show a very deep admiration of Britain and substantial bodies of good feeling for the USA and a number of Western European countries. Feelings about the Soviet Union were on the other hand, overwhelmingly hostile, being almost a mirror image of feelings about Britain. We also explored how far respondents felt it important for Britain to have links with some of these countries.

The degree of symmetry or asymmetry in these distributions for Brazil, Saudi Arabia, Nigeria, Russia, the USA, China and South Africa shown in **Table 2.10** demonstrates a clear patterning of opinion. The marked skew in respect of the USA provides a 'favoured ally' pattern. The near symmetry of the Russian distribution provides a picture of an important antagonist to whom links are nevertheless vital. China and Saudi Arabia provide patterns distinctive to a world power; recognition of their importance outweighs the extent to which they are admired. Nigeria, Brazil and, perhaps surprisingly, South Africa, provide what might be termed a 'third-world minor power' pattern, neither admired nor sought contact with.

References

ABRAMS. M and ROSE, R., *Must Labour Lose?* Penguin, Harmondsworth (1960).

ALFORD, R., *Party and Society,* John Murray, London (1964).

ALMOND, G. A. and VERBA, S., *The Civic Culture,* Princeton University Press, Princeton, N.J. (1963).

BUDGE, I., CREWE, I. and FARLIE, D., *Party Identification and Beyond,* Wiley, London (1976).

CREWE, I., SARLVIK, B. and ALT, J., 'Partisan Dealignment in Britain 1964-1974', *British Journal of Political Science.* (1977) pp 129-190.

HIMMELWEIT, H. T., HUMPHREYS, P., JAEGER, M. and KATZ, M., *How Voters Decide,* Academic Press, London (1981).

KILBRANDON, *'Commission on the Constitution' (Chairman The Lord Kilbrandon) Research Papers 7: Devolution and other Aspects of Government: An Attitudes Survey,* HMSO, London (1971).

MARSH, A., *Protest and Political Consciousness,* Sage Publications, London (1977).

MILLER, W. L., 'Social Class and Party Choice in England: A New Analysis', *British Journal of Political Science 8* (1978) pp 257-284.

SARLVIK, B. and CREWE, I., *Decade of Dealignment,* Cambridge University Press, Cambridge (1983).

In addition, use was made of codebooks provided by the ERSC Data Archive at the University of Essex; those cited here are for British Election Study May 1979 Cross Section (SN1533) and the New Society into the '80's Study (SN1329). Where reference is made to Gallup data, these are derived from *The Gallup Report* of 1981. (Webb and Wybrow, Sphere).

Indices of class polarisation, shown on page 14 are taken from Miller (1978) and from Crewe, Sarlvik and Alt (1977). Figures for 1979 have been calculated from data kindly supplied by Anthony Heath of Jesus College, Oxford.

Acknowledgements

Grateful acknowledgement is made to the ESRC Survey Archive for making available the codebooks for the above and other studies not cited here; and to the former director, Ivor Crewe, who commented most helpfully on earlier versions of the questions.

2.1 PARTY IDENTIFICATION (Q.2)
percentaged by row

	TOTAL	CONSERVATIVE			ALLIANCE						LABOUR			OTHER PARTY	NON-ALIGNED
		Parti-sans	Sympath-isers	Residual Identi-fiers	Parti-sans	Sympath-isers	Residual Identi-fiers	'LIBERAL'	'S.D.P.'	'ALLIANCE'	Parti-sans	Sympath-isers	Residual Identi-fiers	Identi-fiers	
TOTAL	1761	421	163	92	81	96	81	136	106	16	306	191	87	22	221
%	100%	24%	9%	5%	5%	5%	5%	8%	6%	1%	17%	11%	5%	1%	8%

2.2 COMPRESSED PARTY IDENTIFICATION (Q.2)
by social class, age of leaving full-time education and self-assigned social class

	TOTAL	SOCIAL CLASS						AGE LEFT FULL-TIME EDUCATION†		SELF-ASSIGNED SOCIAL CLASS					
		I/II	III non-manual	III manual	IV/V	Looks after home	Other	16 or under	Over 16	Upper middle	Middle	Upper working	Working	Poor	Don't know/ not answered
	%	%	%	%	%	%	%	%	%	%	%	%	%	%	%
Conservative Identifier	39	54	43	34	24	38	36	36	49	(64)	54	46	28	(12)	(38)
Alliance Identifier	15	19	19	14	10	14	11	14	19	(12)	18	15	14	(7)	(12)
Labour Identifier	33	17	26	38	50	33	37	36	20	(12)	18	28	42	(67)	(26)
Non-aligned	8	6	6	9	10	7	12	8	6	(8)	6	6	10	(9)	(13)
Other/don't know	3	3	2	2	4	5	3	3	4	(-)	1	3	4	(2)	(11)
Not answered	2	2	3	2	1	2	1	3	1	(4)	2	2	2	(2)	(6)
BASE: ALL RESPONDENTS Weighted	1719	334	268	365	300	346	106	1338	377	(25)	416	400	783	(53)	(45)
Unweighted	1761	343	281	362	316	353	106	1381	374	(25)	431	411	801	(43)	(48)

For notes on breakdowns, symbols and tabulations, refer to Appendices I and II.

2.3 PARTY IDENTIFICATION (Q.2)
by age within sex

	TOTAL	MALE								FEMALE†							
		TOTAL	18-24	25-34	35-44	45-54	55-59	60-64	65+	TOTAL	18-24	25-34	35-44	45-54	55-59	60-64	65+
	%	%	%	%	%	%	%	%	%	%	%	%	%	%	%	%	%
CONSERVATIVE: Partisans	24	24	13	21	27	28	22	21	28	25	10	12	27	34	25	30	36
Sympathisers	9	11	13	12	12	11	-	18	8	8	10	14	10	3	6	2	6
Residual identifiers	5	5	8	7	4	5	5	3	2	5	11	4	7	5	-	3	5
ALLIANCE: Partisans	5	4	1	3	7	5	3	2	6	5	5	4	4	4	15	8	4
Sympathisers	5	4	2	6	4	3	5	7	5	6	8	9	8	7	3	6	2
Residual identifiers	5	4	8	1	2	6	10	1	3	5	4	8	4	7	5	6	3
LABOUR: Partisans	17	19	11	18	14	19	33	29	22	15	9	15	10	19	15	14	19
Sympathisers	11	12	14	16	14	6	11	11	11	10	13	13	10	6	17	13	6
Residual identifiers	5	3	7	4	4	3	2	-	3	6	12	4	7	6	4	8	5
Non-aligned	8	8	17	10	8	6	2	3	7	8	13	12	5	4	3	7	9
Don't know	2	2	4	-	2	3	-	-	2	3	2	4	2	2	3	-	4
Not answered	2	2	1	-	2	3	5	5	1	3	3	1	5	1	3	5	2
BASE: ALL RESPONDENTS Weighted	1719	793	106	152	166	118	61	51	138	926	116	159	163	146	71	67	199
Unweighted	1761	807	103	153	166	128	64	54	139	954	108	161	173	156	74	69	207

AGE WITHIN SEX

2.4 VIEWS TO BE TAKEN MOST INTO ACCOUNT BY MEMBERS OF PARLIAMENT (Q.7)
by party identification

	TOTAL	PARTY IDENTIFICATION†									
		CONSERVATIVE			ALLIANCE			LABOUR			NON-ALIGNED
		Parti-sans	Sympath-isers	Residual Identi-fiers	Parti-sans	Sympath-isers	Residual Identi-fiers	Parti-sans	Sympath-isers	Residual Identi-fiers	
	%	%	%	%	%	%	%	%	%	%	%
Views of the Party as expressed by the Conferences	16	19	13	20	23	17	8	19	13	10	8
Views of the local Party	8	7	2	7	6	7	4	13	11	19	7
Views of his or her constituents	57	58	64	58	56	59	69	48	58	48	61
Views of fellow MPs in the same Party	8	7	8	12	9	4	9	9	11	10	7
His or her own views	7	6	9	2	5	7	6	10	7	8	8
Other answer	1	1	*	-	-	2	1	1	1	1	2
Don't know	2	1	3	1	1	4	1	1	*	3	6
Not answered	*	*	-	1	1	-	-	1	-	-	1
BASE: ALL RESPONDENTS Weighted	1791	420	157	87	81	92	79	289	190	86	216
Unweighted	1761	421	163	92	81	96	81	306	191	87	221

2.5 VIEWS TO BE TAKEN MOST INTO ACCOUNT BY MEMBERS OF PARLIAMENT (Q.7)
by social class and trade union membership

	TOTAL	SOCIAL CLASS						TRADE UNION MEMBERSHIP			
		I/II	III non-manual	III manual	IV/V	Looks after home	Other	Current	In past but not now	Never	No information
	%	%	%	%	%	%	%	%	%	%	%
Views of the Party as expressed by the Conferences	16	19	15	15	12	15	22	15	15	16	21
Views of the local Party	8	4	7	12	11	8	7	9	10	7	13
View of his or her constituents	57	59	62	54	54	59	56	59	56	58	44
View of fellow MPs in the same Party	8	5	8	9	13	8	7	7	7	10	6
His or her own views	7	11	7	7	7	5	5	8	8	5	11
Other answer	1	1	1	1	1	1	-	1	1	*	-
Don't know	2	1	1	2	2	4	2	1	2	3	3
Not answered	*	*	-	1	-	*	1	-	*	*	1
BASE: ALL RESPONDENTS Weighted	1719	334	268	365	300	346	106	463	484	689	83
Unweighted	1761	343	281	362	316	353	106	474	497	707	83

2.6 MOST IMPORTANT QUALITIES FOR A MEMBER OF PARLIAMENT (Q.8a)
by social class and party identification

	TOTAL	SOCIAL CLASS						PARTY IDENTIFICATION†			
		I/II	III non-manual	III manual	IV/V	Looks after home	Other	Conservative	Alliance	Labour	Non-aligned
	%	%	%	%	%	%	%	%	%	%	%
Be well educated	50	57	51	46	50	50	46	55	48	49	42
Know what being poor means	27	20	26	26	37	24	32	21	25	34	28
Have business experience	22	29	22	21	17	17	27	33	16	13	15
Have trade union experience	14	14	13	14	18	11	15	13	9	20	9
Have been brought up in area he or she represents	48	41	54	49	49	51	40	45	51	48	48
Be loyal to Party he or she represents	42	42	42	38	40	46	55	48	40	42	31
Be independent minded	37	48	43	34	30	34	37	41	43	33	30
None of these qualities	1	1	*	1	-	1	1	1	-	*	2
Other	3	6	4	2	1	4	2	3	5	3	2
Not answered	1	*	-	1	1	1	1	*	*	*	3
BASE: ALL RESPONDENTS											
Weighted	1719	334	268	365	300	346	106	664	252	565	216
Unweighted	1761	343	281	362	316	353	106	676	268	584	221

2.7 PROTEST STRATEGIES IN RELATION TO UNJUST AND HARMFUL LAW (Q.10c) by region and district

	TOTAL	REGION										DISTRICT	
		Scotland	North	N. West	Yorks	W. Midlands	E. Midlands	Wales	S. West	S. East	G.L.C.	Metro-politan	Non-Metro.
	%	%	%	%	%	%	%	%	%	%	%	%	%
ACTIONS:													
Contact my MP	46	33	46	42	40	49	51	33	60	49	51	43	48
Speak to influential person	10	6	11	13	10	11	10	13	10	10	6	10	10
Contact government department	7	4	5	10	8	7	8	9	8	6	8	8	7
Contact radio, TV or newspaper	14	11	10	9	15	11	12	13	20	14	20	14	14
Sign petition	54	56	43	49	53	63	54	59	55	55	54	56	53
Raise issue in organisation already belong to	9	10	8	8	8	7	6	5	14	11	11	10	9
Go on protest or demonstration	8	8	3	10	4	8	6	10	10	7	10	9	7
Form group of like minded people	6	6	5	3	3	4	5	6	7	8	10	6	6
Not answered	1	1	2	2	-	-	3	-	1	1	2	1	1
WOULD TAKE:													
No listed action	14	22	11	12	13	11	17	23	5	12	13	12	14
1 or 2 listed actions	72	66	84	77	77	75	72	61	72	72	66	73	71
3 or 4 listed actions	13	10	5	10	8	11	11	14	21	13	20	13	12
5 or more listed actions	2	2	-	1	2	3	1	2	2	2	2	1	2
BASE: ALL RESPONDENTS													
Weighted	1719	183	95	196	165	157	130	87	149	368	191	615	1104
Unweighted	1761	179	100	209	165	161	130	87	152	383	195	631	1130

2.8 TOLERATED ACTIVITIES OF 'REVOLUTIONARIES' AND 'RACISTS' (Q.5ab) by party identification

		TOTAL	CONSERVATIVE			ALLIANCE			LABOUR			NON-ALIGNED
			Parti-sans	Sympath-isers	Residual Identi-fiers	Parti-sans	Sympath-isers	Residual Identi-fiers	Parti-sans	Sympath-isers	Residual Identi-fiers	
		%	%	%	%	%	%	%	%	%	%	%
'REVOLUTIONARIES' should be allowed to:												
Hold public meetings to express their views	Yes	57	56	57	60	64	69	56	56	58	57	47
	No	42	43	42	40	36	31	43	42	40	42	47
Teach in schools	Yes	25	17	21	27	32	28	12	35	27	38	25
	No	72	82	76	71	67	71	87	62	71	56	68
Teach in colleges or universities	Yes	37	24	37	44	40	45	29	43	43	49	35
	No	60	75	61	56	59	52	69	54	54	47	57
Publish books expressing their views	Yes	74	77	81	78	88	85	76	71	73	66	59
	No	24	22	19	22	12	13	23	27	25	32	36
'RACISTS' should be allowed to:												
Hold public meetings to express their views	Yes	56	57	59	62	66	68	55	54	50	55	50
	No	41	41	38	37	32	29	44	45	49	38	43
Teach in schools	Yes	31	27	31	25	34	35	31	34	30	46	30
	No	66	71	65	71	62	63	69	63	67	52	63
Teach in colleges or universities	Yes	41	33	42	42	47	50	40	44	41	52	39
	No	56	65	55	58	52	46	59	53	56	46	55
Publish books expressing their views	Yes	71	76	80	76	83	81	66	67	62	61	61
	No	27	23	19	24	16	14	33	31	35	34	35
BASE: ALL RESPONDENTS	Weighted	1719	420	157	87	81	92	79	289	190	86	216
	Unweighted	1761	421	163	92	81	96	81	306	191	87	221

PARTY IDENTIFICATION†

2.9 TOLERATED ACTIVITIES OF 'REVOLUTIONARIES' AND 'RACISTS' (Q.5ab)
by social class, age of leaving full-time education and self-assigned social class

	TOTAL	SOCIAL CLASS						AGE LEFT FULL-TIME EDUCATION†		SELF-ASSIGNED SOCIAL CLASS					
		I/II	III non-manual	III manual	IV/V	Looks after home	Other	16 or under	Over 16	Upper middle	Middle	Upper working	Working	Poor	Don't know/not answered
'REVOLUTIONARIES' should be allowed to:	%	%	%	%	%	%	%	%	%	%	%	%	%	%	%
Hold public meetings to express their views — Yes	57	66	64	52	48	55	59	52	75	(67)	58	61	54	64	(52)
No	42	33	35	47	50	42	39	46	25	(33)	41	38	44	33	(42)
Teach in school — Yes	25	29	24	23	25	21	37	22	35	(32)	27	21	25	44	(35)
No	72	69	73	75	71	76	63	75	64	(68)	71	77	72	52	(59)
Teach in colleges or universities — Yes	37	40	34	34	34	37	51	34	48	(39)	39	35	36	52	(40)
No	60	58	62	64	61	59	49	63	50	(61)	59	63	61	44	(55)
Publish books expressing their views — Yes	74	83	84	70	63	72	72	69	91	(75)	79	81	69	77	(73)
No	24	15	15	29	34	25	27	28	9	(25)	20	19	29	23	(24)
'RACISTS' should be allowed to:															
Hold public meetings to express their views — Yes	56	69	61	49	54	52	53	53	68	(55)	59	62	51	71	(61)
No	41	29	39	49	43	44	42	44	31	(45)	38	36	46	29	(34)
Teach in school — Yes	31	36	29	27	37	27	36	31	33	(39)	32	30	31	38	(34)
No	66	61	68	71	60	68	60	66	65	(57)	65	68	66	60	(57)
Teach in colleges or universities — Yes	41	47	36	35	45	38	47	39	45	(43)	41	41	40	45	(46)
No	56	50	61	62	52	58	52	57	53	(53)	56	57	57	53	(49)
Publish books expressing their views — Yes	71	84	80	53	64	66	68	66	87	(68)	76	77	64	67	(78)
No	27	14	19	35	34	30	28	31	12	(25)	22	21	33	33	(17)
BASE: ALL RESPONDENTS *Weighted*	1719	334	268	355	300	346	106	1338	377	(25)	416	400	783	43	(53)
Unweighted	1761	343	281	362	316	353	106	1381	374	(25)	431	411	801	45	(48)

2.10 ADMIRATION FOR AND IMPORTANCE OF LINKS WITH COUNTRIES (Q.201 and Q.15)

	CHINA	SOUTH AFRICA	RUSSIA	BRAZIL	USA	NIGERIA	SAUDI ARABIA	FRANCE	ISRAEL	HOLLAND	WEST GERMANY	BRITAIN
Admiration	-6%	-52%	-66%	-53%	+41%	-60%	-30%	-18%	-25%	+47%	+40%	+77%
Importance of links	+34%	-4%	+32%	-20%	+90%	-11%	+57%					

The figures show the percentage difference between positive and negative evaluations of countries. A minus sign indicates that negative feelings towards the country outweigh positive; a plus sign indicates that positive feelings outweigh negative.

The two rows show the relationship between admiration for a country and the perceived importance of links with that country, as measured by the two questions we asked.

3 Economic policy and expectations

Anthony Harrison*

During 1983 itself, but also during most of the 1979-1983 Conservative Government's period in office, economic issues were at the forefront of political debate. As the economy moved steadily into the worst depression since the war, the Government consciously reversed the conventional wisdom of much of the post-war period and decided that Britain should not attempt to spend its way out of a slump. Extra spending would not produce 'real' jobs, as the Prime Minister was fond of saying. All the Government should do was to get the basic economic circumstances right. Real jobs would be created only if firms and individuals got out and did it themselves.

As the Conservatives won the election at a time when the economy was at its lowest ebb, it might be assumed that they had managed to persuade people that their view of things was right. In fact they appeared to have achieved that success despite, rather than because of, what the electorate thought of their policies.

The public for the most part remained sceptical that the government's policies would work. On many issues they were more inclined to believe in the policies the opposition was offering – a large stimulus through increased public spending, particularly on job creation. Nearly 90% of our sample supported such a policy, and there was more than a two to one majority in favour of reducing unemployment rather than inflation if the two aims were in conflict.

Naturally, on some issues the Government's views and explanations had been accepted. For one thing, few people blamed the Conservative government for Britain's poor economic performance. Most identified several contributory factors and were prepared to identify both management and unions as guilty parties. Like the Government, they thought that poor world trading conditions

---

*Joint Editor of *Public Money*

were largely to blame. Similarly, the prospect of further nationalisation —
although not a very prominent theme in the election campaign that was to
follow our survey — was not popular. Even among Labour identifiers, more
people favoured a reduction in nationalisation than an increase.

In its attitudes towards trade unions, the Government was also in tune with
the majority. Over half of the sample thought that the trade unions had too
much influence, and nearly half of those who were themselves members of trade
unions thought so too. These findings are one indicator that people's membership
of a particular group, party, income, class, trade union does not predict very
well what they are likely to think on many policy issues. We asked, for example,
whether high Government spending had been a cause of Britain's economic
difficulties — a proposition that the Conservative Government had been putting
consistently for four years. The proportions accepting the proposition were
almost identical, regardless of party identification. Similarly, the electorate was
divided almost evenly between supporters and opponents of an incomes policy,
and this dichotomy existed broadly among unionists and non-unionists and
within all social classes.

True, Conservative identifiers were more likely to believe the Government's
general message than others were, but we do not know whether they supported
the government because they believed in its policies or whether they believed in
its policies and therefore supported the government.

On other issues too, traditional class and political loyalties did hold: the
lower paid for instance, were more likely to be critical of British management;
Conservative identifiers were more likely to believe that responsibility for poor
economic performance could be laid at the door of the workers. Even so, the
overall impression from our data is that, on *policy* issues, large measures of
public agreement seem to exist and, where there is disagreement, only in some
cases did political or class allegiance prove to be a good predictor of what
policies would be favoured. By contrast, class and income were more reliable
predicators of *expectations;* the poorer were much more gloomy than the richer,
both about their own and about Britain's economic prospects. In essence, the
relatively rich expected to get relatively richer in the year following our
interview, while the poor did not: indeed, one half of them expected to get
poorer.

Although at national level the majority of people were critical of both
unions and management, when they were asked about their own workplace they
were much less critical. At that level, well over half of workers in establishments
where there were unions thought that union-management relations were very
good or good. An even higher proportion thought that their workplace was well
managed. The minorities who were very critical both of management and unions
were scarcely large enough to give the Government a mandate for major union
reform, or at least not on the basis of local perceptions.

More surprisingly, perhaps, a large majority of our sample regarded the
existing structure of income tax as insufficiently progressive. On balance, both
higher and lower income groups believed that more redistributive taxation
policies were called for.

Probably the most striking difference to emerge from our data was between
the expectations of those in work and those who were unemployed. In some
respects the two groups appeared to inhabit quite distinct labour markets.
Among the working population, for example, not only were over 80% confident

or fairly confident that jobs were secure, but over 60% believed that their wages or salaries would continue to rise by the same or more than the cost of living; and nearly 70% expected their own workplace to maintain or increase its number of employees. Contrast these findings with the expectation by 85% of the total sample that unemployment would stay the same or rise in the coming year. Contrast them too with the expectations of the unemployed about their own prospects of finding work: no more than one in twenty were very confident of their own ability to find a job 'to match their qualifications'; fewer than one in five believed they would find work within two months. Yet the great majority of the unemployed (94%) would still want a job, even if they were to be given a reasonable living income while unemployed. Their prospects, by their own reckoning, were stark indeed.

So, at the time of our survey, economic issues were clearly very much in people's minds. Polls taken in early 1983 confirmed this. The rate of unemployment and the total numbers unemployed were both, as far as the postwar period was concerned, at record levels. On the other hand, the inflation rate was down to a level not seen since the early 1960s. In the run-up to the general election, Conservative ministers continue to argue – as they had done for a number of years – that they needed more time: there were no quick or easy solutions to British economic recovery.

Important though this national debate may have been to the individual, his or her own economic prospects were probably of more immediate significance. The questions we selected were not only those that would measure attitudes in 1983 but those that would also, we felt, bear repetition in 1984 and beyond to give us a picture of change – or lack of it – over a number of years.

We started with a series of questions on people's expectations about the British economic condition, went on to ask about alternative explanations of and possible solutions to economic problems, and finally addressed the individual economic circumstances of different types of respondent. This report starts with our findings on expectations about unemployment and inflation and refers to differing levels of optimism and pessimism among people in different economic circumstances. It then goes on to look at broader economic policy issues.

Economic expectations

Unemployment and inflation

Although the recession had not yet abated in early 1983, the CBI had begun to see prospects of an upturn; but even they did not suggest that the upturn had actually arrived. The Government still had to rely on the assertion that it was getting the conditions right, not that it had actually achieved the results. This was a subtle argument and we wanted to examine whether it had got across to the electorate. Were people expecting things to get better or worse? Did they regard the relatively low inflation level as a stable condition? Did they believe that unemployment would soon peak as the long-awaited recovery began to take effect?

With the Government itself unwilling to commit itself to particular figures, it was scarcely realistic to expect the public to do so. We therefore asked a more impressionistic question about both inflation and unemployment: by how much (a lot or a little) did people expect prices and unemployment to have risen or fallen in a year from now? A five-point scale, which included a 'no change' option, was read out to all respondents.

A large majority of the sample (80% and 68% respectively) expected prices and unemployment to rise over the year. 58% of the sample believed that both would rise. The total distributions were as follows:

	Prices in a year from now	Unemployment in a year from now
Will have :	%	%
gone up by a lot	24	31
gone up by a little	56	37
stayed the same	12	17
gone down by a little	5	12
gone down by a lot	1	1
Don't know	2	2

These findings are scarcely surprising given British experience over the last few years. It would have been interesting to have monitored answers to these questions over, say, the last ten years or so: a major increase in public gloominess (or realism?) has almost certainly taken hold. What is indisputable now is that there is widespread public acceptance of inflation and high unemployment as relatively stable factors in Britain's economic condition.

The sizes of subgroup differences in expectations are much more remarkable, particularly when we confine our attention to those believing that prices and unemployment will go up by *a lot*. The following summary figures show the contrasts. (See **Table 3.1** at the end of this chapter for more details.)

		Prices will rise a lot	Unemployment will rise a lot
Total sample	%	24	31
High household income (£10,000 pa +)	%	13	24
Middle household income (£5,000-£10,000 pa)	%	24	34
Low household income (−£5,000 pa)	%	35	35
White collar (non-manual)	%	16	27
Blue collar (manual)	%	29	33
Conservative identifiers	%	11	14
Alliance identifiers	%	25	35
Labour identifiers	%	34	45
Non-aligned	%	40	42

On the whole, all subgroups were gloomier about unemployment than about inflation. What is striking, however, is the clear relationship between pessimism about both and income, class and politics (obviously associated variables). The poorer that one's own economic circumstances are, the gloomier are one's expectations about both unemployment and inflation. Clearly people on lower or fixed incomes are more likely to find inflation (particularly) and unemployment very threatening; nonetheless, the size of difference between the subgroups is greater than might have been expected and probably reflects experience as well as anxiety. Inflation has affected some groups more than others over the past few years and it is obvious that our question was capturing this experience at least as much as it was eliciting 'objective' forecasts.

There were other interesting subgroup differences in the answers. In particular, women were gloomier than men about the likelihood of large price rises. And the unemployed were notably more pessimistic than the employed about the likelihood of further unemployment, as the figures below show:

	Unemployment will rise a lot
Self-employed	19%
Employees	32%
Unemployed	46%

These findings all relate to expectations about the economy at large. More important, perhaps, how did people view their own prospects over the following year? We asked people in employment how confident they were about pay rises and job prospects at their place of work. And we asked the unemployed about their prospects of finding a job. The answers show a remarkable disparity between the way in which the working population and those seeking to (re) enter it differ in their perceptions of what the future holds. They also show a striking difference *within* the working population between the relatively well off and the relatively poor. In other words, individual expectations split in broadly the same way as expectations about the economy at large.

The following summary table shows the expectations of employees (see **Table 3.2** for details). Optimism about keeping up with inflation increases with income and class; membership of a trade union has little effect on pay expectations; public sector employees are notably more pessimistic about their pay expectations than are private sector employees. The findings can be interpreted in two ways. On the one hand, given the state of the economy, the level of unemployment and the generally poor forecasts of growth, they reveal a remarkably optimistic working population, particularly among the higher paid. On the other hand, about a third of the employees, and more among the lower paid, were expecting their real incomes to fall behind prices during the following year. Moreover, in answer to another question, a further minority (12% of the low household income group, 5% of the rest) were expecting to lose their jobs through redundancy or firm closure during the year following our interview. So one might conclude that the findings hardly suggest a very sanguine or buoyant working population.

Real income will:

		Keep up or rise	Not keep up
Total sample	%	60	36
High household income (£10,000 pa +)	%	67	31
Middle household income (£5,000-£10,000 pa)	%	59	39
Low household income (−£5,000 pa)	%	45	44
White collar (non-manual)	%	65	33
Blue collar (manual)	%	55	40
Private sector employees	%	63	33
Public sector	%	54	43

Nonetheless, when we asked about expectations in respect of staffing levels at the respondent's workplace over the following year, over half of the employees (54%) were expecting staff numbers to remain stable, and a further 16% were expecting them to rise. Again, given our earlier finding that around the same proportion of the population (68%) believed that unemployment would continue to rise during that period, this finding suggests a degree of complacency among the working population that was not mirrored in the sample's forecasts about the economy in general.

Employees in different sectors of the economy show a remarkable awareness of likely trends within their sector. Thus, those in service and distributive sectors were optimistic about stability or expansion, those in manufacturing less so, and those in the public sector still less, as the following figures show. They underline the importance that should be attached to 'sectoral location' as a determinant of attitudes (Dunleavy, 1980).

Number of staff at workplace

		Will increase or stay the same	Will reduce
Total	%	70	29
Private sector: service and distributive	%	81	16
Private sector: manufacturing	%	65	34
Public sector	%	58	41

Interpretation of regional differences in response are impeded not only by associations of region with class, but also by the existence of relatively small, clustered samples within some regions. So we refer to regional differences only in one or two cases where differences are large. Even so, they should be interpreted cautiously. The summary figures below show the proportion of 'optimists' in various grouped regions — that is the minority of employees who believed that their own standard of living would rise in the coming year, or that their workplace would *increase* its staff. The pattern suggests, broadly, that proximity to London is associated with optimism on both fronts.

		My income will rise by more than prices in the coming year	My workplace will increase staff in coming year
Total	%	15	16
Wales and South West	%	6	10
Scotland	%	9	11
Northern England	%	10	13
Midlands	%	16	18
London and South East	%	22	19

Having asked employees to predict their wage or salary increases and workplace staffing levels, we then went on to present them with a hypothetical question:

Suppose you were made redundant or your firm closed down, would you start looking for another job, would you wait for several months or longer before you started looking, or would you decide not to look for another job?

A large majority of employees (84%) said they would start looking for a replacement job without delay. How long in these circumstances, we asked, did they think it would take to find 'an acceptable replacement job'? We list the grouped answers below alongside the answers of the *unemployed* to a similar (in their case not a hypothetical) question. We asked them:

Although it may be difficult to judge, how long from now do you think it will be before you find an acceptable job?

	Employees	Unemployed
	%	%
2 months or less	34	19
3 - 6 months	26	21
7 - 12 months	10	15
Over a year	3	15

In both cases, a large proportion of respondents (more than a third in the case of the unemployed) would not even attempt a prediction. The answers from the remainder suggest that employees are a great deal more sanguine about the availability of alternative jobs than are the unemployed. Indeed, the discrepancy in these forecasts is even greater than it may at first appear when the question wording is taken into account, since the unemployed were being asked to make their estimate *from now,* and many of them (see overleaf) had already been out of work for some time. An interesting sidelight on these contrasts is that those employees (13%) who had themselves experienced at least three months of unemployment in the last five years, were no less optimistic than their counterparts about the speed at which they would reinstate themselves after a job loss.

As far as the unemployed are concerned, we have already shown that they are more pessimistic than employees both about economic prospects in general and about their chances of finding jobs. But their representation in our sample was small and we cannot therefore make too much of their answers. We merely describe their characteristics as a group below.

87% of them were *registered* as unemployed at a benefit office

39% had been unemployed for six months or less at the time of the interview, 25% for 7 to 12 months, and a further 35% for more than a year.

72% of them were male

50% of them were under the age of 35

70% of them were either not very or not at all confident about their prospects of finding 'a job to match their qualifications'. Only 5% were 'very confident'.

We asked them all the following question about their work orientation:

If you received what you would regard as a reasonable living income while unemployed, do you think you would still prefer to get a job or wouldn't you bother?

As many as 94% said that a job would still be preferable. Only among *women* nearing retirement age was there likely to be less insistence on a job in preference to a living income (78%). So if there has ever been a widespread desire among the unemployed to give up looking for work, it is not apparent in the responses we obtained. On the contrary, in answer to further questions — asked only of those who thought they were unlikely to find work within 3 months — 83% said they would be willing to retrain if necessary, and 57% that they would be willing to take an 'unacceptable' job. But only a minority (37%) would be willing to move home in order to find a job. The resistance to mobility in the labour market *apparently* remains strong, though the number in our sample from which to draw any firm conclusion on this subject is much too small.

We also looked at the income expectations of pensioners.

Do you expect your state pension in a year's time to purchase more than it does now, less, or about the same?

Only 5% of pensioners expected real state pensions to increase in value, while a further 35% expected them to remain stable. As many as 45% expected a decrease in real terms, a greater degree of pessimism than that displayed by the working population about their wages or salaries (36% of whom believed wages would not keep up with prices).

Industrial performance

The Government came to office pledged to reduce taxes and public spending. It managed to achieve something else entirely; taxes rose as a proportion of income from 1979-1983, because public spending obstinately failed to come down. The underlying reason was simple. The economy was declining, not growing, so a given level of public spending had to be financed out of a smaller cake. Whether or not the Government could achieve these aims turned on whether the economy would start to grow again, pulling unemployment down (and with it unemployment pay) and pushing tax revenue up. The Government in other words had got itself into a vicious circle of decline: an expanding economy would put it on a virtuous circle. Nonetheless, only 5% of our sample thought industrial performance would improve a lot during the year following the interview, though nearly 40% thought it would improve to some extent. As the following table shows, Conservative identifiers showed themselves to be considerably more optimistic than identifiers with other parties.

	Total	Conservative identifiers	Alliance identifiers	Labour identifiers
	%	%	%	%
Improve a lot	5	8	1	3
Improve a little	39	56	37	29
Stay the same	34	25	44	37
Decline a little	13	6	11	19
Decline a lot	4	2	2	6

Expectations about short term industrial performance do not vary much according to trade union membership, but upper income groups, higher social classes and the self-employed are more likely to be optimistic and, as always, the unemployed are more likely to be pessimistic (see **Table 3.3**). In addition, people living in London and the West Midlands are more optimistic than people living in other regions.

Individual economic circumstances

Income levels

We asked all respondents aged 23 or over to compare their financial position nowadays with that of five years ago. Did they feel they were better off financially now, about the same, or worse off than they were five years ago? The question was, of course, designed only to elicit *feelings* about each respondent's financial position, not to measure real changes.

The findings reveal the same general pattern that we derived in respect of economic expectations. The relatively rich tend to feel they have got richer, while the opposite is true for the poor, as the following summary table demonstrates.

Financial position compared with 5 years ago

	Current income			
	Under £5,000 pa	Between £5,000 and £10,000 pa	Between £10,000 and £15,000 pa	Over £15,000 pa
	%	%	%	%
Better off now	19	35	44	58
About the same	28	24	28	23
Worse off now	52	41	28	19

The low income groups contain most of the unemployed and the pensioners in our sample. So, if we look at the results by employment status, the pattern is partially explained.

	Total	In paid work	Seeking work	Pensioners
	%	%	%	%
Better off now	32	38	19	22
About the same	27	26	13	35
Worse off now	40	37	67	43

As before, membership of a union does not seem to be an important factor in determining the distribution of answers. Nor, in this case, was there much difference between employees and the self-employed. When we asked the latter how their businesses had been doing in the past year (and the past five years), the answers did not, on the whole reflect the fact that they had been living through a recession. Only around one in eight reported a deterioration during the last year and a similar proportion in the last five years. As many as one in three reported an improvement.

We asked further questions of employees about their wage or salary levels and of pensioners about their pensions. As might be expected, on the whole, the lower a respondent's income, the more likely he or she is to *describe* it as low, and vice versa. Once again, trade union members are no different from non-members in their assessment of their wages or salaries. The responses of employees about their wage or salary levels, and of pensioners about their state pension levels, are shown below. They reveal a considerably greater degree of dissatisfaction among pensioners than among those in work about their incomes. Given the fact that the old are, in general, less likely than their younger counterparts to express dissatisfaction in surveys, the differences are striking indeed.

	Employees	Pensioners
	%	%
Very low	13	25
A bit low	28	46
Reasonable	54	28
On the high side	5	*

Management and unions

In our self-completion questionnaire we asked two general questions about unions, as follows:

> *How much influence would you say that trade unions have on the lives of people in Britain these days?*

> *Do you think they have too much influence, about the right amount, or too little influence?*

In answer to the first question, more than two-thirds of the sample thought that unions had a great deal or quite a bit of influence, the remainder saying 'some influence', but hardly anyone saying 'not much'. That broad distribution of answers seems to exist among all groups in the population more or less equally. Manual workers are on the whole, as likely as non-manual workers to express that view, union members are as likely to express it as non-union members are, and so on.

Differences begin to emerge, however, in response to the second question. For instance, Scottish and Welsh respondents were less anti-trade union than were English respondents and, in particular, than those in the South of England (excluding London).

	Total	Scotland/ Wales	North/ Midlands	GLC	South East/ South West
	%	%	%	%	%
Trade unions have:					
too much influence	59	49	57	57	67
about the right amount	34	40	35	34	28
too little influence	5	10	5	5	2

Similar overall results have been obtained regularly in the British Election Studies (see Sarlvik and Crewe, 1983). As expected also, the higher one's social class, the more likely one is to believe that unions have too much influence. But on this question, at last, membership of a union – but not past membership – does distinguish between respondents. Current union members split almost evenly as to whether unions have too much influence (48%) or about the right amount (44%). Even among these union members, however, very few people can be found to support the proposition that unions have too little influence.

On the basis of these answers it can be seen that unions seem to have a poor image, even among a fairly high proportion of their own members. But we also asked specifically about people's trade unions at their place of work, and here the image seems better. Among those who worked in establishments with recognised unions (around two-thirds of the *employees* in our sample), 58% said they did their job well. Moreover, in answer to a further question asked of all employees, as many as 84% considered union-management relations at their workplace to be very good or quite good. A similar proportion (80%) thought, in general, that their workplace was well managed.

The overall impression that people seem to have of trade unions is *not* therefore borne out by people's own experience (or at least not by current experience). The image of overbearing union influence seems to co-exist with a fairly positive evaluation of the work that one's own trade union actually does. Nonetheless, when the two sets of answers are analysed by each other, there is a weak association. A positive evaluation of one's own union is associated with a *less* hostile attitude to trade union influence generally. Among people who are satisfied with their own unions, a majority (52%) believe that trade unions in general have either the right amount or too little influence.

All these questions are scheduled for repetition in future rounds of the series so that changes in attitudes can be measured. For a full treatment of how workplace industrial relations operate in practie, see Daniel and Millward (1983).

Causes of economic problems

In 1983 there could be few who thought the economy was doing well. Government and opposition, industry and unions were agreed on that. Where they differed was on the reason and the remedies.

We look first at the factors people thought important in explaining the reasons for Britain's economic problems. At the political level, the debate was polarised between the Government's argument that the international situation hampered the efforts of the UK to expand, and the opposition's argument that we could take unilateral action and pull ourselves out of the recession.

Naturally, the notion that one factor or even one set of factors was responsible for economic problems is scarcely tenable. For that reason we presented respondents with a number of statements about the possible causes of Britain's economic difficulties and asked them, for each that they considered to be true, how important a factor it had been. One-quarter of the sample thought that all or nearly all (8-10) of the factors given had some importance, and almost two-thirds thought that between 4 and 7 factors were important.

The findings for this series of questions are set out in **Tables 3.4 − 3.7** at the end of this chapter.

Causes of economic problems

	Not true	True and important
	%	%
Decline in world trade	10	82
Energy costs are too high for industry	11	80
British workers reluctant to accept new ways of working	22	69
The Government has not done enough to create jobs	26	67
British industry is badly managed	26	64
Employers are not investing enough	27	63
People are not working hard enough	37	60
Manufacturing industry is not attractive to the best school and college leavers	34	45
Government spending has been too high	45	45
Wages are too high	64	30

The Government's stress on the importance of world trading conditions seems to have impressed a considerable proportion of the public. Of the 82% who consider it to be an important cause of economic difficulties the majority consider it to be very important. This belief is equally likely to be held regardless of social class or party identity. Similarly, the belief that high energy costs are a cause of our present economic difficulties is shared more or less equally by all class and party groupings.

The view that conservatism on the part of British workers in respect of new ways of working is an important factor, is more likely to be held among those in the non-manual than in the manual social classes – though the differences are not particularly marked; even among those in Social Classes IV or V, over 60% consider it to be an important cause of Britain's economic difficulties. There are also differences by party identification: 80% of Conservative identifiers consider this factor to be important, compared with 66% of Alliance identifiers and 60% of Labour identifiers. The self-employed are more likely than others to support this view, but non-members of trade unions are no more likely than members to do so.

The favourite old whipping horse represented in this survey by the statement that 'people are not working hard enough' still attracts strong support. The differences between subgroups on this statement were much the same as those outlined in the paragraph above.

Two of the causes of economic difficulties offered for consideration referred specifically to government action or inaction. Whereas the Conservatives had argued steadfastly that public spending had to be cut in order to release resources for the private sector, the public does not seem wholly to have been persuaded that high public spending has been a *cause* of Britain's economic difficulties in the first place. Less than half of the sample and a similar proportion of Conservative identifiers supported this view.

There were much sharper differences, however, between people with different party identities in respect of the Government's role in creating jobs. Over three-quarters of Labour and Alliance identifiers, but only around one-half of Conservative identifiers, believed that an important cause of our economic difficulties was that the Government had not done enough to create jobs. As will be seen, this omission on the Government's part was not only regarded as an important one, but also one that merited a change in policy.

The remaining possible causes of economic difficulties that we offered referred to the role of British industry. Just over 60% of the population believe that low investment in industry has been important in creating economic problems, and a similar proportion that bad management has been an important factor. Once again, no marked divisions by subgroups are apparent. Conservative identifiers are, however, more likely than others to attribute economic difficulties to high wages, and *much* more likely than others to attribute problems to the inability of industry to attract the best school and college leavers. The following summary figures illustrate the differences.

	Manufacturing industry not attractive to recruits		Wages are too high	
	Not true	True and important	Not true	True and important
	%	%	%	%
Conservative identifiers	28	53	50	44
Alliance identifiers	36	41	67	29
Labour identifiers	39	42	77	19
Non-aligned	37	38	68	23

Economic policies

Wages and prices

For nearly all of the postwar period governments have struggled to find an answer to the problem of combining full employment with stable prices. Both Conservative and Labour governments have declared themselves against income policies and then adopted them. Prices, on the other hand, have not been controlled on a comprehensive basis since the end of the war, though there has been selective action on nationalised industry prices and, during the 1960s, on other prices too through the Prices and Incomes Board.

The Government had put both the control of wages and the control of prices firmly *off* the agenda. Opposition from the Labour Party was muted, partly because the unions had also come out clearly against wage controls. Instead the issue had been wrapped up in the so-called national economic assessment, within which a hidden incomes policy could be found if one was looking for it, and overlooked if one was not.

Our sample reflects these uncertainties about policy: 48% of the population are for and 48% against statutory control over wages. Attitudes varied little with economic position, with social class, or even with party identification. (see **Table 3.8.**) Price controls, however, proved more popular, with 70% favouring them. Support varies according to social class. 60% of those in non-manual occupations, compared with 75% of those in manual occupations, believe that prices should be controlled by legislation. Labour identifiers are more likely to be in favour (78%) of price control than those who identify with other parties. However, even among Conservative identifiers, two-thirds are in favour of price control. The self-employed (51%) are less likely to be in favour than employees or the unemployed.

The choice between the relative emphasis to be placed on counteracting unemployment or inflation is at the heart of the division between the parties on economic policy. We asked a question in terms of government priorities.

If the government had to choose between keeping down inflation or keeping down unemployment, to which do you think it should give the highest priority?

Priorities: inflation v unemployment

	Total	Conservative		Alliance	Labour	Non-aligned
		Total	Partisans			
	%	%	%	%	%	%
Inflation	27	44	50	19	13	21
Unemployment	69	52	45	78	85	73
Can't separate	1	2	2	2	1	2
Other answer	2	2	3	1	2	4

As the table above shows, a strong vote is given in favour of reducing unemployment rather than inflation, if a choice has to be made. There are, however, sharp divisions between members of different parties and social class groups. In fact the difference on this issue between Conservative identifiers and other party identifiers is among the sharpest revealed by the survey. We show Conservative *partisans* separately, because they were the only group among whom a majority was found to be in favour of placing more emphasis on inflation than on employment. The class breakdowns are shown below.

	Social Class			
	I/II	III (non-manual)	III (manual)	IV/V
	%	%	%	%
Inflation	38	26	29	18
Unemployment	57	73	68	79
Can't separate	3	1	1	1
Other answer	2	1	2	2

Policies for economic recovery

If wages and price control were not at the centre of political debate in early 1983, policies for economic recovery certainly were. The Government's policy was one that would in the past have seemed both uncompromising and fundamentalist. They were in favour of 'getting the basic conditions right', and letting the people, in particular workers and managers, do the rest. The opposition parties on the other hand, argued that this policy would simply make things worse: what was needed was a sizeable stimulus to the economy.

Experts too were divided. Some followed traditional Keynesian policies and advocated an increase in government spending to bring about at least some degree of economic recovery. Others broadly supported the Government's policies. There were also groups, such as the Department of Applied Economics at Cambridge, that proposed *import controls,* and this policy was publicly supported by unions in textiles and other industries that were feeling the effect of cheap imported competition.

We did not attempt to force our respondents into any one school of thought. Instead we offered them a series of specific policy measures, including those of wages and price controls, the responses to which we have described above. The sample's policy positions bring little support for the view that the Government has won the economic arguments. (See **Tables 3.8** and **3.9**.)

The most popular policy (with 89% support) was the classic Keynesian solution to widespread unemployment – the setting up of construction projects by the Government to create jobs – a policy that the Government itself had clearly rejected. Next in popular support – again at variance with Government policy – came import controls with 72% support and, surprisingly perhaps, with strong endorsement from among all social classes, economic groups, and political parties.

We have already seen that the Government's claim that public spending reductions are a pre-condition of economic recovery is not widely accepted. We included in our list of policy options two specific possible cuts – spending on defence, and spending on health and education.

Consistently with other findings in this survey, the latter opinion was rejected almost unanimously with only 13% support. Cuts in defence spending were, however, supported by 44% of the population, and among all social classes more or less equally. Less than one-third of Conservative identifiers support such a cut, compared with over half of Labour and Alliance identifiers.

A scheme that the Government has been prepared to promote (though not yet with much success), and which receives support, is 'job sharing'. 61% of the population, with very little difference between social classes or political parties, endorse it as a policy.

The remaining two policy options we offered were increasing Government subsidies to industry and devaluation of the pound, which the Labour Party had been proposing. About two-thirds of the population are in favour of subsidies, again with class, party identity, trade union membership and economic position making little difference to the answers. Devaluation was rejected by a sizeable majority (71%), and by all subgroups more or less equally.

In summary, it seems that the Government's economic policies during the period 1979-1983 commanded little public support at the end of their term of office. Ironically, in the light of the result of the general election, it was the Labour Party that was proposing a good number of policies that had substantial support.

State ownership

Although overall management of the economy was perhaps the most prominent economic issue, the Government was also anxious to claim that it was altering the structure of the economy. 'Rolling back the frontiers of the public sector' had been a slogan during the previous four years. This meant not only a reduction in the Government's direct role in the economy — its ownership of particular industries — but also a reduction in its indirect role, that is the degree to which it intervened in industry. The main chosen instrument for intervention, the National Enterprise Board (now the British Technology Group) and such state-owned public companies as British Leyland and Rolls Royce, were all on a list of assets to be sold off along with many nationalised industries. Although earlier governments had experimented with hiving off, this was the first time that such a sustained attack on the public sector had been launched. We asked:

> On the whole would you like to see more or less state ownership of industry, or about the same amount as now?

49% of the sample thought that state ownership should be reduced with only 11% wanting more of it. But this overall figure disguises quite sharp differences according to party identification.

As the table opposite shows, Alliance identifiers are much closer to Conservative than to Labour identifiers on this issue. Not surprisingly, support for more state ownership is virtually non-existent among the self-employed and is more prevalent among the manual social classes than among the non-manual classes. The differences, however, are small, and though there are sizeable proportions in favour of leaving things as they are, only small minorities want an increase in public ownership. A very similar pattern of answers emerged in response to a question we asked about state intervention in industry. Only 11% wanted to see greater government controls over industry.

Attitudes to state ownership:

Party identification

	Total	Conservative	Alliance	Labour	Non-aligned
	%	%	%	%	%
Should be:					
More	11	5	4	22	8
Less	49	68	55	25	43
Same	33	23	34	46	33
Don't know	7	4	7	7	14

Income distribution

The Goverment had come to office promising lower taxes 'to provide incentives'. Although it did not manage to do so, because of the increasing burden of public spending, it did restructure the incidence of taxes and of benefits in a way that redistributed income in favour of the better off. Perhaps the most significant redistribution that had been taking place in the period since 1979 was between the employed and the unemployed. Despite high levels of unemployment, the earnings of those in jobs were still being pushed up, in many cases faster than the rate of inflation, while the unemployed were barely keeping pace. How then did our sample view the tax system and the distribution of incomes underlying it?

Thinking of income levels in Britain today would you say that the gap between those with high incomes and those with low incomes is too large, about right, or too small?

	Total
	%
Too large	72
About right	22
Too small	3
Don't know	2

By more than a three to one majority the public thinks that the gap between high and low incomes is too large. Predictably those in the non-manual social classes and those with high household incomes are less likely to describe the gap as too large. Nonetheless, even among those in Social Class I/II and among those with a household income of £5,000 or more, over half think that the gap is too large.

Against this background, we moved on to examine people's attitudes to how the Government's current system of taxation affects families of differing income levels. As can be seen from the table overleaf the slogan that 'British taxes are too high' is not accepted as widely as might have been expected. Certainly there is a majority view in all parties that taxes for the *lower paid* are too high, but that is an altogether different proposition from the one implied by the slogan. For the rest, there is no strong move for reducing taxes, even among Conservative identifiers.

Generally how would you describe levels of taxation in Britain today. Firstly for those with high incomes? For those with middle incomes? For those with low incomes? Please choose a phrase from this card.

		Party identification		
	Total	Conservative	Alliance	Labour
	%	%	%	%
Tax on high incomes:				
(Much) too high	29	36	23	22
About right	36	43	38	32
(Much) too low	32	19	37	44
Tax on middle incomes:				
(Much) too high	44	49	40	38
About right	50	47	56	53
(Much) too low	4	2	2	8
Tax on low incomes:				
(Much) too high	79	74	84	83
About right	16	23	12	11
(Much) too low	3	2	4	4

The striking feature of the distribution above is not only that Conservative identifiers display redistributive attitudes, though less so than Labour or Alliance identifiers, but that Alliance and Labour identifiers are, on the whole, very close to each other in their views on this issue.

References

DANIEL, W. W. and MILLWARD, N., *Workplace Industrial Relations in Britain,* Heinemann Educational Books, London (1983).
DUNLEAVY, P., 'The Political Implications of Sectoral Cleavages and the Growth of State Employment', *Political Studies 28,* 1980.
SARLVIK, B. and CREWE, I., *Decade of Dealignment,* Cambridge University Press, Cambridge (1983).

Acknowledgements

Thanks are due to Catherine Hakim and Neil Millward for their valuable advice on the employment related questions.

3.1 LEVELS OF INFLATION (Q.18) AND UNEMPLOYMENT (Q.19) IN A YEAR'S TIME
by sex, social class, gross household income and economic position

	TOTAL	SEX		SOCIAL CLASS						GROSS HOUSEHOLD INCOME					ECONOMIC POSITION					
		Male	Female	I/II	III non-manual	III manual	IV/V	Looks after home	Other	Under £5000 pa	£5,000-£7,999 pa	£8,000-£11,999 pa	£12,000+ pa	No information	Employed	Self-employed	Unemployed	Looks after home	Retired	Other
	%	%	%	%	%	%	%	%	%	%	%	%	%	%	%	%	%	%	%	%
Expect INFLATION to have:																				
Gone up by a lot	24	20	28	12	20	22	36	30	29	35	25	18	13	22	21	13	33	30	27	29
Gone up by a little	56	61	51	68	60	58	44	49	53	45	58	63	67	54	61	62	54	49	48	57
Stayed the same	12	12	13	13	12	13	11	13	6	11	11	14	14	12	12	20	10	13	12	7
Gone down by a little	5	4	5	4	6	4	5	4	5	5	5	3	4	7	4	4	4	4	8	2
Gone down by a lot	1	*	1	1	1	*	1	1	3	1	*	1	1	-	*	-	-	1	*	4
Don't know	2	1	3	1	1	2	3	3	3	2	1	2	1	5	1	2	-	3	5	1
Not answered	*	*	*	*	*	-	-	*	-	*	-	*	-	-	-	-	-	*	*	-
Expect EMPLOYMENT to have:																				
Gone up by a lot	31	29	33	22	32	29	37	34	38	35	35	30	22	28	32	19	46	34	21	40
Gone up by a little	37	39	35	41	34	40	31	36	33	32	34	44	43	34	38	45	30	36	34	31
Stayed the same	17	20	15	21	20	17	16	13	14	14	18	17	22	19	18	23	16	13	18	15
Gone down by a little	12	11	13	14	11	13	13	11	10	15	11	8	12	15	11	11	8	11	23	10
Gone down by a lot	1	1	1	*	-	1	1	1	3	2	1	1	*	1	*	-	-	1	2	5
Don't know	2	1	2	1	1	1	1	4	2	2	1	1	1	4	*	1	-	4	3	1
Not answered	*	*	-	*	-	-	-	-	-	-	-	-	*	-	1	1	1	-	-	-
BASE: ALL RESPONDENTS																				
Weighted	1719	793	926	334	268	365	300	346	106	544	371	307	299	199	803	104	119	346	263	84
Unweighted	1761	807	954	343	281	362	316	353	106	578	378	310	294	201	817	109	127	353	272	83

For notes on breakdowns, symbols and tabulations, refer to Appendices I and II.

3.2 EMPLOYEE'S EXPECTATIONS FOR THE COMING YEAR (Q.32a,b)
by social class, standard industrial classification (SIC 1980,)
gross household income and trade union membership

	TOTAL	SOCIAL CLASS†				S.I.C. (1980)†			GROSS HOUSEHOLD INCOME					TRADE UNION MEMBERSHIP†			
		I/II	III non-manual	III manual	IV/V	Public sector	Private Sector Non-manuf.	Private Sector Manuf.	Under £5,000 p.a.	£5,000-£7,999 p.a.	£8,000-£11,999 p.a.	£12,000+ p.a.	No information	Non-manual Current or past	Non-manual Never	Manual Current or past	Manual Never
	%	%	%	%	%	%	%	%	%	%	%	%	%	%	%	%	%
Expect WAGES or SALARY to rise by:																	
More than cost of living	15	21	16	14	7	11	16	16	10	8	14	23	14	15	26	12	8
Same as cost of living	46	42	52	44	45	43	48	46	35	48	47	48	46	50	41	46	39
Less than cost of living	27	28	21	28	32	34	21	27	31	29	30	22	22	27	19	28	38
Not rise at all	9	8	8	10	10	9	10	7	14	14	7	4	12	7	10	10	12
Will not stay in job	2	*	1	3	3	2	2	2	7	-	2	1	3	1	2	4	1
Don't know	2	1	2	*	2	*	2	1	2	2	1	1	4	1	3	1	3
Expect NUMBER of EMPLOYEES at workplace to be:																	
Increased	16	17	17	17	9	10	18	17	15	14	12	21	15	15	21	13	15
Reduced	29	28	22	30	37	41	16	34	23	33	37	26	13	30	15	39	15
Stay about the same	54	54	60	52	49	48	63	47	60	52	51	51	67	55	62	45	69
Other answer	1	-	*	1	2	*	1	2	2	1	-	1	3	*	-	2	-
Don't know	1	-	1	*	2	*	2	-	1	1	*	-	3	-	2	1	-
Not answered	*	1	-	-	1	*	*	*	-	-	*	1	-	*	1	*	-
BASE: ALL EMPLOYEES																	
Weighted	803	212	205	201	176	226	312	240	99	194	213	218	78	282	132	290	85
Unweighted	817	220	210	196	183	237	315	241	109	203	212	215	78	289	138	292	86

3.3 EXPECTATIONS FOR INDUSTRIAL PERFORMANCE OVER NEXT YEAR (Q.21)
by social class, gross household income and economic position

	TOTAL	SOCIAL CLASS						GROSS HOUSEHOLD INCOME					ECONOMIC POSITION					
		I/II	III non-manual	III manual	IV/V	Looks after home	Other	Under £5000 pa	£5,000-£7,999 pa	£6,000-£11,999 pa	£12,000+ pa	No information	Employed	Self-employed	Unemployed	Looks after home	Retired	Other
	%	%	%	%	%	%	%	%	%	%	%	%	%	%	%	%	%	%
Improve a lot	5	6	4	6	5	4	2	4	6	5	4	6	6	6	2	4	4	5
Improve a little	39	51	41	40	34	30	40	35	38	43	52	30	41	54	32	30	45	39
Stay much the same	34	30	33	35	34	37	31	33	34	36	31	35	36	24	31	37	28	35
Decline a little	13	8	14	13	14	14	17	15	13	11	9	13	12	11	20	14	10	18
Decline a lot	4	2	4	3	5	5	8	6	4	2	2	4	3	1	12	5	3	4
Don't know	5	3	4	3	8	10	3	7	4	3	2	13	3	5	4	10	10	1
BASE: ALL RESPONDENTS																		
Weighted	1719	334	268	365	300	346	106	544	371	307	299	199	803	104	119	346	263	84
Unweighted	1761	343	281	362	316	353	106	578	378	310	294	201	817	109	127	353	272	83

3.4 CAUSES OF ECONOMIC DIFFICULTIES (Q.22i to iii)
by social class, party identification and trade union membership

	TOTAL	SOCIAL CLASS						PARTY IDENTIFICATION†				TRADE UNION MEMBERSHIP			
		I/II	III non-manual	III manual	IV/V	Looks after home	Other	Cons.	Alliance	Labour	Non-aligned	Current	In past but not now	Never	No information
	%	%	%	%	%	%	%	%	%	%	%	%	%	%	%
PEOPLE ARE NOT WORKING HARD ENOUGH															
Very important	36	37	38	39	32	39	27	46	37	27	29	31	39	38	35
Quite important	24	27	22	23	20	28	19	27	24	20	22	23	23	24	29
Not very/not at all important	2	1	1	2	3	2	2	2	2	2	2	1	2	2	2
Not a cause	37	35	37	35	44	29	50	23	37	49	46	44	34	35	30
Don't know/not answered	2	1	2	1	2	2	1	2	*	2	1	1	1	2	4
EMPLOYERS ARE NOT INVESTING ENOUGH															
Very important	34	39	30	40	34	24	36	32	33	39	25	41	37	28	24
Quite important	29	31	30	29	27	28	32	30	31	28	25	30	27	30	30
Not very/not at all important	2	1	2	2	2	3	2	3	2	1	2	2	2	2	4
Not a cause	27	25	30	24	23	33	26	27	30	24	29	21	28	29	28
Don't know/not answered	8	4	7	5	13	13	4	8	5	7	19	7	5	11	13
THERE HAS BEEN A DECLINE IN WORLD TRADE															
Very important	50	60	50	53	42	46	49	57	47	47	42	51	53	48	49
Quite important	31	27	34	30	34	30	36	30	37	30	31	31	31	31	33
Not very/not at all important	4	4	4	2	4	3	5	3	3	4	3	5	2	3	3
Not a cause	10	7	8	10	12	13	5	6	8	14	15	8	10	11	9
Don't know/not answered	5	2	4	4	8	8	2	4	5	6	9	4	4	6	6
BASE: ALL RESPONDENTS															
Weighted	*1719*	*334*	*268*	*365*	*300*	*346*	*106*	*664*	*252*	*565*	*216*	*463*	*484*	*689*	*83*
Unweighted	*1761*	*343*	*281*	*362*	*316*	*353*	*106*	*676*	*258*	*584*	*221*	*474*	*497*	*707*	*83*

3.5 CAUSES OF ECONOMIC DIFFICULTIES (Q.22iv and v)
by social class, party identification and trade union membership

	TOTAL	SOCIAL CLASS						PARTY IDENTIFICATION†				TRADE UNION MEMBERSHIP			
		I/II	III non-manual	III manual	IV/V	Looks after home	Other	Cons.	Alliance	Labour	Non-aligned	Current	In past but not now	Never	No information
	%	%	%	%	%	%	%	%	%	%	%	%	%	%	%
WAGES ARE TOO HIGH															
Very important	14	13	15	16	9	18	14	21	14	9	10	6	16	18	16
Quite important	16	18	20	13	14	17	14	23	14	11	12	14	15	19	11
Not very/not at all important	2	4	2	8	1	1	5	3	1	2	4	2	2	2	4
Not a cause	64	62	61	67	70	59	65	50	67	77	68	76	63	56	69
Don't know/not answered	3	3	2	2	5	5	3	4	4	5	6	2	4	5	-
ENERGY COSTS ARE TOO HIGH FOR INDUSTRY															
Very important	48	47	41	59	48	45	38	51	40	50	40	49	55	43	39
Quite important	32	31	42	26	30	33	29	31	35	30	33	32	30	32	33
Not very/not at all important	3	4	4	1	3	3	5	4	5	1	3	3	2	4	5
Not a cause	11	14	8	8	10	11	22	10	14	11	13	12	8	12	14
Don't know/not answered	6	4	6	7	9	8	5	5	6	7	1	5	5	8	10
BASE: ALL RESPONDENTS Weighted	*1719*	*334*	*268*	*365*	*300*	*346*	*106*	*684*	*252*	*565*	*216*	*463*	*484*	*689*	*83*
Unweighted	*1761*	*343*	*281*	*362*	*316*	*353*	*106*	*676*	*258*	*584*	*221*	*474*	*497*	*707*	*83*

3.6 CAUSES OF ECONOMIC DIFFICULTIES (Q.22vi to viii)
by social class, party identification and trade union membership

	TOTAL	SOCIAL CLASS						PARTY IDENTIFICATION†				TRADE UNION MEMBERSHIP			
		I/II	III non-manual	III manual	IV/V	Looks after home	Other	Cons.	Alliance	Labour	Non-aligned	Current	In past but not now	Never	No information
	%	%	%	%	%	%	%	%	%	%	%	%	%	%	%
GOVERNMENT SPENDING HAS BEEN TOO HIGH															
Very important	23	21	20	22	31	23	22	21	22	27	23	24	28	21	17
Quite important	21	21	24	20	22	23	15	24	26	17	21	19	20	24	20
Not very/not at all important	4	4	5	2	3	3	7	4	2	3	3	3	3	4	2
Not a cause	45	52	45	49	36	41	52	45	45	46	41	50	44	42	51
Don't know/not answered	6	3	6	7	7	10	5	5	6	6	11	4	5	8	11
BRITISH INDUSTRY IS BADLY MANAGED															
Very important	39	34	35	47	45	32	44	36	36	44	35	44	44	34	33
Quite important	25	26	29	21	28	25	19	25	26	25	24	26	26	23	30
Not very/not at all important	3	3	4	1	2	3	8	2	3	3	4	2	1	4	4
Not a cause	26	33	26	24	20	31	23	30	28	22	27	24	25	30	23
Don't know/not answered	6	4	7	7	5	10	6	6	7	5	9	4	5	8	10
BRITISH WORKERS ARE RELUCTANT TO ACCEPT NEW WAYS OF WORKING															
Very important	37	42	39	40	31	30	45	43	34	31	35	35	40	37	29
Quite important	33	33	32	34	31	35	22	37	32	29	31	34	30	33	39
Not very/not at all important	6	6	7	3	5	5	10	5	7	5	7	6	5	6	5
Not a cause	22	16	18	21	30	23	21	11	23	33	23	24	23	19	21
Don't know/not answered	3	2	3	3	3	6	2	3	4	3	4	2	2	4	6
BASE: ALL RESPONDENTS *Weighted*	1719	334	268	365	300	346	106	664	252	565	216	463	484	689	83
Unweighted	1761	343	281	362	316	353	106	676	258	584	221	474	497	707	83

3.7 CAUSES OF ECONOMIC DIFFICULTIES (Q.22ix and x)
by social class, party identification and trade union membership

	TOTAL	SOCIAL CLASS						PARTY IDENTIFICATION[†]				TRADE UNION MEMBERSHIP			
		I/II	III non-manual	III manual	IV/V	Looks after home	Other	Cons.	Alliance	Labour	Non-aligned	Current	In past but not now	Never	No information
	%	%	%	%	%	%	%	%	%	%	%	%	%	%	%
THE GOVERNMENT HAS NOT DONE ENOUGH TO CREATE JOBS															
Very important	45	35	42	52	53	40	51	28	51	62	42	50	51	37	37
Quite important	22	22	24	22	22	24	19	23	24	20	24	22	21	23	25
Not very/not at all important	4	7	3	3	1	3	3	4	5	2	3	4	4	3	1
Not a cause	26	35	29	20	20	27	24	41	17	13	24	21	22	31	32
Don't know/not answered	4	2	3	4	4	6	2	4	3	2	6	3	1	5	5
THE BEST SCHOOL AND COLLEGE LEAVERS DON'T SEEK JOBS IN MANUFACTURING INDUSTRY															
Very important	19	21	20	21	18	15	17	22	20	17	12	21	23	14	26
Quite important	26	28	26	30	22	25	28	31	21	24	26	28	27	25	22
Not very/not at all important	10	11	11	12	10	7	12	11	11	10	9	10	11	10	11
Not a cause	34	31	32	31	39	38	36	28	36	39	37	31	33	38	29
Don't know/not answered	10	9	10	7	11	14	7	9	11	9	16	10	7	12	12
BASE: ALL RESPONDENTS Weighted	1719	334	268	365	300	346	106	664	252	565	216	463	484	689	83
Unweighted	1761	343	281	362	316	353	106	676	258	584	221	474	497	707	83

3.8 POLICIES TO HELP BRITAIN'S ECONOMIC PROBLEMS (Q.23i to v)
by social class, party identification and trade union membership

	TOTAL	SOCIAL CLASS						PARTY IDENTIFICATION†				TRADE UNION MEMBERSHIP			
		I/II	III non-manual	III manual	IV/V	Looks after home	Other	Cons.	Alliance	Labour	Non-aligned	Current	In past but not now	Never	No information
	%	%	%	%	%	%	%	%	%	%	%	%	%	%	%
Control of WAGES by legislation															
Support	48	41	44	49	48	52	59	47	50	50	42	42	50	50	49
Oppose	48	58	53	48	48	40	36	50	46	47	48	57	45	45	44
Don't know/not answered	4	1	4	3	4	8	5	3	5	3	11	1	5	5	7
Control of PRICES by legislation															
Support	70	57	65	76	74	76	75	66	69	78	66	69	73	69	75
Oppose	27	42	33	22	23	19	21	33	29	20	27	30	25	28	18
Don't know/not answered	3	1	2	1	3	5	4	2	2	2	7	2	2	3	7
Reducing the level of Government spending on health and education															
Support	13	11	12	9	19	15	17	15	6	13	19	11	14	14	11
Oppose	85	88	87	90	80	82	81	84	93	86	77	88	85	83	87
Don't know/not answered	1	1	1	1	1	3	2	1	1	1	4	1	1	2	2
Introducing import controls															
Support	72	63	73	81	73	69	72	72	72	73	67	74	73	70	70
Oppose	24	35	25	17	22	20	25	24	24	23	23	24	24	24	20
Don't know/not answered	5	2	2	2	5	11	3	3	4	4	11	3	3	6	10
Increasing Government subsidies for private industry															
Support	64	62	68	64	61	63	65	68	62	60	63	65	62	64	64
Oppose	31	35	29	31	31	27	32	27	32	35	27	32	34	28	26
Don't know/not answered	6	4	3	5	8	9	4	5	5	5	10	3	4	8	10
BASE: ALL RESPONDENTS															
Weighted	1719	334	268	365	300	346	106	664	252	565	216	463	484	689	83
Unweighted	1761	343	281	362	316	353	106	676	258	584	221	474	497	707	83

3.9 POLICIES TO HELP BRITAIN'S ECONOMIC PROBLEMS (Q.23vi to ix) by social class, party identification and trade union membership

	TOTAL	SOCIAL CLASS						PARTY IDENTIFICATION†				TRADE UNION MEMBERSHIP			
		I/II	III non-manual	III manual	IV/V	Looks after home	Other	Cons.	Alliance	Labour	Non-aligned	Current	In past but not now	Never	No information
	%	%	%	%	%	%	%	%	%	%	%	%	%	%	%
Devaluation of the pound															
Support	16	15	15	18	19	13	21	15	18	19	14	18	15	16	15
Oppose	71	76	73	73	69	67	66	75	69	69	67	72	76	67	66
Don't know/not answered	13	9	12	9	13	20	12	10	14	12	19	10	9	17	20
Reducing Government spending on defence															
Support	44	41	47	42	45	43	50	30	52	56	45	51	48	36	44
Oppose	53	58	52	56	52	48	47	68	43	42	50	48	50	59	47
Don't know/not answered	3	2	1	2	2	8	3	2	5	2	5	1	2	4	8
Government incentives to encourage job sharing or splitting															
Support	61	64	69	52	58	67	59	67	64	57	50	56	68	60	66
Oppose	35	33	28	45	38	26	38	30	30	40	41	42	29	34	29
Don't know/not answered	4	3	3	3	4	7	3	3	6	3	9	2	3	6	4
Government to set up construction projects to create more jobs															
Support	89	83	93	92	90	89	91	87	91	93	85	92	91	86	92
Oppose	9	16	6	6	8	6	7	11	7	5	12	7	8	10	3
Don't know/not answered	2	1	1	1	2	5	2	2	2	2	3	1	1	3	6
BASE: ALL RESPONDENTS															
Weighted	*1719*	*334*	*268*	*365*	*300*	*346*	*106*	*664*	*252*	*565*	*216*	*463*	*484*	*689*	*83*
Unweighted	*1761*	*343*	*281*	*362*	*316*	*353*	*106*	*676*	*258*	*584*	*221*	*474*	*497*	*707*	*83*

4 Social policy and the welfare state

*Nick Bosanquet**

This section looks at opinion on an unusually wide and controversial range of issues to do with the future of the welfare state, of health care and of housing. Wherever possible we phrased questions so that they did not force people to take up more definite opinions than they really held. Our results give little support to politicians who claim to have found consistent support for their own positions. On many issues, the drift of opinion is ideologically unorthodox. For instance, on general questions to do with the balance between public spending and taxation, our survey brings little comfort to those who argue that public opinion has turned strongly in favour of more public spending and higher taxation, and still less comfort to those who argue that tax cuts should be made even if it means lower social spending. Similarly, although a sizeable majority of the population is against a two-tier health service with public health provision restricted to those with low incomes, people are quite likely to support both the principle of a health service open to all and a larger role for private health services. Even among opponents of a two-tier health service many believe that the existence of private medical treatment is a 'good thing' for the NHS.

There was a similar range of attitudes to claimants of state benefits. People were convinced that many people were claiming benefits without being entitled to them and that many others were failing to claim benefits to which they were entitled.

Despite a tendency to consensus on several general questions, opinion was sharply divided on many specific issues. There were, for example, clear divisions on whether the current level of unemployment benefit was too high or too low, with Conservative identifiers being much more likely to think it was too high. Similarly, Labour identifiers were much more likely to think that the existence

---

*Lecturer in Economics at The City University.

of private medicine damaged the NHS. There was also division in relation to the redistributive effects of the welfare state. Whereas government spending on social services is widely regarded by politicians as public welfare for the less well off, our sample was more sceptical: fewer than half of the sample thought that people with low incomes were the chief beneficiaries of NHS spending. Labour identifiers in particular were doubtful about the redistributive nature of health, housing and education spending.

The demand for 'privatisation' of welfare exists only, in any strength, where people believe that such a development would not damage the present universal public services. In other words, people are clearly more interested in what they perceive to be the likely consequences of policies and decisions rather than in the principles or doctrines behind them.

Differences by party identification are, on the whole, more important than differences by class. In some ways Britain seems to be becoming an ideologically divided society. A sizeable minority of the population would appear to have very strong opinions that do not seem to be associated with clear class, occupational or income differences. Differences by tenure are also of great importance. Local authority tenants stand out as a group who see themselves – and are seen by others – as living in poor conditions and in an environment which many feel to be deteriorating. This sense of decline is especially felt by tenants in big cities. The recent much stronger identification of the Conservative party with owner occupation has come at a time when differences by tenure may be supplanting (or supplementing) older lines of division by class as an important line of social difference.

Opinion on the importance of government action in the housing field has also shown a clear change. The NHS is popular while spending on housing is less so. The perception corresponds to the decreasing emphasis given to housing programmes by Whitehall.

Previous surveys

There have been recurrent surveys on the general issue of preferences between public spending and taxation. These asked for people's opinions 'if the government had a choice between reducing taxes and spending more on the social services' (Butler and Stokes, 1974). Such a question pushes people towards supporting a *change* in present arrangements; in addition, although it alludes to a connection between increased or reduced public spending and increased or reduced taxation, it does not make the connection very explicit. The answers to such questions have revealed a rising majority in favour of tax cuts until the late 1970s, with recent signs of a reversal in favour of increases in services (*The Economist,* October 8, 1983).

There have also been recurrent surveys of views on education vouchers and private health care, carried out for the Institue of Economic Affairs. These have been interpreted by Harris and Seldon (1979) as showing a rising demand for private services. However, the wording of the preferred options – for example on health care the statement was 'the state should continue the present service but allow people to contract out, pay less contributions and so on and use the money to pay for their own services' – is such that it can hardly support such a strong conclusion.

There have been occasional surveys of attitudes towards the NHS of which the most extensive was undertaken for the Royal Commission on the National Health Service (1978). These have usually found a high level of satisfaction both with the NHS as a whole and with particular aspects of it. Housing has not, on the whole, been well served by attitude surveys, but evidence on current policy issues is usefully summarised in Donnison and Ungerson (1982). There have also been other detailed surveys using local samples. Golding and Middleton (1982), who found that people were biased against scroungers and the undeserving poor, stressed the influence of the mass media on attitudes to the welfare state. Taylor-Gooby (1982) found that attitudes were highly ambivalent with people pulled in one direction by belief in self reliance and self help and in another by their sense of commitment to social services.

Public spending and taxation

We started this section of our questionnaire with a general question about priorities for government spending between a number of different programmes. It is always difficult to decide how to approach such questions. In the economic and political atmosphere of 1983, it might have been sensible to ask people to choose their priorities for *cuts* in spending. On the other hand, since we are, in effect, trying to measure over time the importance that people attach to different government programmes, we decided on balance to take the rather more direct route of asking respondents to select items for *extra* government spending and later of asking them to trade off public spending against taxation. After all, even in 1983, not all government programmes were facing cuts and not all political parties in the pre-election period were advocating cuts. Despite Britain's straitened circumstances, some programmes might still be thought to merit expansion, perhaps at the expense of others. So we asked all respondents:

> *Here are some items of government spending. Which of them, if any, would be your highest priority for extra spending, and which next? Please read through the whole list before deciding.*

Only six respondents nominated none of the items for extra spending. The remainder distributed their priorities (in order) as follows:

	1st priority	1st or 2nd priority
	%	%
Health	37	63
Education	24	50
Help for industry	16	29
Housing	7	20
Social security benefits	6	12
Defence	4	8
Police and prisons	3	8
Roads	2	5
Public transport	1	3
Overseas aid	*	1

Tables **4.1** and **4.2** give further details and breakdowns. An examination of these breakdowns reveals some interesting subgroup differences many of which reflect the preoccupations of people at different stages of the life cycle. So there was a strong vote for education as a first priority among those aged 25-34: 36% of them gave it first priority, compared with 16% of those over the age of 55, and 21% of those under 25. There was a relatively low priority attached to health expenditure by men aged under 34 (27% first priority), but not by women of the same age (35%). There was also a strong vote from young people, particularly young men, for helping industry. Similarly, different interest groups attached higher priority to different areas of expenditure. Thus the unemployed were four times more likely than those in work to choose social security as a first priority.

Even so, the broad ordering of priorities was remarkably similar for all subgroups. No discernible social class patterning emerged, and party identification did not discriminate as much as official party positions might have led us to expect it would. But there were differences, the most striking of which are shown below:

	Conservative	Alliance	Labour
	%	%	%
First priority to:			
Health	34	43	39
Help for industry	20	16	13
Housing	5	6	10
Social security benefits	3	4	9
Defence	6	2	1

So Alliance identifiers were closer to Conservatives on some issues, such as social security and housing, and closer to Labour on others, notably defence and health.

There was little echo in these findings from recent public debates about the shape and balance of public spending. Very few Conservative identifiers (13%) attached any priority (first or second) to defence spending and only around a quarter of Labour identifiers attached any priority to help for industry. There was a widespread feeling among all party identifiers that any further spending should be on the more traditional areas of the social services. Many of the differences that did emerge seemed to be attributable to local economic factors or the preoccupations of different age groups. Thus, young people were more likely to give housing some priority; and people in London and the South East were less likely to give industrial aid any priority.

It is of interest to compare these findings with those we obtained from another set of questions we had asked earlier in the questionnaire (and which are reported in Chapter 3). They were designed to elicit reactions to 'a number of policies which might help Britain's economic problems'. Among the policies we asked about were three that call for comparison: whether people support or oppose 'reducing the level of government spending on health and education', 'increasing government subsidies for private industry', and 'reducing government spending on defence'. It would not have been unduly surprising if the two sets of questions had produced what appeared to be inconsistent answers. After all, one set attempted to measure the level of *support* for reductions (or increases) in spending to help the nation's economy, while the other sought *priorities* for extra spending as a measure of implied importance. Nonetheless, it is comforting that the two questions did produce mutually consistent findings. For example, having taken account of the different question wordings, we find that the proportions of 'sympathetic votes' for expenditure on health and education, aid for industry and defence were cast in the same order at both questions. Moreover, the subgroup differences were in the same direction. Thus Alliance identifiers at both questions were more committed than Labour or Conservative identifiers to expenditure on health and education; Labour and Alliance identifiers were fairly close to each other (at both questions) in their opposition to defence expenditure; and, again at both questions, Conservatives were more sympathetic than Labour or Alliance identifiers to government aid for industry.

So two questions that we asked with different emphasis and in different contexts produced much the same conclusion: a broad preference for any extra government spending to be concentrated on bolstering the welfare state; or, more decisively, for any further cuts not to be directed at health or educational provision.

Social spending

Our general questions on government spending priorities elicited a fairly low vote for social security benefits (12% first or second priority). But we were concerned about what the words 'social security' might actually convey to respondents. We felt it might be interpreted as covering only a fairly narrow range of 'protective' provision for those who are most disadvantaged in society. So we asked a further question to establish levels of support for extra spending on what we referred to as 'social benefits'.

Thinking now only of the government's spending on social benefits like those on this card. Which, if any, of these would be your highest priority for extra spending? And which next?

	1st priority	1st or 2nd priority
	%	%
Retirement pensions	41	64
Benefits for disabled people	24	57
Benefits for the unemployed	18	33
Benefits for single parents	8	21
Child benefits	8	21

The answers revealed the usual strong support for retirement pensions as a social priority and a similarly strong vote for disablement benefits. More remarkable, perhaps, is the fairly strong vote for unemployment benefits: a third of our sample chose it as first or second priority.

In these answers too there was evidence of the influence of particular interest groups. For instance, there is an almost linear relationship between age and first votes for pensions, running from a low of 18% among 18-24 year olds to a high of 55% among those over retirement age. Similarly, there was a stronger than average preference for spending on child benefits among those of child rearing age (especially women), and a markedly stronger than average preference for unemployment benefit among those who were themselves unemployed: for them, retirement pensions and unemployment benefits have almost equal priority.

There were also sharp differences according to party identification. Whereas the identifiers of all three major parties accorded pensions an equally high priority, Conservatives (11%) were less likely than Alliance identifiers (20%) or Labour identifiers (25%) to give unemployment benefit first priority. These findings on social benefit priorities suggest, therefore, that notions of the 'deserving' and 'undeserving' poor have not entirely disappeared. (See Table 4.1 and 4.2 for further details.)

Having introduced the subjects of health spending, education spending and, more important, 'social benefits' to respondents, we then wanted to establish a direct link between spending on these programmes and tax levels. We ignored here the possibility of raising revenue from redistributing expenditure or even from greater efficiency, since we wanted to stress the likely conflict between low tax levels and high social expenditure, given our expectation that people would be inclined to vote for the best of all possible worlds if that option was on offer.

Suppose the government had to choose between the three options on this card. Which do you think it should choose?

	%
Reduce taxes and spend less on health, education and social benefits	9
Keep taxes and spending on these services at the same level as now	54
Increase taxes and spend more on health, education and social benefits	32

At first appearance, these findings seem to contrast with those of other surveys carried out during the past fifteen years or so, but the questions asked have all been different. For instance in the 1970 British General Election Study (Butler and Stokes, 1974), 65% opted for tax cuts in a direct choice against social service increases. But, with the availability to respondents of the *status quo* as a possible option in our survey, it is perhaps not surprising that it was the most popular choice; this is possibly why many studies prefer not to offer it. But we did not wish to perpetuate that omission. In any event, after four years of particularly intense debate about the level of public spending and taxation, fewer than one in ten people choose tax cuts and reduced social spending. In fact, as many as one in three choose the opposite course of increasing them. Whatever differences may be attributable to question wording, it is clear from our results that, while there is no majority support for major increases, there is even less support for major reductions.

It is difficult to interpret the answers of different income groups to this question, because they would probably have been based on some (unstated) model or image of the taxation system which respondents were being asked to consider. How, for instance, would we expect poor people *rationally* to answer the question if their aim was to maximise their own utility? They might legitimately select higher taxes and social spending, or vice versa, depending not only on their individual circumstances, but also on the actual level of tax increase or decrease they had in mind, and on how they thought the tax threshold might be affected in the process. This is not to imply that people do respond rationally in quite this way, simply to note the genuine cross-pressures in considering issues of this sort, some of which may have influenced some respondents.

Nonetheless, we might well have expected (especially with the benefit of hindsight) that the poor would be the least likely to choose the middle of the three options (the *status quo*). And that is what happened. Low income households (less than £5,000 pa) were more likely than others to favour changes in tax and spending — either upwards or downwards. By contrast, more prosperous households (£10,000 pa or more) were more likely to favour the *status quo* but, surprisingly, less likely to favour reductions in tax and spending. The subgroup differences we examined were, however, generally not large at this question and did not follow any clear pattern. The most striking difference was predictably along party political lines: Labour identifiers (42%) were much more likely to favour increases but in tax and spending, followed by Alliance identifiers (35%) and Conservative identifiers (24%). There were also sizeable minorities of Conservative and Labour identifiers who held views that were contrary to their party's positions. (See **Table 4.3** and **4.4**.)

Take-up and level of benefits

The claiming and take-up of social security benefit generates strongly held opinions. Unusually, more than half of the respondents agreed or disagreed *strongly* with each of two propositions we put to them (see below). Moreover, the sample was not just concerned about 'scrounging' or unjustified claims for benefits. Respondents also believed (more strongly and in greater numbers) that many people are not getting the benefits they are entitled to get. We asked whether they agreed or disagreed — strongly or slightly — with each of the following statements:

	Agree strongly	Agree slightly	Disagree slightly	Disagree strongly
	%	%	%	%
Large numbers of people these days *falsely* claim benefits	40	25	13	12
	65		25	
Large numbers of people who are eligible for benefits these days *fail* to claim them	49	32	8	3
	81		11	

Within these overall majorities, however, there were some marked differences by party identification. A high proportion of Conservative identifiers (72%) believed there were many false claimants; by comparison, around 60% of Labour and Alliance identifiers took this view. Conservatives were rather less worried about people's failure to claim benefits to which they were entitled: 44% agreed *strongly* with that proposition, compared with 48% of Alliance identifiers and 57% of Labour identifiers. No other subgroup differences emerged very strongly. In view of these findings, recent Conservative policies designed to prevent scrounging may well be popular. It is quite possible, however, that

policies designed to ensure that people get their entitlements would be even
more popular.

We went on to ask specifically about unemployment benefits, offering two
contrasting statements to respondents and letting them select one or neither of
them. The distribution of answers is shown below, broken down by party
identification.

	Total	Conservative	Alliance	Labour
	%	%	%	%
Benefits for the unemployed are:				
too low and cause hardship	46	30	50	64
too high and discourage people				
from finding jobs	35	50	26	23
Neither	13	13	17	9

These party differences are very great and somewhat surprising. True, the
Labour-Conservative cleavage on this issue was probably predictable, but the
Alliance-Conservative was not. Indeed, the respective positions of Conservative
and Alliance identifiers are almost symmetrically juxtaposed. So, despite a fairly
widespread view among the sample as a whole that unemployment benefits are
too low, there are striking subgroup differences — much greater than on most
other questions. The most striking of these (apart from party identification) are
shown in summary form below. (See Tables 4.3 and 4.4 for further details.)

		Benefits are too low and cause hardship
Total	%	46
People under 25	%	61
People aged 25-64	%	47
People aged 65+	%	32
People in metropolitan areas (cities)	%	51
People in non-metropolitan areas	%	43
Blue collar (manual)	%	51
White collar (non-manual)	%	39
Unemployed	%	76
Employees	%	46
Self-employed	%	26
Current or past union member	%	50
Never a union member	%	40

From these findings there appears to be much greater division of attitudes in
the population towards the level of cash benefits than there is towards social

services in kind. It will be interesting to monitor these results over the next few years, particularly if benefits are reduced (or increased) in real terms during that period. It should be noted, however, that our question forced a choice between two statements that were not quite mutually exclusive; some people may hold the view that benefits are both too low and act as a disincentive to work, and our question would have failed to capture that view. On a number of the questions on public spending we looked to see whether being a member of a trade union had any strong effect on people's attitudes. About a quarter of respondents were currently members of trade unions and about 40% had never been members. The remainder were ex-members, now mostly retired. Much of the difference between members and non-members is probably accounted for by social class differences, but the variations are nonetheless worth recording.

- Current union members were more worried than those who had never been members about people's failure to claim benefits (53% *strongly* concerned against 43%).

- Union members were more concerned about the level of unemployment benefit. 50% thought that it was too low as against 40% of those who had never been members.

- 68% of current members gave priority to more spending on health and education compared to 58% of those who had never been members.

- 37% of union members wanted increased social spending and taxation as against 27% of those who had never been members.

On the whole, ex-members of trade unions were closer in their attitudes to current members than to those who had never been members.

The National Health Service

Previous surveys have suggested general support for the principle of a National Health Service (see, for instance, *The Economist,* October 8, 1983). Surveys have also suggested high levels of satisfaction with its actual operation (Royal Commission on the NHS, 1978). Our survey confirmed that in general there was a high level of support for the principle, although somewhat higher among non-manual groups than among those who are thought to be traditional supporters of the NHS. But the results suggest some dissatisfaction with the actual functioning of the service. As will be seen, whereas the better off see those with low incomes as the chief beneficiaries of the NHS, the relatively poor are not so sure — a doubt shared by recent academic evidence (Le Grand, 1982). This may explain partly why low income groups are less likely than higher income groups to oppose the notion of a two-tier health service. Although we asked respondents about satisfaction and dissatisfaction with the health service before going on to address various policy questions, the findings are produced here in reverse order. We introduced the idea of a 'selective' health service in the following question.

It has been suggested that the National Health Service should be available only to those with lower incomes. This would mean that contribution rates could be lower and most people would then take out medical insurance and pay for health care. Do you support or oppose this idea?

	%
Support	29
Oppose	64
Don't know	7

Thus, the principle of a two-tier health service has substantial public opposition. And that opposition is greatest from those who would be most likely to be excluded from its selective coverage. So, those with household incomes of £10,000 or more (72%), or those in Social Classes I or II (70%) are particularly likely to support a universal NHS. This support translates itself into other subgroup differences also: for instance, Conservative (66%) and Alliance identifiers (68%) are more likely than Labour identifiers (62%) to support the *status quo*. The region of highest level of approval for a universal NHS is Scotland (77%) where waiting lists are relatively short and private medicine almost non-existent. As will be seen, the Scots are also very satisfied with their health service as it is.

So the principle of a universal NHS commands strongest support from people in non-manual occupations. Indeed, some of the highest levels of endorsement for a two-tier health service comes from regions and among groups where Labour identification has been strongest – among ethnic minorities, for instance, and among people in the North of England. Since our fieldwork period in early 1983, there has been intense controversy about the future of the NHS; later surveys will therefore give us a chance to see whether, or how, this controversy has affected attitudes.

The NHS has clearly been embraced by the middle classes in a manner that its pioneers would not have predicted. And it represents a very comfortable object of affection since the better off one is, the more likely one is to believe that the NHS, though available to everyone, is particularly beneficial to the less well off. For evidence that this belief is fallacious, see Le Grand (1982), Social Trends 14 (1984) and the *Black Report* published by the DHSS (1980).

On the whole, which of these three types of family would you say gets best value from their taxes out of the National Health Service...

		Household income		
	Total	Under £5,000	£5,000- £7,999	£8,000 and over
	%	%	%	%
...those with high incomes,	24	35	28	16
those with middle incomes,	14	13	14	16
or those with low incomes?	44	34	44	53

Whereas around a half of the sample saw the NHS as benefiting low income families, and around a quarter as benefiting high income families, there are large differences in perception according to respondents' own incomes. In essence, the richer one is the more likely one is to believe that the NHS is helping the poor, and vice versa. Thus, the NHS is seen to have a tilt, but many people are doubtful about whether the tilt is towards them. The differences in response by income are reflected consistently in other subgroup differences, as shown in summary form below. (See **Table 4.5** for further details.)

		High income families get best value from the NHS
Total	%	24
Conservative identifiers	%	16
Alliance identifiers	%	17
Labour identifiers	%	39
Social Class I and II	%	13
Social Class III (Non-manual)	%	20
Social Class III (Manual)	%	31
Social Class IV and V	%	35
In paid work	%	23
Retired	%	26
Unemployed	%	35
Owner occupiers	%	19
Private tenants	%	31
Local authority tenants	%	35
Whites	%	24
Blacks/Asians/Others	%	36

There were regional differences too, with people in Scotland and the North being more inclined than people in Wales, the Midlands and the South to believe that the tilt was towards high income families.

We also asked two similar questions (*who benefits most?*) about public spending on housing and education. The discussion of these questions comes later, but it is worth noting here that NHS spending is regarded as the *most* redistributive of the three (44% saying that low income families benefit most), followed by housing (36%) and education (30%).

Satisfaction with the NHS

How satisfied or dissatisfied are people both with the NHS as a whole and with different aspects of it? The answers to these sorts of questions have more utility over time than they do for a single reading. Their purpose in 1983 was largely to establish benchmark measures against which we will be able to chart future movements. Another difficulty with such questions is that people have varying levels of familiarity with different sorts of health provision. We considered and rejected confining the satisfaction questions to recent users of each service, preferring in the end to address them to all respondents or − in effect − to all *potential* users, since we felt that the image of a service was probably at least as important as experience in determining consumer preferences and behaviour. Levels of satisfaction with the NHS as a whole were mixed. (See **Table 4.6**.)

	%
Very satisfied	11
Quite satisfied	44
Neither	20
Quite dissatisfied	18
Very dissatisfied	7

It is usual that, on satisfaction questions, older respondents tend to express greater levels of satisfaction than younger respondents do. But this did not apply uniformly to this question. True, if we divided our sample into the under 45s and the over 45s, the older group was more satisfied (58% very or quite) than the younger group (51%). But there is a particularly high level of *dissatisfaction* among women aged 45-59 − a group for whom there may well be experience of long and worsening waiting lists for treatment.

There are also higher than average levels of dissatisfaction in London (especially) and the South East, where the problems of the NHS have received a great deal of press attention during the last few years. By contrast in Scotland the satisfaction ratings (66%) are comfortably higher than in any other region.

There are interesting differences in satisfaction and dissatisfaction with the NHS when analyses by class and income are compared. Whereas class differences show no clear pattern, income differences do. Broadly, the higher the household income, so the more dissatisfaction is expressed.

Income under £5,000 pa	21%
Income between £5,000 and £10,000 pa	26%
Income over £10,000 pa	34%

The division is not therefore between people in manual and non-manual occupations, but between those with higher incomes and those with lower ones; and much of the difference is probably attributable to the low levels of dissatisfaction among pensioner households.

Having established overall ratings for the NHS as a whole, we then went on to ask about satisfaction or dissatisfaction with particular aspects. Whereas around a quarter of the sample had expressed dissatisfaction with the NHS, the proportions expressing dissatisfaction with particular services were generally much lower. Only the hospital out patient service attracted anything approaching the level of discontent attached to the NHS as a whole.

Proportions expressing dissatisfaction with 'the way in which each of these parts of the NHS runs nowadays'.

	%
Local doctors or GPs	13
National Health Service dentists	10
Health visitors	6
District nurses	2
Being in hospital as an in patient	7
Attending hospital as an out patient	21

On most of the services, males tended to express more dissatisfaction than females, and the young more than the old. If we compare these findings with those of the 1978 survey carried out by the Royal Commission on the NHS, we find that out patient treatment was not especially singled out for criticism then. But their findings were based on the responses of those who had been recent patients.

Private medicine

Only 11% of our sample are covered by private health schemes, so that actual experience of these was limited. However, the proportions in membership ranged from 17% in Social Classes I or II to 3% in Social Classes IV or V. 18% of the self-employed were covered, compared with 13% of employees, 11% of those 'looking after the home', 5% of pensioners, and 3% of the unemployed.

Almost a quarter of the people in high income households (£10,000+ pa) are covered by a private health scheme, and these people account for over half of the members we found. Thus, membership was highest among those subgroups of the population most likely to express dissatisfaction with the NHS. For about half of the members, scheme payments were made by their employer.

Although only a small minority of the sample had actually had contact with a private health scheme, nearly everybody was willing to give us their views on the effects of such schemes on the NHS. Were they 'a good thing' or 'a bad thing' for the NHS?

	Total	Conservative identifiers	Alliance identifiers	Labour identifiers
	%	%	%	%
Good thing	37	54	30	20
Bad thing	23	12	24	37
No difference	35	31	42	36
Don't know	5	3	3	7

Similarly, the richer their households and, in general, the higher their social class, the more likely people are to think that private health schemes are good for the NHS. So a minority of the population (even among Labour identifiers) believes that private health schemes actually *damage* the NHS. For the remainder they are almost equally divided between those who think they are beneficial and those who think they are immaterial. What, then, about attitudes to private medical treatment in general?

We presented all respondents with a card containing a range of policy options relating to the NHS and private medical treatment. The proportions choosing each option are shown below and analysed by party identification.

Which of the views on this card do you support? You may choose more than one, or none.

	Total	Conservative identifiers	Alliance identifiers	Labour identifiers
	%	%	%	%
Private medical treatment in Britain should be abolished	10	3	9	19
Private treatment in NHS hospitals should be abolished	26	16	30	36
The present arrangements for private medical treatment and the NHS are about right	41	44	39	39
Private treatment outside NHS hospitals should be encouraged to expand	26	37	26	15
Private treatment generally should be encouraged to expand	20	31	18	10
None of these	4	3	4	3

As can be seen, a number of people chose more than one of the options. Nonetheless, there is a middle bloc within the population, consisting of around 40%, who believe that present arrangements are desirable. The size of this bloc does not vary much according to party identification. Outside this bloc, however, a clear majority of Conservative identifiers favour the expansion of private treatment, while a clear majority of Labour identifiers favour contraction. Around one in five of these favours abolition. Among Alliance identifiers opinion is rather more evenly balanced.

On the issue of private medicine, the division of opinion is much more ideological than demographic. No clear class, age or even income divisions emerged. Apart from party divisions, only the self-employed once again stood out as particular supporters of private medical treatment; and only the Scots once again stood out as particular opponents.

More analyses than we have been able to do so far will certainly reveal further relationships between, and differences within, subgroups of the population. We hope that others will take up the data and do further work. For example, a particularly interesting group to analyse further would be the white collar respondents who were opposed to a two-tier health service, a group that tended to be more satisfied with the functioning of the NHS than others and more likely to believe that low income families were the main beneficiaries of the NHS. They were also more likely to oppose cuts in social spending. These 'Titmussian' middle class respondents could usefully be contrasted with the 'Friedmanite' working class respondents who tended to have contrary attitudes.

Attitudes to housing

Although most respondents expressed satisfaction with their own house or flat, a substantial minority, especially among tenants in big cities and ethnic minorities, is strongly dissatisfied. Attitudes divide between the bulk of people who are content with their accommodation and their local environment but who are apathetic towards government expenditure on housing, and the minority who see themselves facing worsening prospects in a deteriorating environment.

86%	of the sample were satisfied with their house or flat;
77%	said that their local environment had either stayed the same or improved in the last two years;
81%	expected their local environment to remain the same or improve in the next two years;
7%	(as reported earlier) chose housing as a first priority for extra government spending.

Around three-quarters of those who were dissatisfied with their housing were tenants, even though tenants comprised only a third of the sample. We give first a brief profile of the characteristics and attitudes of different tenure groups, with particular emphasis on local authority tenants.

1. Local authority *and* private tenants are about five times more likely than owner occupiers to express dissatisfaction with their accommodation.

	Total	Household Accommodation		
		Owner Occ.	Rented L. A.	Rented other
	%	%	%	%
Satisfied	86	93	74	68
Dissatisfied	9	4	19	21

2. Tenants are more likely than owner occupiers to believe both that their local environment has deteriorated and that it will continue to do so. Whereas owner occupiers show less discontent with their house than with their environment, the opposite is true for tenants, especially council tenants.

	Total	Household Accommodation		
		Owner Occ.	Rented L. A.	Rented other
	%	%	%	%
Local area in **last 2 years**				
Has got better	10	11	8	15
worse	20	16	27	26
Local area in **next 2 years**				
Will get better	11	10	12	14
worse	16	13	23	19

3.   Tenants generally, but council tenants in particular, are becoming decreasingly representative of the population, set apart in their characteristics. Indeed, local authority housing in Britain is getting nearer in character to welfare housing in the USA. Details of the different tenure groups are contained in **Table 4.7**. It is worth noting here, however, that council tenants are much more concentrated in some regions, notably Scotland, the North West and the South East. They are far poorer than owner occupiers, much more likely to be in manual occupations, and more likely to be unemployed or retired. There is growing polarisation in the housing system.

4.   Council tenants were generally convinced that they were unlikely to buy their present flats or houses.

Is it likely or unlikely that you – or the person responsible for paying the rent – will buy this accommodation at some time in the future?

	%
Very likely	5
Quite likely	7
Quite unlikely	4
Very unlikely	76
Not allowed to buy	6
Don't know	1

5.   Half of the Council tenants see themselves as paying *high* rents. In confirmation of this, only 8% of council tenants agreed, at a later question, with the statement that 'Council tenants pay low rents'. About a quarter of the rest of the sample agreed with that statement.

6.   Council tenants tend to believe that they get a poor standard of repairs and maintenance (two in three believe this to be so), but are relatively evenly divided about whether council estates are pleasant places in which to live. Among the rest of the population, one in three believe council estates to be pleasant places to live in, a very poor image of what is still a type of accommodation into which many people are trying to gain entry.

	Total	Owner Occ.	Rented L. A.	Rented other
	%	%	%	%
Councils give a poor standard of repairs and maintenance				
True	56	52	66	58
False	33	37	23	33
Not answered/no self-completion questionnaire	11	11	11	9
Council estates are generally pleasant places to live in				
True	36	33	47	31
False	52	55	41	58
Not answered/no self-completion questionnaire	12	12	12	11

7.   Council tenants views on the effects of current patterns of housing spending
are also rather different from those of the general population. Overall, the
population is evenly divided about whether high, middle or low income
families benefit from the current pattern of government housing expenditure.
This is a more varied response than that given to similar questions in the
field of health and education. The question attempted to elicit people's
perceptions of the relative effects of tax relief on mortgage interest and rent
allowances to different groups. It referred implicitly to the effects of income
support rather than to the distributional effects of the development and
improvement programme. We introduced the question in the self-completion
questionnaire in the following way:

*Central government provides financial support to housing in two main ways. First by
means of allowances to low income tenants; second by means of tax relief to people
with mortgages. On the whole which of these three types of family would you say
benefits most from central government support for housing?*

	Total	Owner Occ.	Rented L. A.	Rented other
	%	%	%	%
Families with high incomes	30	27	37	29
Families with middle incomes	25	25	23	36
Families with low incomes	36	40	30	28
Not answered/no self-completion questionnaire	9	9	10	7

It is interesting to note the tendency of both owner occupiers and council
tenants to believe that the other group benefits more.
   People living in large cities constitute another group who are notably negative about their housing conditions. Although they are relatively content with
their own houses or flats, they are more negative and pessimistic about their
environment. Compared with 20% of the general population, 27% of those living
in cities – and 30% of those living in the GLC area – thought that their
environment had grown worse during the past two years. Similarly 23% of those
living in large cities (compared with 16% of the general population) thought that
their local area would deteriorate in the next two years.
   City dwellers were also more likely to consider that their rents are high.
61% of council tenants living in large cities considered rents to be high, compared
with 46% of those living in other areas. Similarly, they were less likely to consider
that council houses are pleasant places in which to live (30% thought this to be
true, compared with 40% of those living in other areas). People living in the GLC
were especially critical of council estates: as many as 68% considered them to
be unpleasant.
   Given the feelings of residents of large cities, it is hardly surprising that
ethnic minority respondents had a bleak view of their condition and prospects.
They were especially critical of the standard of council estates. Only 21%
of this subgroup thought of council estates as pleasant places to live compared
with 36% of the general population. There is, of course, growing evidence to
suggest that the council estates on which ethnic minorities are concentrated *are*
the most unpleasant of council estates.

Current political lore holds that there is strong majority support in the population for the right to buy council houses. In our survey, however, attitudes were mixed: around one-half of the sample supported such a right. This can probably be attributed to the form of our question, which presented three options rather than a straight choice between a general right and a blanket prohibition. When a range of alternatives is presented, the answers are almost bound to be less polarised.

Which of these views comes closest to your own on the sale of council houses and flats to tenants?

- *council tenants SHOULD NOT be allowed to buy their houses or flats*
- *council tenants SHOULD be allowed to buy but ONLY in areas with no housing shortage*
- *council tenants SHOULD GENERALLY be allowed to buy their houses or flats.*

	Total	Conservative identifiers	Alliance identifiers	Labour identifiers
	%	%	%	%
Should not be allowed	10	6	12	15
Should — if no housing shortage	29	24	39	29
Should generally be allowed	54	63	42	49

Prohibition of council house sales is therefore unpopular, even among Labour identifiers. But, when given the middle option of the right to buy in areas of no housing shortage, a sizeable minority of the population selects it. Once again, the population shows at least a passing interest in the consequences of particular policies rather than in principles alone. Surprisingly perhaps, social class, tenure and other subgroup differences were small in response to this question and showed no clear patterns.

In view of the very small minority of council tenants (as shown earlier) who *expect* to buy, this issue probably has little salience. More important is the general impression we gained of council tenants (and to some extent of private tenants too) as a somewhat excluded, poor and relatively discontented section of society.

Attitudes to poverty

Do people believe that there is 'such a thing as real poverty in Britain today'? In answer to the bald question, a majority (55%) believe there is. The balance of opinion is not dissimilar to that reported by Townsend (62%) in his definitive study of poverty in Britain for which the fieldwork was carried out in 1969 (Townsend, 1979). There are some interesting subgroup differences, notable among which are the following:

		Believe that real poverty exists
Total	%	55
Unemployed	%	69
Employed	%	58
Self-employed	%	43
Aged under 35	%	62
Aged 35 to pensionable age	%	57
Pensioners	%	41
Metropolitan areas (cities)	%	59
Non-metropolitan areas	%	52
Household income of £10,000+ pa	%	62
Household income of £5,000 - £10,000 pa	%	55
Household income of less than £5,000 pa	%	51
Households with children under 5	%	67
Households with school-age children	%	58
Adult only households	%	51
Current or past union member	%	59
Never a union member	%	48
Alliance identifiers	%	64
Labour identifiers	%	60
Conservative identifiers	%	45

It is interesting that belief in the existence of poverty in Britain goes *up* with income, which supports the conclusion that it tends to be seen as a relative condition suffered by those less well off than oneself. The relatively low level of poverty identified by pensioners is probably attributable to the fact that they start from a different reference point of experience between the wars. The unemployed, however, many of whom are only recent entrants to subsistence living, identify a great deal of poverty in Britain.

But what view of poverty did people have in mind? Poverty can be seen in absolute terms as a minimum income required to maintain existence; alternatively it can be seen relative to the living standards that are socially accepted at the time. Our survey suggests that the 'relative' view of poverty is more common now than it was in 1969, and our results are consistent with those reported by Lansley and Weir (1983). We asked respondents which of two views of poverty they held.

There are different views about what real poverty is nowadays. Please look at this card and tell me which of the statements, if either, comes closest to your own views?

	%
Poverty in Britain today is mainly about the shortage of absolute necessities such as food and clothing	26
People in Britain today have enough to eat and wear; the main hardship is not being able to keep up with the living standards most people have	67
Neither of these	4
Not answered	2

Level of assent to the relative definition is now remarkably high. More-over, by and large, the subgroups who tended to deny the existence of poverty were those that supported the relative definition. The notable exceptions were parents of young children and the unemployed, in both cases groups who had probably suffered sharp falls in income fairly recently. Unlike pensioners, they had not yet incorporated low standards of living into their reference points.

Images of the Welfare State

The effect of the welfare state on the 'character' of its citizens is frequently raised in political discussions. Some maintain that people's self reliance and sense of responsibility for their families or neighbours has in some way been lessened by the evolution of the welfare state. They go on to suggest that social workers, doctors and other professionals effectively conspire to increase people's dependence on their services. Those opposing this view would claim that the welfare state has played a key role in integrating society and in deve-loping among its citizens an awareness of their interdependence and a sense of altruism.

We included in the self-completion questionnaire several questions that touch on these issues. They were presented in the form of statements with which respondents were invited to agree or disagree — strongly or slightly. Once again, the questions have more utility over time than they do for a single reading. But we report the answers here to indicate the benchmark positions. It is clear from the pattern of answers that our respondents did not share the passions which politicians bring to these issues.

In presenting the figures here we have elided strong and slight agreement and disagreement, and omitted the neutral category we offered of 'neither agree nor disagree'. The full breakdown can be found in **Table 4.8**. It is however worth noting here that in no case did more than around one in three respondents have strong views either way, and in no case did fewer than around one in six respondents choose the neutral option.

Our statements divided into three broad but overlapping categories. The first category dealt with the role of professionals and consisted of three statements:

	Agree	Disagree
	%	%
People rely too much on doctors instead of taking more responsibility for their own health	52	24
The welfare state makes people nowadays less willing to look after themselves	49	25
Social workers have too much power to interfere with people's lives	44	18

We should stress that some of the statements on other subjects that we offered to respondents did *not* generate more agreement than disagreement. There were wide variations. So the consistency of these answers suggests that worries do exist about the effect of welfare state professionals on the nation's 'moral fibre'; but only small minorities tend to have strong feelings on these issues. Subgroup analyses reveal that they have particular support from those aged over 55, a group for whom the welfare state materialised only about half-way through their lives.

The second category consisted of two statements dealing with the issue of mutual dependence:

	Agree	Disagree
	%	%
Children have an obligation to look after their parents when they are old	39	33
The welfare state encourages people to stop helping each other	35	31

The public is much more equally divided on the extent to which the welfare state replaces family or individual caring. Subgroup variations here are very confused. The most consistent (and surprising) difference that emerges is between men and women − rather than between old and young − on children's obligations towards their parents. Men in all age groups are more likely than women in the same age groups to support the statement. Among people aged 65 or over, there is, finally, a closer correspondence of view and a greater than average level of support. People over 55 are much more likely to support the second statement too.

The final category consisted of three statements about the *operation* of different aspects of health and social service provision.

	Agree	Disagree
	%	%
Social workers should put the child's interests first even if it means taking the child away from its natural parents	61	15
Women should always have their babies in a hospital or nursing home	48	23
People receiving social security are made to feel like second class citizens	46	27

All subgroups we examined shared more or less equal levels of rejection of the importance of the 'blood-bond' between children and their parents. There were, however, some differences on the other two statements. In particular, people under the age of 35 are more likely to agree with the view that social security attaches a stigma to people who can claim it. People over pensionable age, especially women, are much less likely to hold that view.

It is of particular interest to look at sex and age differences in relation to the statement about child birth and hospitals. Whereas a margin of about two to one in the sample were ready to accept medical opinion – or the greater part of it – by agreeing with the statement, among women of the age group most likely to bear children, opinion was almost equally divided. The following table shows the breakdown.

Women should always have their babies in a hospital or nursing home

	Total	All women	Women (18-34)
	%	%	%
Agree strongly	27	24	19
Just agree	21	21	19
Neither agree or disagree	22	21	20
Just disagree	16	18	27
Disagree strongly	7	8	12
Not answered/no self-completion questionnaire	7	7	3

In general the attitudes towards and images of the welfare state we collected show no signs either of fervent idealism in the population or of an emerging strong majority determined to roll back the frontiers and to restrict the activities of professional workers.

References

BUTLER, D. and STOKES, D., *Political Change in Britain* (2nd edition), Macmillan, London (1974).
DHSS, Report of 'Working Group on Inequalities in Health' (Chairman Sir Douglas Black). London (1980).
DONNISON, D. and UNGERSON, C., *Housing Policy*, Penguin, London (1982).
The Economist, 'The Electoral Cost of Welfare Cuts', October 8, 1983, pp 18-19.
GOLDING, P. and MIDDLETON, S., *Images of Welfare*, Martin Robertson, Oxford (1982).
HARRIS, R. and SELDON, A., *Over-ruled on Welfare*, IEA, London (1979).
LANSLEY, S. and Weir, S., 'Towards a Popular View of Poverty', *New Society*, 25 August 1983, pp 283-4.
Le GRAND, J., *The Strategy of Equality*, Allen & Unwin, London (1982).
Royal Commission on the NHS (1978) Research Paper No. 5, 'Patients' Attitudes to the Hospital Service'.
Social Trends 14 p.188, ed. D. Ramprakash, HMSO, London (1984).
TAYLOR-GOOBY, P., 'Two Cheers for the Welfare State; Public Opinion and Private Welfare', *Journal of Public Policy* Vol. 2 Pt 4., October 1982, pp 319-346.
TOWNSEND, P., *Poverty in the United Kingdom*, Penguin, London (1979).

Acknowledgements

Special thanks are owed to the following people who commented on early versions of the questionnaire

    Brian Abel-Smith
    David Donnison
    Alan Lewis
    Peter Taylor-Gooby
    Peter Townsend

4.1 FIRST PRIORITY FOR EXTRA GOVERNMENT SPENDING (Q50a and Q51a) by sex, age, economic position and party identification

| | TOTAL | SEX | | AGE | | | | | | ECONOMIC POSITION | | | | | | PARTY IDENTIFICATION† | | | |
| | | | | MALE | | | FEMALE† | | | | | | | | | | | | |
		Male	Female	18–34	35–54	55+	18–34	35–54	55+	Employee	Self-employed	Unem-ployed	Looks after home	Retired	Other	Cons.	Alli-ance	Labour	Non-alig-ned
	%	%	%	%	%	%	%	%	%	%	%	%	%	%	%	%	%	%	%
Health	37	34	39	27	37	39	35	38	43	37	27	36	38	40	33	34	43	39	33
Education	24	24	24	29	27	16	31	28	15	26	32	21	25	15	26	24	24	24	25
Help for industry	16	17	15	22	16	13	15	16	14	17	17	16	14	13	19	20	16	13	13
Housing	7	7	7	8	6	8	10	5	8	7	10	7	6	9	4	5	6	10	10
Social security benefits	6	5	6	4	4	8	4	4	9	3	1	12	8	8	13	3	4	9	7
Defence	4	5	2	6	4	7	1	1	3	3	3	3	2	6	6	6	2	1	3
Police and prisons	3	3	2	2	2	4	2	3	2	2	4	2	2	5	–	4	2	2	1
Roads	2	2	2	2	1	3	–	3	2	2	4	1	3	2	–	1	2	1	3
Public transport	1	1	*	1	2	2	–	*	1	1	2	–	*	1	–	1	1	1	1
Overseas aid	*	*	*	*	–	–	–	1	*	*	–	–	–	*	1	–	*	*	*
SOCIAL BENEFITS:																			
Retirement pensions	41	44	48	33	41	57	25	37	51	38	50	37	38	54	36	40	40	41	42
Benefits for disabled people	24	23	25	17	28	24	18	25	32	25	28	9	24	28	26	30	24	19	22
Benefits for unemployed	18	18	18	26	15	12	28	17	9	18	8	34	18	10	20	11	20	25	15
Benefits for single parents	8	6	10	9	5	3	14	13	5	9	6	8	9	4	11	11	6	6	7
Child benefits	8	8	7	13	9	2	14	7	2	9	8	10	9	2	8	7	7	8	10
BASE: ALL RESPONDENTS																			
Weighted	*1719*	*793*	*926*	*258*	*285*	*250*	*274*	*309*	*337*	*803*	*104*	*119*	*346*	*263*	*84*	*664*	*252*	*565*	*216*
Unweighted	*1761*	*807*	*954*	*256*	*294*	*257*	*269*	*329*	*350*	*817*	*109*	*127*	*353*	*272*	*83*	*676*	*258*	*584*	*221*

For notes on breakdowns, symbols and tabulations, refer to Appendices I and II.

4.2 SECOND PRIORITY FOR EXTRA GOVERNMENT SPENDING (Q.50b and Q.51b) by sex, age, economic position and party identification

| | TOTAL | SEX | | AGE MALE† | | | AGE FEMALE† | | | ECONOMIC POSITION | | | | | | PARTY IDENTIFICATION† | | | |
		Male	Female	18-34	35-54	55+	18-34	35-54	55+	Employee	Self-employed	Unemployed	Looks after home	Retired	Other	Cons.	Alliance	Labour	Non-aligned
	%	%	%	%	%	%	%	%	%	%	%	%	%	%	%	%	%	%	%
Health	26	25	27	28	24	22	28	29	23	27	26	26	27	21	26	25	24	28	25
Education	26	25	27	24	30	20	29	27	26	28	28	25	27	19	26	25	28	26	26
Help for industry	13	13	13	15	13	11	14	15	12	15	14	12	14	9	7	14	14	12	13
Housing	13	12	14	14	11	13	14	14	13	12	11	19	12	14	17	11	11	16	13
Social security benefits	6	6	7	5	5	9	7	5	7	4	2	10	7	11	17	4	9	8	6
Defence	4	6	3	5	6	7	2	2	3	4	5	1	2	6	5	7	2	2	2
Police and prisons	5	6	5	4	5	8	2	4	7	4	6	3	5	9	2	8	4	3	4
Roads	3	4	2	4	4	5	*	1	3	3	4	2	1	5	2	3	3	2	4
Public transport	2	2	2	1	2	3	1	1	2	1	1	1	2	3	–	1	3	2	1
Overseas aid	1	*	1	*	*	1	1	*	1	1	1	1	1	1	–	*	2	1	–
SOCIAL BENEFITS:																			
Retirement pensions	23	23	24	20	27	21	25	22	25	25	24	20	21	27	19	26	20	23	22
Benefits for disabled people	33	34	33	27	28	47	23	32	42	31	37	27	32	44	36	35	34	32	30
Benefits for unemployed	15	15	15	12	17	15	15	19	12	15	11	21	16	12	11	13	17	16	14
Benefits for single parents	13	11	15	17	11	6	19	15	10	15	11	12	12	8	15	12	15	13	13
Child benefits	13	15	11	21	14	8	17	10	6	12	13	20	15	6	17	11	11	14	13
BASE: ALL RESPONDENTS																			
Weighted	1719	793	926	258	285	250	274	309	337	803	104	119	346	263	84	664	252	565	216
Unweighted	1761	807	954	256	294	257	269	329	350	817	109	127	353	272	83	676	258	584	221

4.3 SOCIAL SPENDING AND THE LEVEL OF BENEFITS (Q.53 and Q.54)
by sex, age, social class and party identification

| | TOTAL | SEX | | AGE | | | | | | SOCIAL CLASS | | | | | | PARTY IDENTIFICATION† | | | |
| | | | | MALE | | | FEMALE† | | | | | | | | | | | | |
		Male	Female	18-34	35-54	55+	18-34	35-54	55+	I/II	III non-manual	III manual	IV/V	Looks after home	Other	Cons.	Alli-ance	Labour	Non-aligned
	%	%	%	%	%	%	%	%	%	%	%	%	%	%	%	%	%	%	%
GOVERNMENT SHOULD:																			
Reduce taxes, lower social spending	9	11	6	10	11	12	5	6	8	9	4	9	13	7	10	10	6	8	10
Keep same as now	54	55	53	56	54	56	54	54	53	59	59	56	49	50	50	63	54	46	49
Increase taxes, increase social spending	32	30	34	30	31	30	35	36	30	28	35	32	33	34	32	24	36	42	29
None/other/don't know	5	3	7	4	3	2	5	4	9	4	1	4	4	8	6	3	4	4	12
Not answered	*	*	*	-	-	-	*	-	*	-	-	-	-	*	2	*	-	*	*
BENEFITS ARE:																			
Too low, cause hardship	46	47	45	54	43	44	59	46	33	34	44	49	54	45	57	30	50	64	43
Too high, discourage job search	35	34	35	27	37	38	24	37	43	44	38	32	29	34	23	50	26	23	31
Neither	13	14	12	16	14	11	13	12	11	16	13	12	11	12	13	13	17	9	16
Don't know	6	5	7	3	6	6	3	5	12	5	4	6	6	8	7	7	7	4	8
Not answered	*	1	1	-	*	*	1	*	-	*	-	1	*	*	1	-	-	1	1
BASE: ALL RESPONDENTS																			
Weighted	1719	793	926	258	285	250	274	309	337	334	268	365	299	346	106	664	252	565	216
Unweighted	1761	807	954	256	294	257	269	329	350	343	281	362	316	353	106	676	258	584	221

4.4 SOCIAL SPENDING AND THE LEVEL OF BENEFITS (Q.53 and Q.54)
by region, district, economic position and trade union membership

	TOTAL	REGION						DISTRICT		ECONOMIC POSITION						TRADE UNION MEMBERSHIP			
		Scotland	North	Midlands	Wales	South	GLC	Metro-politan	Non-metro.	Employee	Self-employed	Unemp-loyed	Looks after home	Retired	Other	Curr-ent	In past	Never	No info.
	%	%	%	%	%	%	%	%	%	%	%	%	%	%	%	%	%	%	%
GOVERNMENT SHOULD:																			
Reduce taxes, lower social spending	9	8	11	10	6	6	9	10	8	8	12	10	7	12	8	7	8	11	5
Keep same as now	54	55	50	56	52	55	59	52	56	57	57	48	50	54	50	54	53	56	56
Increase taxes, increase social spending	32	30	36	29	34	33	27	35	31	32	24	35	34	29	39	37	35	27	30
None/other/don't know	5	7	4	5	8	5	5	4	6	2	7	7	10	6	2	2	4	7	8
Not answered	*	-	*	-	-	*	*	*	*	-	1	-	*	*	1	-	*	-	1
BENEFITS ARE:																			
Too low, cause hard-ship	46	67	50	41	48	38	45	51	43	46	26	76	45	36	61	50	50	40	51
Too high, discourage job search	35	17	34	39	26	41	34	32	36	37	49	11	34	40	21	32	33	38	32
Neither	13	10	10	14	22	13	14	10	14	13	17	9	12	12	15	14	11	13	14
Don't know	6	5	5	6	5	7	8	6	6	4	8	2	8	12	5	4	5	9	2
Not answered	*	1	*	-	-	1	-	*	*	*	1	1	*	*	-	1	*	*	1
BASE: ALL RESPONDENTS																			
Weighted	*1719*	*183*	*456*	*286*	*87*	*517*	*191*	*615*	*1104*	*803*	*104*	*119*	*346*	*263*	*84*	*463*	*484*	*689*	*83*
Unweighted	*1761*	*179*	*474*	*291*	*87*	*535*	*195*	*631*	*1130*	*817*	*109*	*127*	*353*	*272*	*83*	*474*	*497*	*707*	*83*

4.5 FAMILIES WHO GET BEST VALUE FROM TAXES FROM NHS (Q.55)
by region, district, social class and party identification

	TOTAL	REGION						DISTRICT		SOCIAL CLASS						PARTY IDENTIFICATION†			
		Scotland	North	Midlands	Wales	South	GLC	Metro-politan	Non-metro.	I/II	III non-manual	III manual	IV/V	Looks after home	Other	Cons.	Alli-ance	Labour	Non-aligned
	%	%	%	%	%	%	%	%	%	%	%	%	%	%	%	%	%	%	%
High income families	24	28	31	25	18	19	22	29	22	13	20	31	35	23	25	16	17	39	22
Middle income families	14	11	11	16	14	17	18	13	15	16	16	13	13	12	18	14	20	14	13
Low income families	44	42	42	40	48	45	50	45	43	56	47	41	32	42	42	54	46	34	34
Don't know/No difference	16	17	15	17	17	18	9	12	19	13	17	13	18	21	14	15	16	12	30
Not answered	1	3	2	1	3	1	1	2	1	2	1	1	2	1	1	2	-	1	1
BASE: ALL RESPONDENTS																			
Weighted	1719	183	456	286	87	517	191	615	1104	334	268	365	299	346	106	664	252	565	216
Unweighted	1761	179	474	291	87	535	195	631	1130	343	281	362	316	353	106	676	258	584	221

4.6 SATISFACTION WITH NHS (Q.56)
by sex, age, region and district

	TOTAL	SEX		AGE						REGION						DISTRICT	
				MALE			FEMALE†										
		Male	Female	18-34	35-54	55+	18-34	35-54	55+	Scotland	North	Midlands	Wales	South	GLC	Metro-politan	Non-metro.
	%			%			%			%					%	%	%
Very satisfied	11	10	11	10	9	12	5	10	17	17	11	10	11	11	6	10	11
Quite satisfied	44	42	45	35	42	48	50	42	44	49	41	48	59	42	37	40	46
Neither	20	19	20	24	15	17	22	20	20	16	19	23	12	19	22	21	19
Quite dissatisfied	18	21	16	23	24	14	17	19	13	14	21	12	10	20	25	21	17
Very dissatisfied	7	8	7	7	9	8	6	9	6	4	8	7	7	7	9	8	7
Not answered	*	*	*	-	1	-	-	-	1	-	-	*	-	1	*	*	*
BASE: ALL RESPONDENTS																	
Weighted	1719	793	926	258	285	250	274	309	337	183	456	287	87	517	191	615	1104
Unweighted	1761	807	954	256	294	257	269	329	350	179	474	291	87	535	195	631	1130

4.7 HOUSEHOLD ACCOMMODATION (Q.63)
by region, gross household income, social class and economic position of respondent

REGION:

	TOTAL	HOUSEHOLD ACCOMMODATION†		
		Owner occupied	Rented from local authority	Other rented
	%	%	%	%
Scotland	11	6	21	16
North	6	6	3	9
N. West	11	11	14	6
Yorks	10	9	10	11
W. Midlands	9	10	8	6
E. Midlands	8	7	6	16
Wales	5	6	4	4
S. West	9	11	3	6
S. East	21	22	22	16
GLC	11	11	10	13

GROSS HOUSEHOLD INCOME:

	TOTAL	Owner occupied	Rented from local authority	Other rented
Under £5,000 pa	32	21	53	48
£5,000-£7,999	22	21	23	23
£8,000-£11,999	18	21	10	13
£12,000+ pa	17	23	6	9
No information	12	13	8	9
ALL RESPONDENTS: *Weighted*	1719	1123	432	159
Unweighted	1761	1148	462	143

SOCIAL CLASS OF RESPONDENT:

	TOTAL	HOUSEHOLD ACCOMMODATION†		
		Owner occupied	Rented from local authority	Other rented
	%	%	%	%
I/II	19	24	7	19
III non-manual	16	18	7	17
III manual	21	20	25	19
IV/V	17	12	31	19
Looks after home	20	20	23	14
Not classified/other /no occupation	6	5	6	11

ECONOMIC POSITION OF RESPONDENT:

	TOTAL	Owner occupied	Rented from local authority	Other rented
Employee	46	51	35	47
Self-employed	7	8	3	2
Unemployed	7	5	12	8
Looks after home	20	20	23	14
Retired	15	13	21	18
Other	5	4	6	11
ALL RESPONDENTS: *Weighted*	1719	1123	432	159
Unweighted	1761	1148	462	143

BASE: ALL RESPONDENTS

4.8 IMAGES OF THE WELFARE STATE (Q.217)
Percentaged by row

BASE: ALL RESPONDENTS   *Unweighted: 1761*
                            Weighted: 1719

	Agree strongly	Just agree	Neither	Just disagree	Disagree strongly	Not answered	No self-completion questionnaire
People rely too much on doctors instead of taking more responsibility for their own health	% 19	33	18	17	7	1	6
The welfare state makes people nowadays less willing to look after themselves	% 22	27	20	16	9	1	6
Social workers have too much power to interfere with people's lives	% 19	25	30	13	5	1	6
Children have an obligation to look after their parents when they are old	% 18	21	21	18	15	1	6
The welfare state encourages people to stop helping each other	% 13	22	26	22	9	2	6
Social workers should put the child's interests first even if it means taking the child away from its natural parents	% 30	31	17	10	5	1	6
Women should always have their babies in a hospital or nursing home	% 27	21	22	16	7	1	6
People receiving social security are made to feel like second class citizens	% 21	25	19	17	10	1	6

5 Educational issues and priorities

Harvey Goldstein*

The purpose of this chapter, in common with the others, is to provide no more than a brief summary of the principal findings. Only a small part of the data has been analysed so far and there is much of interest still to explore. We have not yet, for example, even analysed attitudes by whether or not respondents had children at school or at what type of school; we have not yet studied the responses of different age groups within social class or political support groups. Our aim here is mainly to provide interested readers with a broad picture of the main results so that they can take the analysis further themselves.

In designing the questions, we hoped to be able to follow previous surveys in Britain and elsewhere so that comparisons across cultures and times could be reported. This has been difficult for a number of reasons.

First, past surveys of attitudes to education have concentrated on educational 'problems', and we have been unwilling to perpetuate such an emphasis. Second, especially in the United States, simple ratings of education have been sought which, while interesting, are probably of less use than attempts to obtain educational priorities. Hence, this discussion of results only occasionally refers to other studies.

In an environment where school-leavers increasingly face the prospect of unemployment, educational priorities seem bound to reflect this. As will be seen, when asked about the priorities in secondary schools between a number of educational goals, easily the most popular choice was 'more training and preparation for jobs' followed by 'stricter discipline'. For primary schools, however, the most popular priorities were 'smaller classes' followed by 'more emphasis on developing the child's skills and interests'.

As far as general priorities for extra educational spending are concerned,

*Professor of Statistics at the University of London Institute of Education.

the group selected as the most in need of attention was 'less able children with special needs', followed closely by 'secondary schoolchildren'. Surprisingly, perhaps, nursery and pre-school children are accorded a low priority for extra expenditure. Less surprisingly, perhaps, students in higher education are seen as equally undeserving of extra expenditure. Nonetheless, when asked about higher education specifically, very few respondents could be found to support the view that opportunities for young people in Britain to go on to higher education should be reduced. Similarly, only a minority (though a much more sizeable one) would like to see the system of grants for students changed to a loan system.

Attitudes to private education are predictably polarised. Those who have experienced it or are probably in a position to afford it for their children are, on the whole, fairly well disposed to its existence, even to its expansion, while those who have no experience or little prospect of private education are less enthusiastic. Although only one in five of the population would actually like to see a reduction in the number of private schools, the majority of these favour abolition. Nonetheless, a clear majority of our sample believed that a reduction in private education would have no impact on the state system.

As far as multi-cultural education is concerned, we found fairly positive attitudes towards some policies and a negative attitude towards others. There is, for example, strong support for including in the general curriculum more emphasis on the history and culture of countries from which ethnic minority pupils originate. Similarly there is strong support for special classes in English for those who require them. But when asked about special dispensations to pupils from different ethnic backgrounds — such as allowing separate religious instruction if requested, allowing traditional dress to be worn, allowing mother tongue lessons in school hours — the votes in favour decreased substantially. On the whole, there is strong support for measures that will incorporate cultural diversity and little support for those that will encourage cultural separateness.

Previous surveys

Few previous attempts have been made to carry out representative surveys of attitudes to education in Britain. Most previous studies have been small, local and unrepresentative (e.g Chuman and Gallop 1981, Luckham 1972). In 1979 and 1980, however, the National Consumer Council carried out a large survey of 2000 adults using a probability sample (National Consumer Council, 1981). Unfortunately, this survey was directed mainly towards eliciting consumer concerns about services. Of the 16 questions dealing with education, almost all asked about the respondent's 'worries' or 'complaints'. While of interest, such questions inevitably represent only one aspect of public attitudes.

Over and above such limitations, there is the more general problem in surveys of the subtle effects of question wording on response. It is well known, for example, that by wording questions negatively as opposed to positively, or by adding a 'neutral' response to a preference scale, responses can be altered — both in terms of marginal frequencies and associations between variables (Kalton & Schuman, 1982). This awareness has informed the design of the present enquiry.

Surveys in other countries

In the United States and Canada there has been somewhat more activity. Since 1969 the US Gallup organisation has conducted an annual probability-based survey involving about 1500 adults to study attitudes towards American public (i.e. non-private) schools (Gallup, 1982). Similar questions are asked each year permitting simple analyses of trends, and it has become a major source for commentators on the state of US schooling. Many of the Gallup attitude questions ask respondents to 'grade' aspects of education – for example, teachers – or to 'rate' the amount of attention paid to a number of listed school subjects. Gallup's starting point, however, is to ask about major problems facing schools, with the risk that the 'response set' thus created might have a negative impact on respondents' attitudes to subsequent issues.

In Canada, the Ontario Institute for Studies in Education has carried out four surveys of attitudes to education from 1978 to 1982 (Livingstone *et al*, 1983). Several questions asked people to express satisfaction or dissatisfaction with issues such as discipline, contact with parents etc. Other questions asked people to agree or disagree with statements, for example about relations between school and work. There were also priority questions both on relative government spending, and on spending within the educational system.

Necessarily, surveys in other countries are difficult to use comparatively because of different educational and cultural traditions which in turn create problems for question wording. In addition, we were conscious that our survey was being conducted at a time of major budgetary cuts in Britain, so we wanted to avoid formulating questions that allowed respondents to opt for unconstrained improvements. Instead we concentrated initially on priorities.

The findings

Resource allocation

Our first two questions in this section were designed to establish the perceived importance of different aspects of education. The first sought a ranking of different levels of education by asking for respondents' two major priorities for extra public spending on education. The items we presented and the overall results were:

	First priority for extra spending
	%
Nursery or pre-school children	10
Primary school children	16
Secondary school children	29
Less able children with special needs	32
Students at colleges, universities and polytechnics	9

Table 5.1 at the end of this chapter includes the principal breakdowns. It shows that women, the elderly, Labour identifiers and those who left school at 16 or under all attach a relatively higher priority to the needs of less able children at the expense of secondary school children. The breakdowns also show that women attach greater priority than men to pre-school education at the expense of higher education; among those with personal or household experience of private education, this relative preference is reversed. The strong vote for children with special needs may in part reflect the concentration of local education authorities on special needs provision following the 1981 Education Act. But the overall preference for less able children and secondary school children, in comparison with all other listed groups, is very clear.

In the event, although the question was principally concerned with different levels of education, we inserted the option of special needs provision in order to explore preferences for particular groups of children within the system. The results we obtained suggest that further research could usefully be undertaken to explore priorities between different groups of children within each level of education.

Factors in improving schools

In our second question on priorities, we asked our sample to select what they considered to be the most important factor which could lead to improvements first in primary schools, then in secondary schools (see **Tables 5.2** and **5.3**). A list of thirteen possible improvements was given to respondents, from which they were asked to select only the single most important.

'Smaller classes' were most highly rated for primary schools (31%), followed by 'more emphasis on developing the child's skills and interests' (19%), and 'more resources for books and equipment' (15%). 'More discussion between parents and teachers' and 'stricter discipline' accounted only for about 10% each, and a number of other factors achieved 3% or less — better buildings, better pay for teachers, involvement of parents in governing bodies, emphasis on preparation for exams, preparation for job training, more emphasis on arts, maths or English. Some interesting age patterns emerge, the older respondents being more inclined to choose stricter discipline at the expense, for instance, of developing skills and interests. There was also less concern with smaller classes among ethnic minorities while those who stayed in full-time education after the age of 16 tended to give a relatively higher priority to developing a child's skills and interests. Women were particularly concerned about smaller classes.

The pattern of answers for secondary schools was very different. Here 'smaller classes' was given first priority by only 10% of the sample, the same proportion who favoured 'more spending on books and equipment'. For secondary schools, 'more training and preparation for jobs' was given the greatest support (27%), followed by 'stricter discipline' (19%) and 'more emphasis on developing skills and interests' (13%). 'More discussion between parents and teachers' was an even smaller priority (5%) than it was for primary schools. Only 7% chose 'more emphasis on exam preparation', while items such as better buildings, better pay for teachers, involvement of parents in governing bodies and emphasis on arts, maths or English all achieved a very low priority (less than 3%).

Unlike the priorities for primary schools, we found no major sex differences in the results, but there were age differences. The younger age groups placed even greater emphasis on training for jobs at the expense mostly of stricter discipline.

It would be wrong to make too much of direct comparisons of priorities between primary and secondary schools in Britain, because we allowed respondents to select only one improvement for each. Nevertheless, it does appear that job training and stricter discipline are the clear priorities for secondary schools, while smaller classes and the related item of developing individual skills and interests are the priorities for primary schools. In both cases it was surprising that so few people gave priority to so-called 'basic' subjects such as mathematics and English, given the continuing public commentary on these. If we had asked directly about 'basic skills' it is possible that a somewhat larger percentage would have chosen this option. In the 1982 US Gallup poll, about 26% of the sample felt there should be more emphasis on the 'basics', while in Ontario 'basic' and 'everyday' skills were ranked only third behind 'job training and career preparation', and 'development of creativity'. More relevant, perhaps, when asked about basic reading, writing and arithmetic, 93% of the US public were opposed to any cuts. Unfortunately these questions were not asked in terms of priorities and therefore have only limited utility here. In any case the differences between America and Britain seem to be large: for example the NCC survey in Britain found that only 9% of respondents regarded discipline as a problem compared with 70% in the US Gallup poll.

The thirteen options we presented to respondents in this question clearly do not represent similar levels of additional expenditure or resource allocation. But the question was framed primarily in order to understand how educational objectives are viewed in primary and secondary schools. In summary it appears that at secondary level the specific issue of job training tends to overwhelm most other issues, while at primary level somewhat broader educational objectives are still allowed scope.

State and private schools

With private schooling continuing as a political issue, and often linked to the possible consequences of reduced resources for state schools, it is interesting to estimate the support for different levels of private schooling and the possible effect of a reduction in their number on state schools. Two questions were asked. The first obtained people's views on the relative number of private schools in Britain (more, fewer, the same), and the second on the likely impact of their existence on state schools. It seemed most useful to obtain views about the effect of a change in the number of private schools, so we sought opinions on the effect of fewer private schools. We could − instead or in addition − have asked for opinions on the effect of more private schools and this might well have produced a different picture. But resource limitations prevented our doing so.

The majority of respondents (67%) favoured the *status quo* and thought in any case that a reduction in private schools would make no difference to the state system (59%) (see **Tables 5.4** and **5.5**). But the balance among the minority who wanted a change was in favour of a reduction in private education (19%) as opposed to an expansion (11%). Moreover, the majority of those who wanted a reduction favoured abolition of the private school system. This balance of opinion was reflected among different age groups. Not surprisingly, among those with household experience of private education, those in the higher social classes and Conservative identifiers (which are related characteristics), the balance of opinion was more favourable to private schools. Conversely, among those in manual occupations and Labour identifiers a stronger vote against private schools is apparent; around one in three Labour identifiers, for instance, would favour a reduction in the number of such schools, and one in five would favour abolition. Alliance identifiers had intermediate views both on the number of private schools and on the likely impact of a reduction.

Overall, as many respondents (18%) thought that state schools would benefit as those who thought they would suffer if private schools were reduced, the majority believing that the state schools would not be affected. The same proportion of Conservative identifiers (12%) as of labour identifiers held 'non-conforming' views on this issue.

A related issue is the question of who benefits most from present public expenditure on education. The question we asked was:

> On the whole, which of these three types of family would you say gets best value from their taxes out of government spending on education . . . those with high incomes, those with middle incomes, or those with low incomes?

We asked similar questions on health and housing, and it is interesting to compare the answers.

	Government spending on		
	NHS	Housing	Education
Who benefits most:	%	%	%
High income families	24	30	34
Low income families	44	36	30

There is, however, a strong class and income effect here: on the whole, those with high incomes believe that low income families benefit more, and vice versa. But it is interesting to note that, of the three areas of expenditure we investigated, education was viewed as the most regressive. It will be instructive to monitor these answers over the years as the debate on resources for both the health and education services continues.

Educational standards

The question of changes over time in educational 'standards' has continued to dominate media discussions of education, despite the dubious relevance of any research evidence to support a particular view, or even to supply a generally accepted definition of 'standards'. Nevertheless, only 4% of the sample failed to express a view on this issue, and overall about the same number (39%) thought that standards had improved since their own schooldays as thought they had deteriorated (41%). Not surprisingly, those most recently in school were less likely than others to believe that standards had either improved or declined, since there would not have been time. There is, however, a large social class difference in the answers: the middle classses, Conservatives, those who left school beyond the minimum age, and those with household experience of private schooling all had majorities who believed that standards had declined since they were educated. On the whole, the opposite was true for working class respondents, Labour identifiers and early school leavers (see **Table 5.6**).

There seems to be no good previous data with which to compare the present findings and this makes them somewhat difficult to interpret. During the 1970s the US Gallup Poll found a downward trend in the high ratings, but it had ceased by the end of the 1970s. Likewise, in Ontario there was a decline in 'satisfaction with schools' from 1978 to 1979 but little change after that. Once again, this question is essentially more useful as a monitoring device than it is for a single reading.

Publication of examination results

The 1981 Education Act has required schools to make public examination results publicly available from 1982. It is too early to assess the importance of this development. Nevertheless, it seemed useful to establish a baseline level of opinion so that changing views can be monitored by future surveys.

About two-thirds of people think such information would be useful for parents of present or future pupils, but only about half of these think it would be *very* useful. These figures may simply reflect a general feeling that publication of hitherto unavailable information ought to be useful; so it would be rash to read too much into the answers. There were some minor age differences in the distribution of answers, with younger respondents less likely to be enthusiastic than those in the 35-44 age group, a group for whom such information is probably most relevant to their assessment of secondary schools.

Opportunities for higher education

In our earlier question about overall educational priorities, only 9% chose higher education as their first priority for extra educational spending (see Table 5.1). Nevertheless 44% feel that opportunities for young people to go on to higher education should be increased. At a time when such opportunities are decreasing as a result of government cuts only 5% felt that there should be fewer such opportunities. This is not necessarily contradictory. After all, education spending is given a high ranking (24%, second only to health) by respondents (see Chapter 4) in relation to government spending in general. This is true incidentally of the USA as well, where education was the most popular first priority (21%), just ahead of health and in Canada it was third (13%) behind both health and job creation.

The younger age groups, Labour identifiers, and those with full time education after the minimum school leaving age were more favourably disposed towards increased opportunities for higher education than were the elderly, Conservative and Alliance identifiers, and those who left school before 16. Ethnic minorities were strongly in favour of increased opportunities (60%) with only a third believing opportunities were currently at about the right level (see **Table 6.7**). The cluster of groups in favour of promoting higher education

— the younger, the better educated and Labour identifiers — is unusual and ought to be examined in further work.

   Although not currently an issue, there had in 1982/3 been discussion of giving loans rather than grants to students in higher education, so we included a question to establish public support for such a change. A majority of respondents (57%) were in favour of retaining the grant system, and there was a clear age trend from those under 35 (66%) to those 55 and over (45%) and a trend also from Labour (66%) through Alliance to Conservative (51%) (see **Table 5.8**). Those with full time education beyond 16 (and therefore more likely to have experienced grants) were also more likely to opt for grants in preference to loans.

Provision for cultural diversity in schools

In the self-completion part of the questionnaire, respondents were asked whether or not they thought that schools containing many children whose parents come from other countries and cultures should adopt special policies. Such policies included:

	% agreeing
providing special classes in English if required	77
teaching *all* children about the history and culture of these countries	74
allowing those for whom it is important to wear traditional dress at school	43
teaching children (from different backgrounds) about the history and culture of their parents' countries of origin	40
providing separate religious instruction if their parents request it	32
allowing these children to study their mother tongue in school hours	16

Table 5.9 contains more detailed breakdowns. The responses suggest considerable support for making some provision for minority cultures in schools, but rather more support for policies that will enhance uniformity rather than diversity. Thus, for instance, there is little support for separate religious or mother tongue instruction while there is strong support for teaching English and for the overall curriculum to include more about different cultures. As always, however, there are subgroup differences. Principally, women are somewhat more favourably disposed than men towards separate religious instruction, traditional dress and a curriculum expansion to include lessons to all children about different cultures; the oldest age group was more sympathetic towards separate religious instruction, while the non-manual group was more sympathetic towards provision of English classes. Ethnic minority groups were more sympathetic towards almost all aspects, but primarily towards mother tongue provision and curriculum expansion for minority ethnic groups. On all the policies, Labour and Alliance identifiers were more sympathetic than Conservative towards allowances being made for cultural minorities in schools, particularly towards steps to encourage diversity rather than those, such as English classes, that enhance standardisation.

References

LUCKHAM, B., 'The Image of Adult Education', *Studies in Adult Education, 4,* (1972) pp 1-20.
CHUMAN, P. A. S. and GALLUP, R., 'Educational Attitudes of Bengali Families in Cardiff', *Journal of Multilingual and Multicultural Development, 2,* (1981) pp 127-144.
NATIONAL CONSUMER COUNCIL *An Introduction to the Findings of the Consumer Concerns Survey,* NCC, London (1981).
KALTON, G. and SCHUMAN, H., 'The Effect of the Question on Survey Responses; a Review', *Journal of Royal Statistical Society, A, 145,* (1982) pp 42-73.
LIVINGSTONE, D. W., HART, D. J. and McLEAN, C. D., *Public Attitudes Toward Education in Ontario 1982,* Ontario Institute for Studies in Education, Informal Series/51.

Acknowledgements

Special thanks are owed to the following people who provided help and comment on early versions of the questions:

Tessa Blackstone
James Cornford
Barbara Goldstein
Caroline Gipps
Stephen Steadman
William Taylor
Barbara Tizard
Jenny Tuson
Alison Wolfe

5.1 HIGHEST PRIORITY FOR EXTRA GOVERNMENT SPENDING ON EDUCATION (Q.65a)
by sex, age, social class, ethnic group, age of leaving full-time education, schooling of household members and party identification

	TOTAL	SEX		AGE†			SOCIAL CLASS				ETHNIC GROUP		AGE LEFT FULL TIME EDUCATION†		SCHOOLING OF HOUSEHOLD⁰		PARTY IDENTIFICATION†			
		Male	Female	18-34	35-54	55+	Non-manual	Manual	Looks after home	Other	White	Black/Asian/Other	16 or under	16 or Over	State Only	Private (any member)	Cons.	Alliance	Labour	Non-aligned
	%	%	%	%	%	%	%	%	%	%	%	%	%	%	%	%	%	%	%	%
Nursery/pre-school children	10	7	13	13	12	7	9	10	15	7	10	12	10	11	11	6	9	8	13	9
Primary school children	16	18	15	14	17	18	15	18	16	17	16	18	16	17	17	11	16	16	18	14
Secondary school children	29	33	25	33	30	22	33	29	22	21	29	24	26	36	27	37	34	34	23	21
Less able children with special needs	32	27	37	30	29	37	29	32	38	36	32	38	35	21	33	30	28	27	37	41
Students at colleges, universities or polytechnics	9	12	7	9	11	9	11	9	5	17	10	7	8	14	9	14	11	11	7	9
None of these/don't know	3	3	3	1	2	6	3	2	5	2	3	1	3	2	3	3	3	4	2	5
Not answered	*	*	*	*	1	1	*	*	*	2	*	-	*	-	*	-	*	-	-	1
BASE: ALL RESPONDENTS Weighted	1719	793	926	533	593	587	602	664	346	106	1631	88	1338	377	1491	228	664	252	565	216
Unweighted	1761	807	954	525	623	607	624	678	353	106	1677	84	1381	374	1529	232	676	258	584	221

For notes on breakdowns, symbols and tabulations, refer to Appendices I and II.

5.2 MOST IMPORTANT FACTOR TO IMPROVE PRIMARY SCHOOLS (Q.66a)
by sex, age, social class, ethnic group, age of leaving full-time education, schooling of household members and party identification

	TOTAL	SEX		AGE +			SOCIAL CLASS				ETHNIC GROUP		AGE LEFT FULL TIME EDUCATION +		SCHOOLING OF HOUSEHOLD		PARTY IDENTIFICATION +			
		Male	Female	18-34	35-54	55+	Non-manual	Manual	Looks after home	Other	White	Black/Asian/Other	16 or under	Over 16	State Only	Private (any member)	Cons.	Alli-ance	Labour	Non-aligned
	%	%	%	%	%	%	%	%	%	%	%	%	%	%	%	%	%	%	%	%
More resources for books and equipment	15	17	14	19	16	12	14	16	17	12	15	21	16	15	16	12	13	18	19	11
More discussion between parents and teachers	9	9	10	9	8	11	8	11	10	8	10	8	10	7	10	8	9	10	11	9
Smaller classes	31	27	34	32	37	23	35	7	32	21	31	16	30	34	30	37	31	31	26	39
More emphasis on developing child's skills and interests	19	21	17	26	17	15	21	18	16	26	19	15	17	26	20	17	19	18	19	21
Stricter discipline	11	10	12	6	11	16	11	10	12	17	11	15	12	9	11	15	14	11	9	10
Other factor	11	14	8	6	10	18	9	14	10	10	11	17	12	7	11	10	12	10	13	6
None of these/don't know	2	2	3	1	2	5	1	3	3	-	2	5	3	2	2	2	2	2	2	4
Not answered	1	*	1	*	-	1	*	*	*	6	*	4	1	-	1	*	*	*	1	2
BASE: ALL RESPONDENTS																				
Weighted	*1719*	*793*	*926*	*533*	*593*	*587*	*602*	*664*	*346*	*106*	*1631*	*88*	*1338*	*377*	*1491*	*228*	*664*	*252*	*565*	*216*
Unweighted	*1761*	*807*	*954*	*525*	*623*	*607*	*624*	*678*	*353*	*106*	*1677*	*84*	*1381*	*374*	*1529*	*232*	*676*	*258*	*594*	*221*

5.3 MOST IMPORTANT FACTOR TO IMPROVE SECONDARY SCHOOLS (Q66b)
by sex, age, social class, ethnic group, age of leaving full-time education, schooling of household members and party identification

	TOTAL	SEX		AGE [+]			SOCIAL CLASS				ETHNIC GROUP		AGE LEFT FULL TIME EDUCATION [+]		SCHOOLING OF HOUSEHOLD [°]		PARTY IDENTIFICATION [+]			
		Male	Female	18-34	35-54	55+	Non-manual	Manual	Looks after home	Other	White	Black/Asian/Other	16 or under	Over 16	State Only	Private (any member)	Cons.	Alliance	Labour	Non-aligned
	%	%	%	%	%	%	%	%	%	%	%	%	%	%	%	%	%	%	%	%
More resources for books and equipment	10	10	9	12	10	7	12	8	7	14	10	6	9	13	10	10	9	13	9	10
More discussion between parents and teachers	5	4	5	5	3	6	3	5	6	7	4	7	5	4	5	3	4	7	6	3
Smaller classes	10	12	9	9	13	10	12	10	9	9	11	6	9	15	10	15	11	8	10	13
More emphasis on preparation for exams	7	7	6	7	6	8	6	8	6	8	7	5	7	5	7	5	8	4	7	6
More emphasis on developing child's skills and interests	13	13	13	16	16	8	15	12	14	14	13	16	12	17	13	15	14	18	12	9
More training and preparation for jobs	27	26	28	35	24	27	24	28	32	23	27	28	28	25	28	23	24	27	30	26
Stricter discipline	19	17	20	11	21	24	20	19	19	14	19	13	20	15	18	21	21	16	17	19
Other factor	6	8	5	5	6	9	6	8	5	8	6	10	7	5	6	6	6	6	7	7
None of these/don't know	2	2	3	1	1	5	1	3	3	-	2	3	2	1	2	1	2	1	2	4
Not answered	1	*	1	*	*	1	*	*	*	6	*	4	1	-	*	*	*	*	1	1
BASE: ALL RESPONDENTS Weighted	1719	793	926	533	593	587	602	664	346	106	1631	88	1338	377	1491	228	664	252	565	216
Unweighted	1761	807	954	525	623	607	624	678	353	106	1677	84	1381	374	1529	232	676	258	584	221

5.4 PROPORTION OF PRIVATE SCHOOLS (Q67a)
by sex, age, social class, ethnic group, age of leaving full-time education, schooling of household members and party identification

	TOTAL	SEX		AGE†			SOCIAL CLASS				ETHNIC GROUP		AGE LEFT FULL TIME EDUCATION†		SCHOOLING OF HOUSEHOLD°		PARTY IDENTIFICATION†			
		Male	Female	18-34	35-54	55+	Non-manual	Manual	Looks after home	Other	White	Black/Asian/Other	16 or under	Over 16	State only	Private (any member)	Cons.	Alliance	Labour	Non-aligned
	%	%	%	%	%	%	%	%	%	%	%	%	%	%	%	%	%	%	%	%
More	11	12	10	8	12	12	12	11	9	10	11	13	10	15	9	25	19	7	4	8
About same as now	67	65	69	69	69	64	71	65	68	57	67	68	68	67	68	63	73	74	59	66
Fewer	8	8	9	9	9	8	6	9	9	12	9	5	9	8	9	5	3	9	14	9
None at all	11	12	10	11	10	12	8	12	11	19	11	11	11	9	12	5	4	8	20	10
Other answer/don't know	2	2	2	2	2	4	2	2	3	-	2	3	3	1	2	2	2	2	2	6
Not answered	*	*	*	1	*	*	*	*	-	2	*	-	*	*	*	-	*	*	*	1

5.5 EFFECT ON STATE SCHOOLS IF FEWER PRIVATE SCHOOLS (Q.67b)
by sex, age, social class, ethnic group, age of leaving full-time education, schooling of household members and party identification

STATE SCHOOLS:	TOTAL	SEX		AGE†			SOCIAL CLASS				ETHNIC GROUP		AGE LEFT FULL TIME EDUCATION†		SCHOOLING OF HOUSEHOLD°		PARTY IDENTIFICATION†			
		Male	Female	18-34	35-54	55+	Non-manual	Manual	Looks after home	Other	White	Black/Asian/Other	16 or under	Over 16	State only	Private (any member)	Cons.	Alliance	Labour	Non-aligned
	%	%	%	%	%	%	%	%	%	%	%	%	%	%	%	%	%	%	%	%
would benefit	18	19	17	18	19	17	17	17	19	24	18	8	17	20	17	20	12	18	25	15
would suffer	18	17	20	21	21	14	23	15	16	22	18	17	17	23	18	24	26	16	12	14
It would make no difference	59	61	58	59	57	62	58	64	58	47	59	65	60	57	60	54	59	63	57	63
Don't know	4	3	6	2	3	7	2	4	8	5	4	10	5	1	4	3	3	2	5	7
Not answered	*	*	*	*	-	1	*	*	-	2	*	-	*	-	*	-	*	*	*	1
BASE: ALL RESPONDENTS																				
Weighted	*1719*	*793*	*926*	*533*	*593*	*587*	*602*	*664*	*346*	*106*	*1631*	*88*	*1338*	*377*	*1491*	*228*	*664*	*252*	*565*	*216*
Unweighted	*1761*	*807*	*954*	*525*	*623*	*607*	*624*	*678*	*353*	*106*	*1677*	*84*	*1381*	*374*	*1529*	*232*	*676*	*258*	*584*	*221*

5.6 STANDARDS NOW COMPARED WITH THOSE DURING RESPONDENT'S SCHOOLING (Q.69)
by sex, age, social class, ethnic group, age of leaving full-time education,
schooling of household members and party identification

	TOTAL	SEX		AGE†			SOCIAL CLASS				ETHNIC GROUP		AGE LEFT FULL TIME EDUCATION†		SCHOOLING OF HOUSEHOLD[0]		PARTY IDENTIFICATION†			
		Male	Female	18-34	35-54	55+	Non-manual	Manual	Looks after home	Other	White	Black/Asian/Other	16 or under	Over 16	State only	Private (any member)	Cons.	Alliance	Labour	Non-aligned
	%	%	%	%	%	%	%	%	%	%	%	%	%	%	%	%	%	%	%	%
Higher now	39	38	41	20	46	51	32	44	46	36	41	26	44	22	41	27	33	36	49	38
About the same	15	17	13	30	11	6	15	17	11	21	15	15	14	18	16	11	12	16	15	21
Lower now	41	41	40	44	40	38	50	35	37	34	41	35	37	53	38	54	50	43	31	33
Not educated here/don't know	5	4	5	6	4	5	3	5	5	10	3	24	4	7	4	7	4	5	4	8
Not answered	*	1	*	*	1	1	1	*	*	*	1	-	*	1	1	*	*	-	1	1

5.7 OPPORTUNITIES TO GO ON TO HIGHER EDUCATION (Q.71a)
by sex, age, social class, ethnic group, age of leaving full-time education,
schooling of household members and party identification

	TOTAL	SEX		AGE†			SOCIAL CLASS				ETHNIC GROUP		AGE LEFT FULL TIME EDUCATION†		SCHOOLING OF HOUSEHOLD[0]		PARTY IDENTIFICATION†			
		Male	Female	18-34	35-54	55+	Non-manual	Manual	Looks after home	Other	White	Black/Asian/Other	16 or under	Over 16	State only	Private (any member)	Cons.	Alliance	Labour	Non-aligned
Should be increased	44	44	43	47	48	37	42	45	41	53	43	60	42	49	44	45	38	44	54	35
About right now	49	48	49	48	47	51	51	47	50	42	50	33	50	46	49	48	54	48	41	53
Should be reduced	5	5	5	4	4	7	5	5	5	2	5	2	5	5	5	5	6	6	3	6
Don't know	2	2	3	1	2	5	2	2	4	-	2	5	3	1	2	2	2	2	2	5
Not answered	*	*	*	*	-	1	*	*	*	2	*	-	*	-	*	*	*	*	*	1
BASE: ALL RESPONDENTS																				
Weighted	1719	793	926	533	593	587	602	664	346	106	1631	88	1338	377	1491	228	664	252	565	216
Unweighted	1761	807	954	525	623	607	624	678	353	106	1677	84	1381	374	1529	232	676	258	584	221

5.8 STUDENTS SHOULD GET GRANTS OR LOANS (Q.71b)
by sex, age, social class, ethnic group, age of leaving full-time education, schooling of household members and party identification

	TOTAL	SEX		AGE†			SOCIAL CLASS				ETHNIC GROUP		AGE LEFT FULL TIME EDUCATION†		SCHOOLING OF HOUSEHOLD⁰		PARTY IDENTIFICATION†			
		Male	Female	18-34	35-54	55+	Non-manual	Manual	Looks after home	Other	White	Black/Asian/Other	16 or Over	under 16	State Only	Any member private	Cons.	Alliance	Labour	Non-aligned
	%	%	%	%	%	%	%	%	%	%	%	%	%	%	%	%	%	%	%	%
Grants	57	58	56	66	61	45	58	56	56	63	57	66	63	55	58	52	51	58	66	50
Loans	38	38	38	30	36	47	37	39	37	34	39	31	32	39	37	45	45	36	30	39
Don't know/other answer	4	4	5	3	3	7	4	4	6	2	5	2	5	3	5	1	3	4	4	10
Not answered	1	1	1	*	1	1	1	1	1	2	1	-	1	1	1	1	*	1	1	1

5.9 PROVISIONS FOR CULTURAL DIVERSITY IN SCHOOLS (Q.216)
by sex, age, social class, ethnic group, age of leaving full-time education, schooling of household members and party identification

	TOTAL	SEX		AGE†			SOCIAL CLASS				ETHNIC GROUP		AGE LEFT FULL TIME EDUCATION†		SCHOOLING OF HOUSEHOLD⁰		PARTY IDENTIFICATION†			
		Male	Female	18-34	35-54	55+	Non-manual	Manual	Looks after home	Other	White	Black/Asian/Other	16 or Over	under 16	State Only	Any member private	Cons.	Alliance	Labour	Non-aligned
Provide special English classes if required	77	77	77	81	78	74	82	74	78	76	77	80	75	87	77	82	77	84	78	70
Provide separate religious instruction if requested by parents	32	29	35	32	29	36	29	33	34	42	32	41	31	36	32	34	27	41	36	30
Allow traditional dress if important	43	40	46	47	45	38	44	40	45	49	43	48	41	52	42	49	38	53	45	41
Study mother tongue in school hours	16	17	16	16	15	18	18	15	15	24	16	32	14	25	16	20	12	16	20	18
Teach history and culture of parents' country	40	39	42	42	34	42	42	39	37	50	40	53	39	47	40	43	36	46	45	34
Teach history and culture of these countries to all children	74	70	77	75	75	71	76	71	74	71	74	71	72	79	73	76	73	78	74	68
No self-completion questionnaire	6	7	6	4	5	9	6	7	5	7	6	10	7	5	7	5	6	4	6	12
BASE: ALL RESPONDENTS Weighted	1719	793	926	533	593	587	602	664	346	106	1631	88	1338	377	1491	228	664	252	565	216
Unweighted	1761	807	954	525	623	607	624	678	353	106	1677	84	1381	374	1529	232	676	258	584	221

6 Social and moral values

Colin Airey[*]

Our survey suggests a widespread public belief that Britain is far from an equal opportunity society. Race and class prejudice and discrimination are seen to exist in large measures and are regarded as important obstacles to advancement. Around 90% of the population believe there is prejudice against Asians and blacks; around 70% that a person's social class affects his or her opportunities. Moreover, around a third of the total sample described themselves as prejudiced against people of other races.

Prospects for improvement during the 1980s are somewhat mixed. Over 40% of the population believe that race prejudice will increase during the 1980s and a further third that it will remain at its present level. Younger people (those aged 18-34), who are less likely than older people to express prejudice themselves, are particularly pessimistic about the growth of race prejudice in Britain. The outlook for class prejudice is arguably less bleak. A third of the population see it as a problem of declining importance. 16% believe that it will increase.

We did not ask respondents directly about gender or sex discrimination. But we did ask of married people which partner performed various household tasks and of unmarried people (both formerly married and never married) which partner *should* perform them. The answers were decisive: for married people a woman's exclusive domain includes washing and ironing (89%), making the evening meal (77%), and household cleaning (72%), while the man's exclusive domain includes the household repairs (82%).

People who have never been married are likely to take a somewhat different view of what ought to happen. Most of the tasks are seen by this group as ones that ought to be shared equally. The most interesting difference is between the young married and unmarried (aged 18-24). The unmarried are more or less

---

[*]Joint Deputy Director of Social and Community Planning Research.

completely egalitarian in their allocation of tasks, while the married have already taken on the tasks of their older counterparts.

So there is clearly strong resistance to male participation in household duties – or at least widespread acquiescence in traditional household divisions of labour.

We also examined attitudes towards a number of personal moral issues, among which were divorce, pre- and extra-marital sex, abortion and pornography. If public attitudes to these issues were to be classified on a permissiveness continuum, we would find relatively permissive attitudes towards divorce, pre-marital sex and abortion, and relatively censorious attitudes towards extra-marital sex, homosexuality and pornography. But there are large differences between subgroups and varying gradations of permissiveness and censoriousness according to circumstances. We come to these issues in the final section of this chapter.

Race prejudice and discrimination

The verb 'to be prejudiced' is not commonly used in the first person singular. Most people consider prejudice to be an attitude held by others. A social survey does not therefore lend itself easily to the measurement of prejudice. There are, nonetheless, a number of major studies of racial attitudes and prejudice among the British population, that form the background to any further research.

Banton (1959) reporting on fieldwork carried out in 1956 identified a proportion of about 1 in 10 of the population with rooted beliefs in the inferiority of black and coloured people. This finding is noteworthy particularly because the study was carried out in areas of low ethnic minority concentration and before urban race disturbance of the later 1950s focused public attention on the race issue.

In *Colour and Citizenship* (ed. Rose, 1969) Abrams reported the findings of a survey designed to measure the extent of race prejudice in Britain. The survey was conducted in five local authority areas – all with a high incidence of black and Asian residents – and identified indirectly, through a number of attitude questions, a proportion of the population (10%) that Abrams described as racially prejudiced and a further 17% that he described as prejudice-inclined. Abrams' findings were subject to some criticism on two counts. First his identification of the prejudiced as being 'authoritarian' (including the conclusion that they were therefore relatively unchangeable in their attitudes) was disputed. Second his description of the majority as tolerant or tolerant-inclined, despite evidence to the contrary in his other findings, was the subject of some debate. See Banton (1983) and Lawrence (1974).

Nonetheless, our first thoughts were to repeat some of the attitude measures that had been used 15 years previously in the widely reported Abrams study. That we could not do so is an indication of the extent to which the way in which we talk about race issues has changed in the intervening period. Both in terminology and content, the four questions on which Abrams mainly built his measurement of prejudice are now wholly inappropriate: some are concerned with attitudes to acts that would now be unlawful; some are simply offensive.

For purpose of illustration, Abrams' questions were:

"If you had any choice would you particularly avoid having neighbours from any of these places – West Indies, India, Pakistan? IF YES . . . even if they were professional people working at the hospital or university?"

"Do you think the authorities should let or refuse to let a council house or flat to a family born in the West Indies, India or Pakistan? IF REFUSE . . . even if the family had been on the waiting list for the right length of time?"

"Do you think a private landlord should let or refuse to let accommodation to a family born in the West Indies, India or Pakistan? IF REFUSE . . . even if he knew that the coloured family would look after the accommodation property?"

"Do you think the majority of coloured people in Britain are superior, equal or inferior to you?"

We chose instead to investigate the extent of race prejudice and discrimination by four groups of questions. The first referred to the extent to which race prejudice was thought to be a problem in Britain nowadays, whether it has been increasing and how it was likely to change. The second group referred to the extent to which respondents saw both themselves and others as prejudiced. The third referred to perceived discrimination and attitudes to legislation. And the fourth group referred to immigration and settlement issues. We also asked a series of questions about multi-cultural education, the results of which have been reported in Chapter 5.

Prejudice in Britain

The first two questions we asked on this topic were:

First of all, thinking of Asians – that is people originally from India and Pakistan, who now live in Britain. Do you think there is a lot of prejudice against them in Britain nowadays, a little, or hardly any?

And black people – that is West Indians and Africans – who now live in Britain. Do you think there is a lot of prejudice against them in Britain nowadays, a little or hardly any?

	Perceived prejudice against:	
	Asians	**Blacks**
	%	%
A lot	54 } 91	50 } 90
A little	37	40
Hardly any	6	7
Don't know/other answer	3	3

These figures show a striking degree of agreement that Britain is a prejudiced country. Such unanimity is rare, as other findings from the survey suggest.

There are no differences in the extent to which men and women believe Britain to be a prejudiced society (see **Table 6.1**). There is, however, a slight tendency for belief in race prejudice to be associated with age: the older a person is the less likely he or she is to believe that prejudice exists nowadays. Whereas prejudice is equally likely to be perceived by people in different occupational groups, it is less likely among those in low income households (who tend also to be older). Members of ethnic minority groups in the sample (there were only 84) were less likely than whites to perceive – or report – prejudice.

Most respondents (75%) did not differentiate in their perception of prejudice suffered by Asians and by blacks.

	%
A lot of prejudice against Asians; a lot against blacks	43
A little prejudice against Asians; a little against blacks	28
Hardly any prejudice against Asians; hardly any against blacks	4
More prejudice against Asians than blacks	12
More prejudice against blacks than Asians	9
Don't know/other answer	3

We then went on to ask about respondents' perception of the level of race prejudice in the past ('five years ago') and in the future ('in five years time'). The distribution of answers is also shown in Table 6.1. 45% of the sample took the view that race prejudice had become more widespread in Britain during the past five years, and 42% that it would become more prevalent than it is now during the next five years. Pessimism about the trend in race prejudice was strongest among those who perceived 'a lot' of prejudice nowadays, as the following figures illustrate.

Perceived prejudice against blacks nowadays

	Total	A lot	A little	Hardly any
	%	%	%	%
Racial prejudice in Britain:				
More now than 5 years ago	45	59	33	18
Less now than 5 years ago	16	10	22	36
Same as now	36	30	44	44
Will be more in 5 years	42	52	34	23
Will be less in 5 years	17	14	20	30
Same as now	36	31	44	40

Not only are young people (18-34) more likely to perceive race prejudice now, but they are also more likely to believe that its level will increase during the next five years. (Table 6.1.)

Self-rated prejudice

Calling into question the maxim that prejudice has no first person singular, we then asked all respondents:

How would you describe yourself. . . as very prejudiced against people of other races, a little prejudiced, or not prejudiced at all? IF AT ALL PREJUDICED: Against any race in particular?

It was never likely that the first category ('very prejudiced') would attract much support — and so it proved. It was inserted in order to make the second category ('quite prejudiced') more palatable — and seemed to do so. (See table below.) In framing our questions we had assumed, perhaps wrongly, that the word 'prejudice' would almost universally have a pejorative connotation. That is why we asked respondents about *other people's* prejudice before asking about their own, with a view to making any admission of prejudice on their part appear less deviant. In other words, we shared the long-standing scepticism of many researchers in this field about the prospect of getting people to admit to prejudice. In the event it is remarkable that over a third of our sample did so.

It would have been particularly interesting to have monitored answers to a question like this over the last ten years or so. In a society apparently committed to racial equality and tolerance, we would expect the proportion describing themselves as prejudiced to have declined. But we wonder whether the opposite trend has not been establishing itself — with expressed prejudice becoming more and more acceptable, or at least less and less inadmissible. We cannot tell. It is interesting, however, that Abrams classified 27% of the population as prejudiced or prejudice-inclined. Now, some fifteen years later, and on a self-rating question — which would be expected to underestimate the incidence of prejudice — we have found 35%. The full distribution of answers is shown below and the detailed breakdowns appear in **Table 6.2** at the end of this chapter.

Self rated prejudice

		Total
		%
Yes, very prejudiced		4
Yes, a little prejudiced		31
* Against:	Asians Pakistanis Indians Sikhs	} 10
* Against:	Blacks West Indians Africans	} 6
* Against:	Coloured, other racial groups	4
* Against:	No particular race	20
Not prejudiced at all		64
Other answer		1

The breakdowns show that women are less likely than men to describe themselves as prejudiced; older people (55+) are less likely than others to describe themselves as prejudiced; respondents in manual occupations are slightly less likely than those in non-manual occupations to describe themselves as prejudiced. The breakdowns also show large differences according to party identification. Alliance

---

* More answers than one were accepted.

and Labour identifiers (28%) are much less likely than Conservative identifiers (46%) to describe themselves as prejudiced. Self-rated racial prejudice is at a considerably lower level in Scotland and Wales than in England – where there is little regional variation.

Abrams also found that there were relatively more prejudiced men than women. He found, however, that Liberal supporters were less prejudiced than Labour, who in turn were less prejudiced than Conservative supporters. Now the cleavage appears to exist only between Conservative identifiers and the rest.

The greater the degree of self-rated racial prejudice the higher is the perceived level of racial prejudice in Britain. This may be because those who believe that prejudice is widespread are more likely to be open about their own prejudice. Or it may be that the more prejudiced one is, so the more convinced one is that others share one's views. (Table 6.1.)

As a further measure of prejudice and, to some extent, of integration, we asked four further hypothetical questions which we thought might capture greater levels of prejudice than the self-rating question was likely to do.

Do you think most white people would mind or not mind if a suitably qualified person of Asian (black or West Indian)* origin were appointed as their boss? IF WOULD MIND: A lot or a little?

And you personally? Would you mind or not mind? IF WOULD MIND: A lot or a little?

Do you think most white people would mind or not mind if one of their close relatives were to marry a person of Asian (black or West Indian)* origin? IF WOULD MIND: A lot or a little?

And you personally? Would you mind or not mind? IF WOULD MIND: A lot or a little?

The pattern of answers was similar whether respondents were asked about Asians or blacks. In confirmation of our earlier finding that, on the whole, people perceive more prejudice in others than in themselves, our sample believed the rest of the population to be much less accepting of ethnic minorities than they were. Whereas over half thought that the population at large would object to an Asian or black boss, around 20% said they would object personally. Whereas over three-quarters thought that the population at large would object to an Asian or black marriage to a close relative, between 50% and 60% of them said they would object personally (see **Tables 6.3** and **6.4**).

The table facing illustrates the extent to which individuals differentiate between what they consider to be most people's opinions and their own.

In each case, approximately 40% differentiated between their own and other people's opinions. In the great majority of these cases, the respondent considered other people to be more prejudiced than himself or herself. The questions about an Asian or black marriage revealed a much greater degree of prejudice than those about an Asian or black boss. Subgroup differences here are particularly interesting. (See Tables 6.3 and 6.4.) Whereas there are no substantial differences between men and women on this question, age continues to differentiate respondents. Although young people (aged 18-34) are hardly less likely than other age groups to believe that 'most people' would mind an Asian or black boss, they are less likely to mind themselves. And in response to the question

---

*Half of the sample was asked about Asians; half about blacks or West Indians.

about marriage there was a particularly marked difference. Among those aged 18-34 approximately two-thirds of both men and women would not mind an Asian marriage in the family, while among those aged 55 or over the position was reversed.

	Asian boss	Black boss	Asian marriage	Black marriage
	%	%	%	%
Most people would mind a lot; I would mind a lot	8	7	24	26
Most people would mind a little; I would mind a little	5	6	11	12
Most people would not mind; I would not mind	41	40	16	15
Most people would mind more than I would	38	40	35	35
I would mind more than most people would	4	3	9	8
Other answer/don't know	4	4	5	5

Among the non-manual occupational groups, the prospect of a black boss is more likely to be acceptable than the prospect of an Asian boss. Among the manual occupation groups, however, blacks and Asians are equally acceptable.

We felt it was important to check whether or not people who described themselves as prejudiced at our earlier question were also more likely to adopt a discriminatory stance at this question. If they had turned out to express attitudes that were similar to the rest of the population's, we would certainly have begun to doubt the utility of the self-rating question. In the event, as the summary table below shows, the self-rated 'prejudiced' are *much* more likely than the 'non-prejudiced' to express antipathy towards an Asian or black boss or relative. They are also more likely to attribute prejudice to 'most people' though the differences are less clear cut.

Self-rated prejudice

	Total	Prejudiced	Non-prejudiced
	%	%	%
Asian or black boss:			
I would mind (a lot or little)	20	38	9
Most people would mind	54	58	52
Asian or black marriage:			
I would mind (a lot or little)	54	77	41
Most people would mind	78	85	74

Discrimination

The existence of prejudice is one thing (and, as we have said, the term is not necessarily pejorative to everybody) but to what extent does it seem to have translated itself into discrimination?

Daniel (1968) reported on surveys carried out to evaluate the effectiveness of the 1965 Race Relations Act. His research established conclusive evidence of widespread discrimination against blacks and Asians in employment opportunities, housing and the provision of services. The study was widely reported and was influential in creating the climate of public opinion that led to the passing of more stringent anti-discrimination legislation in 1968.

In our survey we asked specifically about job discrimination.

On the whole, do you think people of Asian origin in Britain are not given jobs these days because of their race... a lot, a little or hardly at all?

And on the whole do you think people of West Indian origin in Britain are not given jobs these days because of their race... a lot, a little or hardly at all?

	Against Asians	Against West Indians
	%	%
Discrimination in employment:		
A lot	20	25
A little	40	40
Hardly at all	31	27
Don't know/other answer	9	9

So just under two-thirds of the population believe that Asians and West Indians suffer job discrimination, much lower proportions than those believing prejudice to exist in Britain but still a remarkable commentary on the extent to which people perceive Britain to be denying equal opportunities to ethnic minorities. Moreover, there were few subgroup differences of any size in the answers. (See **Table 6.5**.) Whereas younger people are more likely than older people to perceive prejudice, they are just as likely to perceive discrimination. There are few regional differences, except that Londoners are more likely than others to believe that there is discrimination in employment against blacks.

Smith (1976) found that 73% of the adult male population believed that employers discrimination against Asian and black employees and applicants. Our finding, though lower, is depressingly close to that figure some eight years later. Smith also found that Asian men (45%) were less likely than whites to perceive discrimination. We had too few Asians in our sample to analyse separately, but, among ethnic minorities as a whole there was a higher than average perception of discrimination, despite their lower than average perception of prejudice that we reported earlier. (See Table 6.5.)

Having completed our questioning about perceptions and expressions of prejudice and discrimination, we turned to the issue of race relations laws.

There is a law against racial discrimination, that is against giving unfair preference to a particular race in housing, jobs and so on. Do you generally support or oppose the idea of a law for this purpose.

	%
Support race law	69
Oppose race law	28
Other answer	3

It is interesting to note here that a slightly greater proportion of our sample (76%) supported a law against sex discrimination, and that 59% of the population supported both laws. As is the case with all such questions, however, much of the support may well be disguised support for the present situation, whatever it happens to be. Having told people that a law exists, a proportion of the population will tend to endorse its existence.

Nonetheless, there appears to be considerably more support for legislation against racial discrimination now than when Rose (1969) examined the question. He reports a number of opinion polls taken in 1967 and 1968 in which support for legislation averaged 45%. Most of these polls were taken near to or after the passing of the 1968 Race Relations Act. Since then there has been further legislation on race and a law against sex discrimination. So we would expect people to have become used to the idea of anti-discriminatory legislation. In that context, the fact that a quarter of the population still opposes such a law is, perhaps surprising. It is instructive to note that those who describe themselves as 'prejudiced' are more than twice as likely, as those who do not, to oppose the legislation.

On the whole, opposition to a law against discrimination increases with age; it is also greater among manual occupational groups than among non-manual ones; and it is greater among Conservative and Labour identifiers than among Alliance identifiers. (See **Table 6.6**.)

Immigration and settlement

We asked two questions in the self-completion questionnaire about immigration.

Britain controls the number of people from abroad that are allowed to settle in this country. Please say, for each of the groups below, whether you think Britain should allow more settlement, less settlement, or about the same as now?

Four groups were listed: Australians and New Zealanders, Indians and Pakistanis, people from common market countries, West Indians. Very few people could be found to support the notion of *more* settlement by any of the groups, but Australians and New Zealanders (15%) were more popular as potential immigrants than any of the other groups. The proportions wanting *less* settlement are decisively anti-Asian and anti-black.

Less settlement by:	Indians and Pakistanis	67%
	West Indians	62%
	People from common market countries	42%
	Australians and New Zealanders	26%

Even among the ethnic minority respondents in our sample, the proportion favouring less settlement by Indians and Pakistanis or by West Indians was as high as 45%. The pattern of answers to this question was remarkably consistent throughout all subgroups of the population: black or Asian immigration is generally unpopular and — as we would expect — decidedly so among those who describe themselves as prejudiced.

We also wanted to find out whether people distinguished between immigration in general and settlement by dependents. So we asked:

Now thinking about the families (husbands, wives, children, parents) of people who have already settled in Britain, would you say in general that Britain should. . . be stricter in controlling the settlement of close relatives, or less strict. . ., or keep the controls about the same as now?

It might have been expected that the majority would choose the third option. Yet only a third of the sample (32%) responded in this way, the majority (53%) opting for stricter control and only 8% for less strict control. Ethnic minority respondents comprised the only group we identified within which a sizeable vote for less strict control of dependents could be found; but even here the vote was not overwhelming at 24%.

Conservative identifiers (62% favouring stricter controls) are markedly more hawkish than Labour identifiers (49%) or Alliance identifiers (44%). They were also more inclined, in answer to a further question, to believe that Asian and West Indian immigrants in Britain are given 'too much help'. The majority view (55%) was that present arrangements are about right, with a third of the population believing that too much was being done already.

Social class

Britain is frequently referred to as a class-bound society. But do the British public share that impression? According to our survey, the majority does. Not only did around 70% of the sample believe that British people are aware of social class differences nowadays, but the same proportion believed that a person's social class still affects his or her opportunities. 58% held *both* of these beliefs. So class prejudice or discrimination, though regarded as less prevalent than race prejudice (90%), is nonetheless still seen to be an important factor in British society. More important, for around one half of the population, class discrimination is seen to be an unchanging feature of British life. 46% of our sample believed that social class is as important now in affecting people's opportunities as it was ten years ago, and 49% predicted that it would continue to be as important for the next ten years. A futher 16% thought it would become more important in the next decade. The summary table facing shows how these beliefs are interrelated.

Thus it appears that about a third of the population could be decribed as being optimistic about Britain's movement towards a classless society, the remainder being either sceptical or pessimistic. This distribution of answers is less gloomy than that on racial discrimination, where Britain was more widely perceived to be in the middle of a worsening trend.

%

Class discrimination now is:

worse than past – will get still worse	10	
same as past – will get worse	5	16
better than past – will get worse	1	
worse than past – will stay same	8	
same as past – will stay same	32	49
better than past – will stay same	9	
worse than past – will get better	4	
same as past – will get better	8	32
better than past – will get better still	20	
Don't know	3	

The extent to which these opinions are held by various subgroups of the population is shown in **Table 6.7**. Broadly speaking, the higher one's own social class (whether Registrar General determined or self-assigned) the less likely one is to consider social class important today, but the more likely one is to think that it used to be more important than now and that its importance will continue to diminish. These differences are reflected in differences by party identification. Thus, Labour identifiers are more likely than others to consider social class important today, to believe that class discrimination now is worse than it used to be and that it is likely to become still worse in the future. Whereas younger people (18-34) were shown to be more likely than other age groups to perceive race as an obstacle to advancement, it was those aged 35-54 who were more likely than other age groups to perceive class as an obstacle to a person's advancement.

Having asked respondents about the importance of social class, we went on to ask them to classify themselves into one of five groups, both now and when they were children.

Most people see themselves as belonging to a particular social class. Please look at this card and tell me which social class you would say you belong to.

And which social class would you say your parents belonged to when you started at primary school?

	Own	Parents
	%	%
Upper middle class	1	2
Middle class	24	16
Upper working class	23	12
Working class	46	58
Poor	2	9
Don't know	3	2

The description 'working class' or 'poor' was therefore thought to be appropriate for two-thirds of the population when at primary school age, but for half the population now. The older the respondent, the more likely he or she was to describe his or her background as being 'poor'. The overall distribution of

self-assigned class does not seem to have changed much in the past fifteen years
or so. In the 1966 British Election Survey, for instance, when people were asked
a similar question, two-thirds of the sample also assigned themselves to one or
other of the 'working class' categories. When we compare how people assigned
themselves at primary school age with how they assign themselves now, we find
that somewhat over half of the sample selected much the same category at each
age. If we compress the five class categories we offered into four, the following
pattern emerges.

Self-assigned class

**At start of
primary school**

	%			%
Upper middle or middle class	14			
Upper working class	5	No change	=	56
Working class	36			
Poor	1			
Upper middle or middle class	4			
Upper working class	2	Now lower	=	7
Working class	1			
Upper working class	4			
Working class	20	Now higher	=	32
Poor	8			
Don't know	4			

Table 6.8 relates self-assigned social class (own and parents) both to the Registrar
General's Social Class categories, and to income and age. The relationships are
complex and interesting. For example, the tendency to describe one's own social
class as 'higher' than one's parents varies with age. It is more likely to be true of
those born, broadly speaking in the 1930s and 1940s (ie aged 35-54) than either
those born earlier, or those born in the 1950s or later. Moreover, those in the
youngest two age groups are more likely than those in the oldest to describe
their own social class as 'lower' than their parents.

Not surprisingly, the higher a person's current household income, the more
likely he or she is to claim to have moved upward. Only 22% of those with a
household income under £5,000 described their social class as higher than their
parents, compared with 47% of those with a household income of £12,000 or
more. Income, and self-assigned social class are, however, only tenuously related.
For instance, nearly one in five of those with household incomes of under
£5,000 described themselves as middle or upper middle class. Similarly, we
found self-assigned social class to be a poor proxy for Registrar General's Social
Class. For instance 50% of those who would be classified by the Registrar
General as Social Classes I or II describe themselves as upper working or
working class.

Sex and gender discrimination

Household divisions of labour

Duncan, Schuman and Duncan (1974), writing about Detroit and Chicago, showed that very little change had occurred in the allocation of household tasks between men and women during the sixteen years from 1955 to 1971. Despite a substantial increase in women's employment in that period, household cleaning, washing dishes and shopping were still seen substantially as the wife's tasks. Indeed the 1971 data showed shopping to be even more exclusively a wife's task than it had been in 1955, while household repairs remained substantially the husband's job. Keeping track of money and bills was the single task that wives and husbands seemed to share equally, both in 1955 and 1971. Pahl (forthcoming, 1984) also deals with this topic, using British data.

Using the Detroit items as a starting point, we listed eight everyday household tasks and asked married respondents (or those living as married) how they actually shared each task with their partners. We asked unmarried respondents how they thought each task *should* be shared. The results for the total sample are presented on the next page.

An egalitarian division of household labour would be one in which either the great majority of married couples shared each of the tasks equally, or where the balance between husbands, wives and joint responsibility was more or less even. Only one of our eight tasks – the organisation of money and bills – qualified by this criterion for married couples. Our findings suggest that husbands rarely play the major role in most everyday and time consuming household jobs – the cleaning (3% mainly the man), the cooking (5%) and the washing and ironing (1%). They play a slightly larger role in household shopping, in decisions about decorating, and in washing dishes. But they only finally come into their own – predictably – as the major participants in household repairs. Whether or not the contemporary British family is symmetrical in other respects (see Young and Willmott, 1973), it is far from symmetrical in the allocation of household tasks.

According to our figures, however, single people (those who have never married) would arrange things differently. For all but two of the tasks – the washing and ironing and the repairs – the majority of this group favours equal participation by men and women (and this was not primarily a function of age differences – see below).

The formerly married (who were not living with a partner) were less egalitarian than the single people, but more so than married couples were in their actual allocation of tasks. Their preferred allocation has, perhaps, been tempered by experience. We did not ask married people how each of the tasks should be allocated but will make good that omission in the next round of interviewing.

When we examined the pattern of answers among different subgroups of the population, we found few differences between men and women in the way they reported the allocation of household tasks. There were some differences between occupational groups but these were not substantial. We did find, however, that households with young children were relatively inegalitarian, perhaps reflecting the fact that women in these households were less likely to be in paid employment. (See **Table 6.9**.)

		Married	Formerly married	Never married
		'Does'	'Should do'	'Should do'
		%	%	%
Washing and ironing:	Mainly man	1	–	–
	Mainly woman	89	81	66
	Shared equally	10	17	32
Preparation of evening meal:	Mainly man	5	–	–
	Mainly woman	77	60	45
	Shared equally	17	38	53
Household cleaning:	Mainly man	3	*	*
	Mainly woman	72	54	37
	Shared equally	24	44	61
Household shopping:	Mainly man	5	2	2
	Mainly woman	51	42	28
	Shared equally	44	55	69
Choice of living room colour:	Mainly man	5	3	1
	Mainly woman	48	38	23
	Shared equally	46	58	74
Evening dishes:	Mainly man	17	9	10
	Mainly woman	40	23	16
	Shared equally	40	66	73
Organisation of household money and bills:	Mainly man	29	26	21
	Mainly woman	39	22	12
	Shared equally	32	49	65
Repairs of household equipment:	Mainly man	82	80	73
	Mainly woman	6	2	*
	Shared equally	10	16	25

Taken as a whole, the pattern of answers was very similar to that of the American data. It is also probably similar to the pattern that would have been produced if we had asked the same questions in Britain at any time during the past thirty years or so. We searched for indications of potential change in the answers given by younger respondents (aged 18-24). As can be seen in **Table 6.10**, people in this age group seem to be much more egalitarian than the general population. If, however, we divide them according to sex and marital status, we find that the unmarried are, by a considerable margin, more egalitarian in their attitude to household tasks than the married are in their performance of them. In particular it is the unmarried – notably unmarried women – who give this age group its egalitarian character. The pattern of answers from the married 18-24 year olds is not dissimilar to that of the general population.

These differences are illustrated in the summary table facing which shows the answers for four household tasks. The first two rows contain the answers of all married people and of young married people in respect of their *actual* allocation of tasks; the last two rows contain the answers of young unmarried people and of young unmarried women in respect of their *preferred* allocation of tasks. As will be seen, the differences are large and the pattern consistent. Marriage somehow turns out to entail rather more household responsibilities for women than their unmarried counterparts think it ought to do. Or could it be perhaps, that early marriage is likelier amongst those women who are more inclined to assume a housewife's role?

		Preparation of evening meal	Household cleaning	Household shopping	Washing and ironing
Total married: task **is** shared equally	%	17	24	44	10
Married 18-24 task **is** shared equally	%	21	24	56	22
Total unmarried 18-24: task **should be** shared equally	%	51	60	68	31
Unmarried women 18-24: task **should be** shared equally	%	60	61	79	40

Sex discrimination

Three-quarters of our sample supported a law against sex discrimination, a slightly higher level of support than for a law against race discrimination. Particularly high levels of support came from young women (18-24), people in Social Class III non-manual occupations and from Alliance identifiers. On the whole also, the higher the level of education and income, the greater is the level of support for a law against sex discrimination.

A number of the scale items in our self-completion questionnaire attempted to measure what might be called traditionalist attitudes towards women, work and marriage. The answers will be more interest over time than they are for a single reading, but we report them here as benchmark measures. These measures will be supplemented in the 1984 fieldwork round by more direct questions on sex roles and on perceived sex discrimination.

In the case of each scale item, respondents were invited to agree or disagree, (strongly or slightly) with a statement; a neutral category was also provided. In the summary figures overleaf, we compress each of the two categories of agreement and disagreement and omit the (sometimes substantial) proportions who selected the neutral option. In the last column, we produce the margin by which the mean score for each statement differed from the midpoint score of 3.0. A *minus* sign refers to a more traditionalist leaning. A *plus* sign refers to a more egalitarian or feminist leaning.

Only the first two statements produced reasonably strong support for a more feminist position, the remainder producing either marginal support or opposition. We have doubts, however, as to whether the second and fourth statements in the list actually worked as agree/disagree items. A third of the sample selected the neutral option for the second statement and nearly half did so for the fourth statement, indicating perhaps that the degree of generalisation inherent in them was too great for many respondents to overlook.

		Agree	Disagree	Mean difference from mid-point
A wife should avoid earning more than her husband does	%	14	57	+.78
More women should enter politics	%	52	8	+.71
Children are essential for a happy marriage	%	29	41	+.20
Women generally handle positions of responsibility better than men do	%	22	25	−.03
It is wrong for mothers of young children to go out to work	%	42	32	−.24
It should be the woman who decides how many children a couple has	%	27	42	−.26

Each statement produced its own − usually small − subgroup differences in the level of agreement or disagreement. The tendency, however, was for women, the young (particularly the unmarried), and the non-manual social classes to adopt a more feminist position than their counterparts.

Personal and moral values

Sexual relationships

Surveys of sexual behaviour and attitudes have been somewhat specialized in their content of coverage. For example, Schofield's studies (1965, 1973) were carried out among young people; three OPCS studies by Woolf (1971), Bone (1975) and Dunnell (1979), dealing as they were, mainly with family planning and fertility questions, confined their coverage to women under 50; Gorer's (1971) study of sexual attitudes and behaviour excluded people aged 45 or over. Since our survey was based on interviews with a representative sample of the total population, we decided to include a number of attitudinal items that had been tested and used effectively over the past ten years or so in similar surveys in the USA.

We started with the following series of questions to indicate the strength of disapproval (or otherwise) of various classes of extra-marital relationships.

> *If a man or a woman have sexual relations before marriage what would your general opinion be? Please choose a phrase from this card. '*

> *What about a married man having sexual relations with a woman other then his wife?*

> *What about a married woman having sexual relations with a man other than her husband?*

> *What about sexual relations between two adults of the same sex?*

There were no differences in the distribution of answers for a husband or wife's extra-marital relationships. In fact 96% of the sample answered in the same terms for both. This finding seems to confirm recent assertions about the decline in the notorious 'double standard' of morality for husbands and wives. Thus, the distribution below refers only to the three main categories of relationship and includes in each case the American data in response to a similar question in 1982.*

	Pre-marital relationship		Extra-marital relationship		Homosexual relationship	
	Britain	USA	Britain	USA	Britain	USA
	%	%	%	%	%	%
Always wrong	16	28	58	72	50	70
Mostly wrong*	11	9	25	13	12	5
Sometimes wrong	17	21	11	10	8	6
Rarely wrong	8	x	1	x	4	x
Not wrong at all	42	40	2	3	17	14
Other answer	5	3	4	2	9	5

* USA 'Almost always', Britain 'Mostly'.

The General Social Survey has been asking similar questions to these intermittently over the past ten years or so. Yet the only change in attitude during that period has been towards pre-marital sex, strong disapproval having gone down from 46% to 37% or, put the other way around the proportion saying 'not wrong at all' having risen from 26% to 40%. American attitudes to extra-marital sex and to homosexuality have remained more or less constant since 1973.

We do not have past data of the same kind with which to compare British attitudes over time. It is interesting, however, that the British public appears to be less censorious than the US public in its attitudes towards pre-marital sex and homosexuality. Even so, nearly two thirds of the British population in 1983 considered homosexual relations to be always or mostly wrong with only 17% expressing no reservations about such relationships. Extra-marital relationships generate even higher levels of disapproval both here and in the USA.

Our findings on attitudes to pre-marital sex offer partial confirmation of Dunnell's (1979) conclusion that one of the traditional functions of marriage as a precondition of sexual relations is fast disappearing. She found, for instance, that among the cohort of women who had married in the late 1950s, 35% reported having had sexual relationships with their husbands before marriage. Among the cohort who had married in the early 1970s, however, the proportion was 74%. Our data show that age has a strong bearing on *attitudes* too. Thus, while only 6% of those aged 18-34 consider pre-marital sex to be always or almost always wrong, over half of those aged over 55 hold this view. Similar differences emerged in respect of attitudes to extra-marital and homosexual

*Source: General Social Survey (GSS) by National Opinion Research Centre (NORC), Chicago, 1982.

relationships. **Tables 6.11** and **6.12** indicate the extent to which various subgroups of the population have differing attitudes towards each type of sexual relationship. In addition to showing that permissiveness is much more likely among young people than among older people, the breakdowns reveal that, in general, men are more likely than women to hold permissive attitudes, but the reverse is true in respect of homosexual relationships. They also show that professional people, and others from the non-manual social classes, hold relatively less censorious attitudes, particularly in respect of homosexual relationships.

Some of these differences are reflected in other subgroups. For instance, people who have never been married (and tend to be young) are more likely to have liberal attitudes than those who are currently married, while people who have formerly been married (and tend to be older) are more likely to have disapproving attitudes. On the whole, permissive or censorious attitudes to the various categories of sexual relationships are associated. Thus those who said that pre-marital sexual relationships are always or almost always wrong are likely to have similar views on extra-marital or homosexual relationships. A similar pattern obtains among those who consider one or other relationship to be rarely or not at all wrong. This finding is in close accord with that reported by Gorer (1971), who noted a strong correlation between hostile attitudes to homosexuality and to pre-marital sex.

In essence, our findings give little support to those who assert that marriage is somehow becoming a less and less important institution in Britain. It is true that marriage is no longer seen by many people to be the starting point for sexual relationships but, once entered into, it is certainly seen by the great majority of the population to be an *exclusive* relationship for men and women equally.

As far as reactions towards homosexuality are concerned (but not towards other sexual relationships), attitudes varied somewhat according to party identification and region. Alliance identifiers are less censorious in their attitudes towards homosexual relationships than are either Conservative or Labour identifiers; people living in the South (particularly London and the South West) tend to be less censorious than people living in Scotland, Wales or Northern England.

Having dispensed with the question of personal morality (approval or disapproval) in respect of homosexual relationships, we then went on to the rather more important practical question of discrimination against homosexuals on the grounds of their sexual preference. Again, our intention was to establish a benchmark figure against which changes could be measured in future years. The questions and answers were:

I would like you to tell me whether, in your opinion, it is acceptable for a homosexual person. . .

		Yes	No
to be a teacher in a school?	%	41	53
to be a teacher in a college or university?	%	48	48
to hold a responsible position in public life?	%	53	42

Around half of the population therefore would wish to bar homosexuals from teaching posts and nearly as many would bar them from a wider range of occupations. This suggests a widespread public belief that homosexuals are somehow sufficiently threatening (or vulnerable) to be denied access to important areas of British life. The General Social Survey, which has regularly included the question about teaching in colleges and universities, shows a slightly higher level of tolerance; 55% in 1982 said that it was acceptable for homosexuals to hold such posts.

The greatest intolerance towards homosexuals comes from among older respondents, those in manual occupations, those who are most censorious of homosexual relationships anyway. Younger people, particularly younger women, and people with no religious affiliation are much more accepting on all three items. For instance, on the question of whether homosexuals should be able to hold responsible public positions, some two-thirds of people under 45 saw no objection.

We also asked a further question which, in the event, proved to be of doubtful validity. Should homosexual couples be allowed to adopt a baby under the same conditions as other couples? The answer, decisively, was 'No'; only 8% of people saw no objection. But it is likely that many respondents interpreted the question as referring only to male couples.

Divorce

The Divorce Law Reform Act came into effect in 1971. In allowing divorce on grounds of irretrievable breakdown of marriage within three years of the date of marriage, it made divorce considerably easier to obtain than it had previously been. Since then the number of divorces has doubled (from 80,000 per annum to 159,000*) and it is now estimated that one in every three marriages ends in divorce.

Our survey suggests that further liberalisation of the divorce laws would not be popular. Indeed, 31% of the population think that divorce in Britain should be more difficult to obtain than it is now, and 55% that it should remain as it is. Only 11% of the population think that divorce should be made easier. Women are more resistant than men to further liberalisation and older people more resistant than younger people.

| | USA | | Great Britain |
	1974	1982	1983
	%	%	%
Divorce should be:			
Easier to obtain	32	22	11
More difficult	42	51	31
Things should remain as they are	21	21	55
Don't know/other answer	5	6	3

This pattern of opinion differs markedly from that in the USA where the

---

*Source: Social Trends, 1984.

proportion of marriages ending in divorce is even higher than in the UK. Opinion there polarised to a greater extent: whereas over half of the American population would prefer to see divorce made more difficult, there is a sizeable minority (around 20%) who would prefer to see it made easier. Resistance to liberalisation of the divorce laws in the USA has increased in recent years, as shown by the figures on the previous page (taken from the GSS and presented alongside our own figures).

The Law Commission in Britain has recently recommended the principle of a clean financial break at the end of a marriage with a time limit set for maintenance. This principle is incorporated in the Matrimonial and Family Proceedings Bill currently before Parliament. We included some questions that bear on this issue. Each one was designed to elicit whether divorced men are seen to have financial responsibilities towards their ex-wives and children in different circumstances.

Only 10% of the population believe that a man should make maintenance payments to his ex-wife where there are are no children of the marriage and where both partners (aged about 35 in our examples) are working. The same proportion of men and women hold this view. Only among respondents aged 55 or over was there substantially greater support for maintenance payments in these circumstances. In the same situation (both partners working, same age), except for the fact that the couple have children, the level of support for maintenance payments to support the ex-wife rises to 26%. Again the pattern of answers is the same for both men and women, and older people are more likely than younger people to support maintenance for the wife. There is near unanimity in the sample (92%) that a divorced father should make maintenance payments to support his children.

We asked also about an *unmarried* couple without children who had been living together for 10 years at the time of separation; once again both partners were working. Only 4% of the sample felt that a man should make maintenance payments in these circumstances, less than half the proportion who supported maintenance for an ex-wife in the same circumstances.

On each of these questions, including the last one, people with a religious affiliation are more likely than those with no affiliation to favour continued financial support for the woman after separation. They are also more likely than those with no religious affiliation to think that divorce should be more difficult to obtain.

Abortion and contraception

In the self-completion questionnaire we presented respondents with a list of circumstances in which a woman might wish to have an abortion. In each case we asked simply whether or not an abortion should be allowed by law. The list of circumstances was similar to one that had been included on a number of occasions as part of the General Social Survey. Our results are presented in ascending order of agreement, alongside the American results for 1972 and 1982.

	USA		Great Britain
	1972	1982	1983
Abortion should be allowed by law, when:	%	%	%
The woman decides on her own she does not wish to have the child*	NA	39	35
The woman is not married and does not wish to marry the man	40	47	42
The couple agree they do not wish to have the child†	38	46	43
The couple cannot afford any more children	46	50	44
There is a strong chance of a defect in the baby	74	81	77
The woman became pregnant as a result of rape	74	83	80
The woman's health is seriously endangered by the pregnancy	83	89	82

* GSS wording: 'When the woman wants it for any reason'.
† GSS wording: 'If she is married and does not want any more children'.

The answers divide attitudes into two distinct groups. Where there is danger to health of either mother or baby, or where the pregnancy results from rape, approximately 80% of the population consider that legal abortion should be available. Where, however, the desire to have an abortion is simply a matter of preference or even of financial need, only around 35% to 45% of the population consider that legal abortion should be available.

The same grouping of answers is apparent in the American data. In general a slightly higher proportion of the US population supports the availability of legal abortion in the listed circumstances. Part of this difference may, however, be accounted for by the slightly lower proportion of older people who completed our self-completion questionnaire. Certainly, as they stand, the British figures are generally closer to the American figures of 1972 than they are to those of 1982. **Table 6.13** gives the full range of answers by various subgroups of the population.

Surprisingly, perhaps, the breakdowns show that men are more inclined than women to favour the availability of legal abortion for reasons of preference (even the woman's singular preference), but less inclined than women to favour its availability for reasons of health (or rape). In general also, the younger a person is, male or female, the more likely he or she is to favour the availability of legal abortion.

People who claim a religious affiliation are, on the whole, less sympathetic towards legal abortion. Interestingly, however, even among Roman Catholics, around a quarter support legal abortion for each of the reasons of preference, and at least 70% support it if the mother's health is endangered or if the pregnancy has resulted from rape.

We also included in the self-completion questionnaire a single scale item on contraception. Respondents were invited to agree or disagree (strongly or just) with the statement that *'Contraceptive advice and supplies should be available to all young people, whatever their age'*. The statement was, we thought, likely to be seen as a fairly extreme position on the issue, but we were wrong. More than half of those who expressed a view agreed with the statement.

	%	
Strongly agree	20	} 44
Just agree	24	
Strongly disagree	21	} 38
Just disagree	17	
Neither agree nor disagree	12	
Did not complete self-completion questionnaire	6	

As we have come to expect on this sort of issue, young people are much more likely than older people to agree with the statement. For instance, 52% of people aged under 35 agreed, compared with only 27% of retired people. Alliance (48%) and Labour identifiers (50%) were more likely than Conservative identifiers (37%) to agree with the statement, but social class did not discriminate on this issue.

The availability of pornography

Attitudes to such issues as pornography are clearly difficult to investigate by means of a social survey. One problem is that the word has come into common use only in the last ten years or so yet its definition is constantly changing. Twenty years ago, for instance, the term would probably have included nudity in the theatre and photographs that now appear routinely in some daily newspapers. Now, for many people, it probably refers to more explicit sexual material of the kind that is available in 'adult' video tapes and magazines.

We experimented with a fairly simple question in our self-completion questionnaire. All but a few respondents were able to answer it and, more importantly, the answers seemed to fall into intelligible patterns. This suggests that most people attach some meaning to the term pornography, though it is doubtful that they all attached the same meaning. We recognise also that we were probably measuring reactions based more on impressions than on knowledge. Our question and the answers, analysed by age within sex, are set out opposite.

As the table shows, around a third of the population, and more than half of people over 55, would favour an outright ban on pornographic films and magazines. This view is more likely to be held by women than by men in all age groups. But it is a view that people under 35 are very unlikely to hold. The most popular view among all except those aged 55 or over is that pornographic magazines and films should be available in special shops *without* public display. Unrestricted availability is supported by fairly small minorities of both men and women in all age groups.

Restrictions on the display of pornographic material would find favour among Conservative *and* Labour identifiers more or less equally, but less so among Alliance identifiers. There were also regional differences in attitude: people living in Scotland and the North of England are more likely to be in

favour of an outright ban; people living in the South of England are less likely
to hold that view.

*Which of these statements come closest to your views on the availability of pornographic
magazines and films?*

	Total	Sex		Age		
		Male	Female	18-34	35-54	55+
	%	%	%	%	%	%
They should be banned altogether	31	23	37	8	25	56
They should be available in special adult shops but not displayed to the public	48	53	44	66	54	27
They should be available in special adult shops with public display permitted	6	8	5	11	7	2
They should be available in any shop for sale to adults only	6	7	5	9	6	4
They should be available in any shop for sale to anyone	1	1	1	*	1	1

Permissiveness in respect of pornography is associated with permissive
sexual attitudes. For example 60% of those who think that pre-marital sex is
always or mostly wrong, also think that pornographic material should be banned
altogether. By contrast, only 15% of those who consider pre-marital sex to be
rarely or not wrong hold this view.

References

BANTON, M., *White and Coloured,* Cape, London (1959).
BANTON, M., *Racial and Ethnic Competition,* Cambridge University Press, London (1983).
BONE, M., *The Family Planning Services; Changes and Effects,* HMSO, London (1978).
DANIEL, W. W., *Racial Discrimination in England,* Penguin London (1968).
DUNCAN, O. D., SCHUMAN, H. and DUNCAN, B., *Social Change in a Metropolitan Community,* Russell Sage Foundation, New York (1973).
DUNNELL, K., *Family Information,* HMSO, London (1979).
General Social Surveys Cumulative Codebook, 1972-1982, National Opinion Research Center, Chicago, USA (1982).
GORER, G., *Sex and Marriage in England Today,* Nelson, London (1971).

LAWRENCE, D., *Black Migrants, White Natives: a study of Race Relations in Nottingham*, Cambridge University Press, London (1974).

PAHL, R. E., *Divisions of Labour*, Blackwell, Oxford (forthcoming 1984).

ROSE, E. J. B., *et al*, *Colour and Citizenship: a Report on British Race Relations*, Oxford University Press, London (1969).

SCHOFIELD, M., *The Sexual Behaviour of Young People*, Allen Lane, London (1965).

SCHOFIELD, M., *The Sexual Behaviour of Young Adults*, Allen Lane, London (1973).

SMITH, D. J., *The Facts of Racial Disadvantage*, Political & Economic Planning, Vol. XLII, Broadsheet No. 560, (1976).

Social Trends 14, HMSO, London (1984).

WOOLF, M., *Family Intentions*, HMSO, London (1971).

YOUNG, M. and WILLMOTT, P., *The Symmetrical Family*, Routledge & Kegan Paul, London (1973).

Acknowledgements

I am grateful to the following persons for their comments and suggestions arising from earlier versions of the questionnaire:

Peter Brierley
Martin Bulmer
Malcolm Cross
Nicholas Deakin
Catherine Hakim
Robert Hutchison
Mark Johnson
Mavis MacLean
Catherine Marsh
Aubrey McKennell
Muriel Nissel
Ray Pahl
Michael Quine

6.1 EXTENT OF PREJUDICE AGAINST BLACKS AND ASIANS (Q.80a,b,c,d) by sex, age, social class, ethnic group and self-assigned prejudice

	TOTAL	SEX		AGE†			SOCIAL CLASS						ETHNIC GROUP		SELF-ASSIGNED RACIAL PREJUDICE†		
		Male	Female	18-34	35-54	55+	I/II	III non-manual	III manual	IV/V	Looks after home	Other	White	Black/ Asian/ Other	Very little/	A little	Not at all
AGAINST ASIANS:	%	%	%	%	%	%	%	%	%	%	%	%	%	%	%	%	%
A lot	54	55	52	59	54	49	52	58	57	55	48	52	54	44	81	57	50
A little	37	37	37	37	39	36	41	38	35	34	39	34	37	45	16	38	39
Hardly any	6	5	7	3	6	10	5	3	6	9	8	9	6	7	3	4	8
Other/don't know/not answered	3	2	3	2	2	6	3	1	2	3	5	5	3	4	-	2	3
AGAINST BLACKS:																	
A lot	50	52	49	51	47	49	52	53	50	52	45	54	51	39	76	54	47
A little	40	40	40	43	41	35	42	40	39	37	42	33	39	49	18	41	41
Hardly any	7	6	7	4	6	10	5	5	8	8	8	9	7	9	6	3	9
Other/don't know/not answered	4	3	4	2	2	5	2	2	3	3	5	4	3	3	-	1	3
FIVE YEARS AGO:																	
Less than now	45	47	43	48	43	45	37	43	51	49	45	49	46	39	60	49	43
More than now	16	18	14	16	15	18	21	15	15	14	13	23	16	19	13	16	16
About the same	36	33	39	35	40	34	40	41	32	36	38	25	36	39	25	34	38
Other/don't know/not answered	3	2	3	1	3	3	2	1	2	1	4	4	3	3	2	1	3
IN FIVE YEARS TIME:																	
More than now	42	46	38	47	42	38	36	44	51	43	37	37	42	36	77	50	36
Less than now	17	19	15	18	15	20	23	14	16	18	14	22	17	21	4	16	19
About the same	36	31	41	34	40	36	36	39	30	35	42	36	36	37	19	31	40
Other/don't know/not answered	4	3	5	2	4	7	4	3	3	4	7	6	4	6	-	3	5
BASE: ALL RESPONDENTS																	
Weighted	*1719*	*793*	*926*	*533*	*593*	*587*	*334*	*268*	*365*	*300*	*346*	*106*	*1631*	*88*	*76*	*537*	*1095*
Unweighted	*1761*	*807*	*954*	*525*	*623*	*607*	*343*	*281*	*362*	*316*	*353*	*106*	*1677*	*84*	*75*	*559*	*1114*

For notes on breakdowns, symbols and tabulations, refer to Appendices I and II.

6.2 SELF-ASSIGNED PREJUDICE (Q80e,f)
by sex, age, region, district, social class and party identification

	TOTAL	SEX		AGE[†]			REGION						DISTRICT		SOCIAL CLASS				PARTY IDENTIFICATION[†]			
		Male	Female	18-34	35-54	55+	Scot-land	North	Mid-lands	Wales	South	GLC	Metro-politan	Non-metro	Non-man-ual	Man-ual	Looks after home	Other	Cons.	Alli-ance	Labour	Non-aligned
	%	%	%	%	%	%	%	%	%	%	%	%	%	%	%	%	%	%	%	%	%	%
Very prejudiced against people of other races	4	5	4	6	5	3	1	5	7	3	4	4	5	4	4	6	3	2	6	1	4	5
A little prejudiced	31	34	29	31	34	28	22	31	31	23	35	33	32	31	36	28	29	31	40	27	24	30
AGAINST: (Asians Pakistanis Indians or Sikhs)	10	10	10	14	9	6	4	10	13	5	11	8	10	10	10	11	10	4	12	9	8	9
(Blacks W.Indians or Africans)	6	7	5	6	7	5	3	2	9	3	6	12	8	5	7	5	5	8	8	4	5	3
(Coloureds/ Other speci-fied races)	4	4	3	3	4	5	5	3	5	5	3	2	3	4	4	4	2	7	5	4	3	3
(No particu-lar race/ other answer)	20	23	18	20	24	17	10	21	19	17	24	20	20	20	23	19	19	16	26	14	16	22
Not prejudiced at all	64	61	66	63	61	67	77	64	61	73	59	61	62	64	59	65	68	65	54	70	72	62
Other/Not answered	1	1	1	*	*	1	-	*	1	-	1	2	1	1	*	1	*	2	*	*	*	2
BASE: ALL RESPONDENTS																						
Weighted	1719	793	926	533	593	587	183	456	286	87	517	191	615	1104	602	665	346	106	664	252	565	216
Unweighted	1761	807	954	525	623	607	179	474	291	87	535	195	631	1130	624	678	353	106	676	258	284	221

6.3 EXTENT TO WHICH ASIAN OR BLACK BOSS WOULD BE ACCEPTABLE (Q.83a,b) by age within sex

ASIAN BOSS:

	TOTAL	SEX Male	SEX Female	MALE 18-34	MALE 35-54	MALE 55+	FEMALE† 18-34	FEMALE† 35-54	FEMALE† 55+
	%	%	%	%	%	%	%	%	%
SELF									
Mind a lot	11	12	10	8	13	14	7	9	1
Mind a little	8	10	7	10	9	10	6	10	6
Not mind	79	78	81	80	77	76	85	80	78
Other answer	2	1	1	2	1	1	1	-	2
Not answered	*	1	-	-	-	-	1	1	1
MOST PEOPLE									
Mind a lot	23	22	25	26	19	21	25	24	25
Mind a little	30	30	30	29	30	30	38	27	27
Not mind	43	46	41	44	46	46	34	46	42
Other answer	2	1	3	1	2	1	1	2	5
Not answered	1	1	1	-	2	1	2	1	1
BASE: ALTERNATE RESPONDENTS									
Weighted	892	404	488	118	149	137	152	155	177
Unweighted	920	414	506	115	157	142	150	166	187

BLACK BOSS:

	TOTAL	SEX Male	SEX Female	MALE 18-34	MALE 35-54	MALE 55+	FEMALE† 18-34	FEMALE† 35-54	FEMALE† 55+
	%	%	%	%	%	%	%	%	%
SELF									
Mind a lot	9	11	6	7	10	17	3	4	11
Mind a little	12	10	13	16	5	7	10	12	17
Not mind	79	79	79	77	84	76	85	82	71
Other answer	1	-	1	-	-	-	2	1	1
Not answered	*	-	*	-	-	-	-	*	-
MOST PEOPLE									
Mind a lot	25	24	26	22	20	33	20	26	30
Mind a little	29	28	30	39	27	15	36	29	28
Not mind	42	44	41	34	48	50	43	42	38
Other answer	2	3	2	3	5	1	1	2	2
Not answered	1	1	1	2	1	1	-	1	2
BASE: ALTERNATE RESPONDENTS									
Weighted	798	375	423	136	132	107	119	153	149
Unweighted	809	379	430	136	134	109	116	161	151

6.4 EXTENT TO WHICH ASIAN OR BLACK MARRIAGE PARTNER WOULD BE ACCEPTABLE (Q.83c,d) by age withing sex

ASIAN MARRIAGE PARTNER:

	TOTAL	Male	Female	MALE 18-34	MALE 35-54	MALE 55+	FEMALE† 18-34	FEMALE† 35-54	FEMALE† 55+
	%	%	%	%	%	%	%	%	%
SELF									
Mind a lot	31	31	32	18	30	43	17	30	46
Mind a little	20	18	22	19	18	16	16	28	20
Not mind	47	50	45	63	50	38	66	40	33
Other	1	1	1	-	1	2	*	1	2
Not answered	1	1	*	-	1	1	-	1	-
MOST PEOPLE									
Mind a lot	42	42	42	35	45	44	40	43	44
Mind a little	35	32	37	40	32	26	42	34	34
Not mind	20	22	17	22	17	28	18	18	17
Other	3	2	3	4	3	-	1	4	4
Not answered	1	2	1	-	3	3	-	1	1
BASE: ALTERNATE RESPONDENTS									
Weighted	892	404	488	118	149	137	152	155	177
Unweighted	920	414	506	115	157	142	150	166	187

BLACK MARRIAGE PARTNER:

	TOTAL	Male	Female	MALE 18-34	MALE 35-54	MALE 55+	FEMALE† 18-34	FEMALE† 35-54	FEMALE† 55+
	%	%	%	%	%	%	%	%	%
SELF									
Mind a lot	33	33	33	24	34	44	18	32	46
Mind a little	24	22	27	20	24	20	22	33	24
Not mind	41	43	39	55	38	34	58	34	28
Other	2	2	2	1	4	2	2	1	2
Not answered	-	-	-	-	-	-	-	-	-
MOST PEOPLE									
Mind a lot	49	46	51	43	47	50	42	57	52
Mind a little	30	28	32	30	27	27	38	29	31
Not mind	18	21	16	24	20	18	20	12	15
Other	2	4	1	2	5	4	1	1	1
Not answered	1	1	1	*	1	2	-	1	1
BASE: ALTERNATE RESPONDENTS									
Weighted	798	375	423	136	132	107	119	153	149
Unweighted	809	379	430	136	134	109	116	161	151

6.5 RACIAL DISCRIMINATION IN EMPLOYMENT (Q.81a,b)
by sex, age, region, ethnic group and part identification

	TOTAL	SEX		AGE†			REGION						ETHNIC GROUP		PARTY IDENTIFICATION†			
		Male	Female	18-34	35-54	55+	Scotland	North	Midlands	Wales	South	GLC	White	Black/Asian/Other	Cons.	Alliance	Labour	Non-aligned
TOWARDS ASIANS:	%	%	%	%	%	%	%	%	%	%	%	%	%	%	%	%	%	%
A lot	20	21	20	21	20	21	.21	22	17	19	21	21	20	20	17	20	25	19
A little	40	41	39	44	40	38	36	36	45	31	44	42	40	48	44	43	37	33
Hardly at all	31	30	31	32	32	28	32	34	30	29	26	34	31	23	31	29	30	33
Don't know	8	7	9	4	7	13	10	7	8	21	8	3	8	9	8	7	7	13
Not answered	*	1	1	*	*	1	1	*	*	-	1	*	1	-	*	*	1	1
TOWARDS BLACKS:																		
A lot	25	27	23	24	26	24	22	23	20	21	26	37	24	28	22	23	30	21
A little	40	40	39	45	37	37	36	37	45	36	41	37	39	48	44	44	35	33
Hardly at all	27	26	29	28	30	24	29	34	27	24	24	22	28	16	27	25	28	31
Don't know	8	7	9	3	6	14	13	6	7	19	8	4	8	8	7	8	7	13
Not answered	*	1	*	*	*	*	1	*	*	-	1	*	*	*	*	*	*	2
BASE: ALL RESPONDENTS																		
Weighted	1719	793	926	533	593	587	183	456	286	87	517	191	1631	88	664	252	565	216
Unweighted	1761	807	954	525	623	607	179	474	291	87	535	195	1677	84	676	258	584	221

6.6 LEGISLATION AGAINST RACIAL DISCRIMINATION (Q.82a)
by sex, age, class, ethnic group and party identification

	TOTAL	SEX		AGE†			SOCIAL CLASS						ETHNIC GROUP		PARTY IDENTIFICATION†			
		Male	Female	18-34	35-54	55+	I/II	III non-manual	III man-ual	IV/V	Looks after home	Other	White	Black/Asian/Other	Cons.	Alliance	Labour	Non-aligned
	%	%	%	%	%	%	%	%	%	%	%	%	%	%	%	%	%	%
Support	69	68	70	76	68	64	76	71	63	61	74	70	68	81	66	79	69	67
Oppose	28	31	26	22	30	33	22	26	36	34	23	28	29	18	31	20	29	29
Other answer	2	1	3	2	2	2	1	2	1	4	2	-	2	1	3	1	2	3
Not answered	1	*	1	*	*	1	1	*	*	1	1	2	1	-	1	*	*	1
BASE: ALL RESPONDENTS																		
Weighted	1719	793	926	533	593	587	334	268	365	300	346	106	1631	88	664	252	565	216
Unweighted	1761	807	954	525	623	607	343	281	362	316	353	106	1677	83	676	258	584	221

6.7 IMPORTANCE OF SOCIAL CLASS (Q.76b,c,d)
by age, social class, party identification and self-assigned social class

	TOTAL	AGE†			SOCIAL CLASS						PARTY IDENTIFICATION†				SELF-ASSIGNED SOCIAL CLASS					
		18-34	35-54	55+	I/II	III Non-manual	III manual	IV/V	Looks after home	Other	Cons.	Alli-ance	Labour	Non-aligned	Upper Middle	Middle	Upper Working	Working	Poor	Don't know/not answered
	%	%	%	%	%	%	%	%	%	%	%	%	%	%	%	%	%	%	%	%
AFFECTS OPPORTUNITIES IN BRITAIN TODAY:																				
A great deal	25	22	29	24	23	17	30	33	18	34	19	24	33	22	(25)	20	27	28	(28)	(12)
Quite a lot	45	49	47	39	44	51	44	38	47	44	48	51	41	39	(52)	47	46	44	(38)	(33)
Not very much	25	25	20	29	28	29	22	22	27	12	28	22	21	27	(19)	27	24	23	(23)	(39)
Not at all	3	3	3	3	3	1	2	2	5	5	3	1	3	6	(-)	3	2	4	(8)	(-)
Other/don't know	2	1	1	4	1	1	1	4	4	3	2	2	2	4	(4)	2	1	2	(2)	(9)
Not answered	*	*	*	*	*	*	-	1	1	2	*	*	*	1	(-)	*	-	*	(-)	(8)
TEN YEARS AGO:																				
Less important	22	21	23	22	17	15	27	28	20	22	17	14	30	23	(16)	21	19	25	(28)	(5)
More important	30	35	30	26	44	39	21	20	30	29	38	37	21	23	(58)	40	33	22	(34)	(34)
No change	46	41	46	50	38	44	50	50	47	46	44	48	46	48	(22)	38	46	51	(35)	(49)
Don't know	*	*	*	1	-	-	1	1	1	-	-	*	1	2	(-)	*	1	*	(-)	(4)
Not answered	2	2	1	1	1	2	1	2	3	3	1	1	2	4	(4)	1	1	2	(2)	(8)
IN TEN YEARS TIME:																				
More important	16	19	15	14	10	10	19	22	17	19	14	8	22	16	(8)	16	15	18	(21)	(2)
Less important	32	32	33	31	43	35	26	27	31	29	38	34	26	25	(48)	36	34	28	(36)	(27)
No change	49	46	50	51	45	53	53	47	48	49	46	55	49	53	(32)	46	49	51	(40)	(56)
Don't know	2	2	2	3	1	3	2	3	4	1	1	2	3	2	(8)	2	2	2	(2)	(8)
Not answered	1	*	*	1	1	*	-	1	1	2	*	1	*	1	(4)	*	-	*	(-)	(8)
BASE: ALL RESPONDENTS																				
Weighted	1719	532	594	587	334	268	365	300	346	106	664	252	565	216	(25)	416	400	783	(43)	(53)
Unweighted	1761	525	623	607	343	281	362	316	353	106	676	258	584	221	(25)	431	411	801	(45)	(48)

6.8 SELF-ASSIGNED SOCIAL CLASS AND PARENTS' SOCIAL CLASS AT AGE 5 (Q.77)
by age, social class of respondents and gross household income

	TOTAL	AGE†			SOCIAL CLASS						GROSS HOUSEHOLD INCOME				
		18-34	35-54	55+	I/II	III non-manual	III manual	IV/V	Looks after home	other	Under £5,000 p.a.	£5,000-£7,999 p.a.	£8,000-£11,999 p.a.	£12,000+ p.a.	No information
	%	%	%	%	%	%	%	%	%	%	%	%	%	%	%
OWN SOCIAL CLASS:															
Upper middle	1	1	1	2	4	1	*	1	2	1	1	-	1	4	2
Middle	24	22	26	25	43	25	14	13	26	24	18	17	26	41	26
Upper working	23	25	26	19	27	34	24	15	19	17	14	24	34	31	20
Working	46	44	43	49	23	36	58	64	45	46	58	55	37	20	45
Poor	2	3	2	3	*	-	1	1	4	7	6	1	*	-	2
Don't know/not answered	3	4	2	3	3	5	2	1	4	4	3	2	2	4	5
PARENTS' SOCIAL CLASS AT AGE 5:															
No change { Middle/upper middle	14	11	13	14	21	15	5	7	14	19	10	8	12	22	16
Upper working	5	7	4	5	8	8	4	3	4	6	4	3	7	7	7
Working	36	36	33	38	17	29	46	51	34	39	46	42	31	14	35
Poor	1	1	1	1	-	-	1	2	2	1	3	1	-	-	-
Own higher than parents	32	30	37	32	42	38	33	26	31	19	22	34	41	47	27
Own lower than parents	7	10	9	6	8	6	7	8	11	12	11	10	6	5	7
Don't know/other/not answered	4	5	3	4	4	4	4	3	5	6	4	3	2	5	8
BASE: ALL RESPONDENTS															
Weighted	*1719*	*533*	*593*	*587*	*334*	*268*	*365*	*300*	*346*	*106*	*544*	*371*	*307*	*299*	*199*
Unweighted	*1761*	*525*	*623*	*607*	*343*	*281*	*362*	*316*	*353*	*106*	*578*	*378*	*310*	*294*	*201*

6.9 DIVISION OF FAMILY JOBS (Q.88)
by sex, age and social class

	TOTAL	SEX		AGE						SOCIAL CLASS					
				MALE†			FEMALE†				III	III		Looks after home	Other
		Male	Female	18-34	35-54	55+	18-34	35-54	55+	I/II	non-manual	manual	IV/V		
HOUSEHOLD SHOPPING	%	%	%	%	%	%	%	%	%	%	%	%	%	%	%
Man mainly	5	4	5	2	3	7	3	3	10	3	3	5	8	4	(8)
Woman mainly	51	49	53	43	55	47	47	59	50	53	49	48	54	54	(32)
Shared equally	44	46	42	55	42	45	49	38	39	43	47	47	38	41	(60)
MAKES EVENING MEAL															
Man mainly	5	5	5	4	4	6	6	5	5	2	?	6	7	3	(8)
Woman mainly	77	75	79	73	75	76	75	83	78	82	68	73	76	87	(50)
Shared equally	17	20	15	22	20	18	20	11	17	15	24	20	17	9	(42)
DOES EVENING DISHES															
Man mainly	17	18	16	14	17	22	16	14	20	16	22	21	14	13	(16)
Woman mainly	40	37	44	44	36	34	45	46	39	37	34	38	38	53	(30)
Shared equally	40	43	38	39	44	44	38	36	40	43	42	39	46	32	(55)
DOES HOUSEHOLD CLEANING															
Man mainly	3	4	3	1	3	6	4	2	4	4	5	5	2	2	(3)
Woman mainly	72	69	74	67	72	66	77	78	66	70	73	70	66	80	(50)
Shared equally	24	27	22	31	24	27	18	19	29	25	22	24	31	17	(47)
DOES HOUSEHOLD WASHING AND IRONING															
Man mainly	1	2	*	2	2	1	*	-	*	1	3	1	*	*	(-)
Woman mainly	89	88	90	88	91	84	88	92	89	86	89	90	90	93	(68)
Shared equally	10	10	9	10	7	14	11	7	10	13	7	9	10	6	(32)
REPAIRS HOUSEHOLD EQUIPMENT															
Man mainly	82	86	79	80	84	88	80	80	76	78	88	86	87	75	(81)
Woman mainly	6	4	9	4	5	3	6	7	13	8	3	5	7	10	(3)
Shared equally	10	8	11	5	11	8	14	11	9	12	9	9	5	13	(16)
ORGANISES MONEY AND PAYS BILLS															
Man mainly	29	28	30	30	28	27	29	33	26	36	30	22	21	36	(23)
Woman mainly	39	38	40	35	38	41	36	40	44	29	38	43	47	37	(51)
Shared equally	32	33	30	35	33	32	35	27	29	34	32	34	33	27	(26)
DECIDES ON COLOUR OF LIVING ROOM															
Man mainly	5	6	4	9	6	3	4	4	4	3	5	8	4	4	(3)
Woman mainly	48	54	43	42	51	66	33	44	51	50	47	54	55	37	(51)
Shared equally	46	40	52	49	42	30	63	52	42	46	47	38	40	58	(46)
BASE: *Weighted*	1209	587	622	138	251	198	181	260	180	251	179	265	201	274	(38)
Unweighted	1210	590	620	133	255	202	167	271	180	253	180	260	211	268	(38)

BASE: *RESPONDENTS MARRIED NOW OR LIVING AS MARRIED*

6.10 DIVISION OF FAMILY JOBS AMONG THOSE AGED 18-24 (Q.88)
by sex and marital status

| | TOTAL | SEX | | MARITAL STATUS† | | | |
| | | Male | Female | Married now or living as married *(who does ...?)* | Never married *(who should do ...?)* | | |
					Total	Male	Female
	%	%	%	%	%	%	%
HOUSEHOLD SHOPPING							
Man mainly	2	2	2	2	2	3	2
Woman mainly	33	39	34	43	27	34	19
Shared equally	63	56	70	56	68	59	79
MAKES EVENING MEAL							
Man mainly	3	3	3	9	-	-	-
Woman mainly	55	56	54	70	46	52	38
Shared equally	40	38	42	21	51	43	60
DOES EVENING DISHES							
Man mainly	12	10	14	15	11	10	12
Woman mainly	26	25	27	45	15	18	12
Shared equally	60	62	58	40	72	68	76
DOES HOUSEHOLD CLEANING							
Man mainly	5	3	6	11	1	1	-
Woman mainly	48	44	51	65	37	39	33
Shared equally	46	51	42	24	60	56	61
DOES WASHING AND IRONING							
Man mainly	*	1	-	1	-	-	-
Woman mainly	70	73	68	77	67	71	60
Shared equally	27	23	31	22	31	23	40
REPAIRS HOUSEHOLD EQUIPMENT							
Man mainly	79	87	72	86	76	85	62
Woman mainly	*	-	1	1	-	-	-
Shared equally	19	11	27	12	23	12	36
ORGANISES MONEY AND PAYS BILLS							
Man mainly	25	28	23	29	23	28	16
Woman mainly	23	18	27	38	13	13	14
Shared equally	51	52	49	33	62	58	63
DECIDES ON COLOUR OF LIVING ROOM							
Man mainly	5	4	5	11	1	1	-
Woman mainly	24	27	22	31	21	27	14
Shared equally	69	67	72	58	77	70	86
Weighted	222	106	116	82	137	79	58
Unweighted	211	103	108	70	137	78	59

BASE: *RESPONDENTS AGED 18-24*

6.11 ATTITUDES TO SEXUAL RELATIONSHIPS (Q.89) by sex, age, social class and marital status

	TOTAL	SEX		AGE MALE†			FEMALE†			SOCIAL CLASS					MARITAL STATUS†		
		Male	Female	18-34	35-54	55+	18-34	35-54	55+	I/II	III non-manual	III manual	IV/V	Looks after Other home	Married now	Separated/divorced/widowed	Never married
BEFORE MARRIAGE:	%	%	%	%	%	%	%	%	%	%	%	%	%	%	%	%	%
Always/mostly wrong	28	22	33	5	18	44	7	25	60	26	24	20	32	36	26	44	19
Sometimes wrong	17	15	19	15	17	14	19	24	14	23	17	15	14	18	19	13	11
Rarely wrong/not wrong at all	50	58	43	78	61	33	70	46	20	47	54	60	48	40	49	35	68
Depends, varies/not answered	5	5	6	2	4	8	4	6	7	4	5	5	6	5	5	7	3
HUSBAND OUTSIDE MARRIAGE:																	
Always/mostly wrong	83	81	85	75	78	89	80	83	91	79	77	84	85	89	84	86	78
Sometimes wrong	11	12	9	19	14	4	13	11	5	13	18	9	8	7	11	7	14
Rarely wrong/not wrong at all	3	3	2	3	4	2	4	2	1	4	2	4	3	1	2	2	5
Depends, varies/not answered	4	4	4	3	4	5	4	4	4	4	3	3	5	3	3	5	2
WIFE OUTSIDE MARRIAGE:																	
Always/mostly wrong	84	83	86	78	80	90	80	83	93	80	78	85	86	89	85	87	80
Sometimes wrong	10	12	9	17	13	5	15	12	3	14	17	8	7	9	10	7	13
Rarely wrong/not wrong at all	2	2	2	3	4	1	3	2	2	3	2	3	3	-	2	1	5
Depends, varies/not answered	3	3	3	2	4	4	4	4	4	3	3	3	5	4	3	5	2
SAME SEX:																	
Always/mostly wrong	62	67	57	57	63	82	45	51	73	52	48	70	70	70	61	70	58
Sometimes wrong	8	6	10	9	8	2	15	10	6	12	13	5	4	3	9	4	10
Rarely wrong/not wrong at all	21	20	22	28	22	10	30	28	10	27	27	18	17	21	22	13	26
Depends, varies/not answered	9	6	11	6	7	6	11	12	12	8	12	9	10	7	9	13	6
BASE: ALL RESPONDENTS																	
Weighted	1719	793	926	258	285	250	274	309	337	334	268	365	300	346	1209	252	255
Unweighted	1761	807	954	256	294	257	269	329	350	343	281	362	316	353	1210	287	260

6.12 ATTITUDES TO SEXUAL RELATIONSHIPS (Q.89)
by region, religion, ethnic group and party identification

	TOTAL	REGION							RELIGION					ETHNIC GROUP		PARTY IDENTIFICATION†			
		Scotland	North	Midlands	Wales	S. West	S. East	GLC	Roman Catholic	C. of E./Anglican Christian	Other Christian	Non-christian	No religion	White	Black/Asian/Other	Cons.	Alliance	Labour	Non-aligned
	%	%	%	%	%	%	%	%	%	%	%	%	%	%	%	%	%	%	%
BEFORE MARRIAGE:																			
Always/mostly wrong	28	33	30	24	30	30	25	27	32	31	49	(32)	10	28	26	29	27	26	30
Sometimes wrong	17	13	16	20	19	19	15	20	12	21	17	(19)	15	17	20	20	19	14	13
Rarely wrong/not wrong at all	50	48	51	50	46	50	54	46	52	43	30	(41)	70	50	45	46	48	55	50
Depends, varies/not answered	5	6	4	7	5	1	7	7	4	5	4	(15)	5	5	10	5	6	4	7
HUSBAND OUTSIDE MARRIAGE:																			
Always/mostly wrong	83	82	85	82	86	90	83	74	80	87	90	(59)	77	84	69	84	84	85	76
Sometimes wrong	11	12	9	9	5	7	11	20	14	8	7	(21)	14	11	13	11	11	10	13
Rarely wrong/not wrong at all	3	2	3	4	2	2	2	2	2	2	1	(9)	4	2	6	3	2	3	3
Depends, varies/not answered	4	4	2	5	7	1	5	4	3	3	2	(15)	5	3	10	3	3	3	8
WIFE OUTSIDE MARRIAGE:																			
Always/mostly wrong	84	83	86	84	85	90	83	77	85	87	90	(74)	77	84	81	85	83	86	77
Sometimes wrong	10	11	9	9	9	8	11	18	11	8	7	(12)	15	11	6	11	12	9	12
Rarely wrong/not wrong at all	2	2	3	3	-	1	2	2	1	2	1	(-)	3	2	3	2	2	2	3
Depends, varies/not answered	3	4	2	5	6	1	4	4	3	2	2	(15)	5	3	10	2	3	3	7
SAME SEX:																			
Always/mostly wrong	62	66	65	63	72	58	61	47	67	63	74	(47)	53	61	68	61	48	67	66
Sometimes wrong	8	8	8	6	6	9	9	12	6	8	5	(20)	10	8	5	9	13	5	8
Rarely wrong/not wrong at all	21	15	21	23	11	30	19	28	16	19	14	(21)	29	21	16	20	30	21	14
Depends, varies/not answered	9	11	7	9	9	4	11	14	10	10	8	(18)	8	9	11	9	10	7	12
BASE: ALL RESPONDENTS																			
Weighted	1719	183	456	286	87	149	368	191	164	684	293	(34)	544	1631	88	664	252	565	216
Unweighted	1761	179	474	291	87	152	383	195	170	708	300	(33)	551	1677	84	676	258	584	221

6.13 CIRCUMSTANCES IN WHICH ABORTION SHOULD BE LEGALISED (Q.204)
by sex, age, religion, marital status and ethnic group

	TOTAL	SEX		AGE						RELIGION					MARITAL STATUS†			ETHNIC GROUP	
				MALE			FEMALE†												
		Male	Female	18-34	35-54	55+	18-34	35-54	55+	Roman Catholic	C of E/ Anglican	Other Christian	Non christian	No religion	Married now	Separated/ divorced/ widowed	Never married	White/ Other	Black/ Asian/ Other
	%	%	%	%	%	%	%	%	%	%	%	%	%	%	%	%	%	%	%
The woman decides on her own she does not wish to have the child	35	39	32	48	36	32	40	33	25	23	33	21	(30)	50	35	27	41	35	29
The couple agree they do not wish to have the child	43	48	39	63	47	34	52	41	28	25	44	22	(42)	60	45	30	50	44	37
The woman is not married and does not wish to marry the man	42	44	40	53	43	36	50	41	30	23	43	23	(29)	56	43	31	46	42	31
The couple cannot afford any more children	44	46	42	51	47	39	51	44	33	27	46	27	(40)	55	45	36	48	44	44
There is strong chance of a defect in the baby	77	74	79	78	76	68	88	82	69	51	82	69	(60)	82	79	69	74	77	67
The woman's health is seriously endangered by the pregnancy	82	82	82	88	84	74	91	86	71	70	86	73	(71)	86	84	73	84	82	77
The woman becomes pregnant as a result of rape	80	78	81	86	76	74	88	85	73	71	84	72	(53)	85	81	75	81	81	66
BASE: ALL RESPONDENTS																			
Weighted	1719	793	926	258	285	250	274	309	337	164	684	293	(34)	544	1209	252	255	1631	88
Unweighted	1761	807	954	256	294	257	269	329	350	170	708	300	(32)	551	1210	287	260	1677	84

Appendix I
Technical details of the survey

Sample design

The survey was designed to yield a representative sample of people living in Britain aged 18 or over at the time of the survey.

For practical reasons, the sample was confined to those living in private households whose addresses were included in the electoral registers. Thus we excluded people living in institutions and those living in private households whose addresses were not on the electoral registers. Owing to the timing of fieldwork (March/April 1983), it was necessary to sample from registers that had just reached the end of their period of currency.

The sampling method involved a multi-stage design, with four separate stages of selection.

Selection of parliamentary constituencies

103 of the 552 constituencies in England and Wales were selected with probability proportionate to their electorates.

Prior to our selection of constituencies they were stratified according to the classification of the Centre for Environmental Studies Planning and Applications Group (PRAG). This system groups constituencies into 'clusters' (30) and ultimately into 'families' (6), that are broadly homogeneous in terms of demographic, socio-economic and other characteristics derivable from census data.

For Scotland a different procedure was followed. The local authority districts there were grouped into 12 strata, on the basis of region and degree of urbanisation. Districts within the Highlands and Islands Region (one stratum) were excluded. From the remainder, 11 districts were selected with probability proportionate to their electorates.

Selection of polling districts

Within each of the selected constituencies/districts a single polling district was selected, again with probability proportionate to electorate.

Selection of addresses

Twenty-three addresses were sampled in each of the 114 polling districts. The sample issued to interviewers was therefore $114 \times 23 = 2,622$ addresses. The selection was made from a random starting point and, treating the list of electors as circular, a fixed interval was applied to generate the required number of addresses for each polling district. By this means, addresses were chosen with probability proportionate to their number of listed electors. The name of the elector whose selection had led to the inclusion of each address was noted (to be handed over to interviewers), as were the names of all other electors listed at each address.

Selection of individuals

The selection of individuals for interview was made by interviewers, who initially identified all persons currently aged 18 or over and resident at the selected household. Where the listing revealed a difference between the register entry and the current position, because members aged 18 or over had either joined or left the household, all persons were listed and the respondent selected by means of a random selection grid. In households where there had been no change, the person on whose account the address had been selected was chosen for interview. Where there were two or more households at the selected address, interviewers were required to identify the household of the elector whose name had led to the inclusion of that address, or the household occupying that part of the address where he or she used to live, before following a similar procedure.

Prior to analysis, the data were weighted to take account of any differences between the number of eligible persons on the register and at the address. This occurred in approximately 30% of cases, in each of which the data were weighted by the number of persons aged 18 or over living at the household divided by the number of electors listed on the registers for that address. A few extreme values were reduced so that all weighting fell within a range of between 2.0 and 0.33. In the remaining 70% of cases, the two figures matched, so the effective weight was one.

Fieldwork

Interviewing was carried out largely during the months of March and April 1983. Approximately 10% of interviews, mainly those generated from reissued addresses, were completed during May and the first few days of June.

The interviews were carried out by 116 interviewers drawn from SCPR's regular interviewing panel, all of whom attended a one-day briefing about the questionnaires and sampling procedures.

The response achieved is shown below:

	No.	%
Addresses issued	2,622	
Vacant, derelict, out of scope	90	
In scope	2,532	100
Interview achieved	1,761	70
Interview not achieved	771	30
Refused	565	22
Non contact	105	4
Other non response	101	4

There were some variations in response by region. The highest levels of response were achieved in East Anglia (79%) and the East Midlands (76%), the lowest levels in the South East (66%), Wales (66%) and Greater London (63%).

In 109 instances (6% of the total), the self-completion questionnaire was not returned by the respondent and is therefore absent from the dataset. Those not returning a self-completion questionnaire included a higher proportion (11%) of respondents aged 65 or over.

Analysis variables

A number of standard analyses were used in the tabulation of the data. Many of these appear in the tables included in this report; some are used only in the tables available on microfiche.

Where appropriate, we set out below the definitions used in creating these analysis groups.

Region

The Registrar General's Standard Regions (11) have been used. Sometimes these have been grouped. In addition we divide Metropolitan Counties (including Glasgow) from other areas.

Social class

For all respondents classified as being in paid work at the time of interview, *or* as waiting to take up a job already offered *or* seeking work *or* retired from work, the occupation (present, future or last as appropriate) was classified

according to the OPCS *Classification of Occupations 1980.* Employment status
was also coded so as to generate six Social Classes.

I	—	Professional	
II	—	Intermediate	Non-manual
III (non-manual)	—	Skilled occupations	
III (manual)	—	Skilled occupations	
IV	—	Partly skilled occupations	Manual
V	—	Unskilled occupations	

The remaining respondents were grouped either as 'looking after the home'
or 'no paid occupation/not classifiable'.

Industry

All respondents for whom an occupation was coded were allocated a Standard
Industrial Classification code (CSO as revised 1980). Two digit class codes were
applied. Respondents with an occupation were also divided into Public Sector,
Private Sector (Non Manufacturing) and Manufacturing. This division was on the
basis of the *1968* Standard Industrial Classification. Orders II – XIX were
categorised as Manufacturing; Orders I, XX-XXVI (with the exception of MLH
701, 708, 872 and 874) as Private Sector (Non-Manufacturing). The four
excepted MLHs and Order XXVII were classified as Public Sector.

Trade union membership

Respondents in employment were subdivided by Social Class (I, II, III, Non-
Manual/III Manual, IV, V) and then by whether they had ever been members
of a trade union (Q.96a,b).

Party identification

Respondents were classified as identified with a particular party on one of
three counts: if they considered themselves as supporters of the party (Q.2a,b)
or as closer to it than to others (Q.2c,d) *or* as most likely to support it in the
event of a general election (Q.2e). These three groups are described respectively
(in both text and tables) as 'partisans', 'sympathisers' and 'residual identifiers'.

Alliance identifiers included those nominating the Social Democratic Party or the Liberal Party or the Alliance. Those who failed to nominate a party at all of these three questions were classified as non-aligned.

Other analysis groupings

These were taken directly from the questionnaire and are self explanatory.

Sex (Q.91a)

Age (Q.91b)

Household income (Q.99a)

Employment status
     (Q.28, 29, 30)

Religion (Q.79a)

Accommodation (Q.63)

Marital status (Q.87)

Household type (Q.91a,b)

Ethnic group (Q.94)

Age of completing full time
     education (Q.93)

Types of school attended (Q.92)

Self assigned social class (Q.77a)

Self rated racial prejudice (Q.81e)

Sampling errors

As with all sample surveys, this survey presents only estimates of the characteristics of the population it represents. Imprecision arises both from sampling errors and from other errors in the process of data collection and analysis.

The sampling error associated with a sample-based estimate (such as the proportion holding a certain opinion) can be assessed by calculating a quantity known as the 'standard error'. There is (for example) a 95% chance that the true population figure is within two standard errors of the sample-based estimate.

For a simple random sample, in which all members of the population have equal and independent chances of selection, the standard error of a proportion is calculated by the formula $\sqrt{p(1-p)/n}$, where p is the sample-based proportion and n is the sample size. For complex (multi-stage stratified) designs of the type used in this survey, the standard error is generally (though not always) larger than that for a simple random sample of the same size. The ratio of the standard error of a complex design to that of a simple random sample is commonly referred to as 'deft' (a contraction of the term 'design factor'). It is not the same for each variable within a survey. The table overleaf shows ten examples of 'defts' and standard errors applicable to this design. They have been calculated by SCPR's Survey Methods Centre using the World Fertility Survey 'Clusters' program.

The 95% confidence limits (calculated as twice the standard error on either side of the estimated proportion) are also shown. Alternative confidence limits can be calculated by using different multiples of the standard error.

It should be noted that all these calculations are based on the total sample (n = 1,761), and that errors for proportions based on sub-groups would be larger.

		% of total sample	Deft	Standard error (complex)	95% confidence limits %
Man should maintain children after divorce	(Q.84a(i))	92.0	1.071	0.7	90.6–93.4
Covered by private health insurance	(Q.58a)	10.8	1.134	0.8	9.1–12.5
Lot of discrimination in employment against Asians	(Q.81a)	20.5	1.125	1.1	18.3–22.7
Oppose law against sex discrimination	(Q.86)	21.7	1.431	1.4	18.9–24.6
Support law against racial discrimination	(Q.82a)	69.5	1.382	1.5	66.4–72.5
Government should increase taxes/spend more on benefits	(Q.54)	32.2	1.259	1.4	29.4–35.0
First priority to retirement benefits	(Q.51a)	40.8	0.970	1.1	38.6–43.1
Would vote for party regardless of candidate	(Q.3)	57.7	1.089	1.3	55.1–60.3
Sexual relations before marriage not wrong	(Q.89a)	50.4	1.314	1.6	47.2–53.5
Agree strongly that many people fail to claim benefit	(Q.52a)	49.2	1.513	1.8	45.6–52.8

Appendix II
Notes on the tabulations

1. The following symbols appear in the tables:

    *   =   less than 0.5%

    —   =   zero

    †   =   Certain respondents are omitted from some tables because of missing data unclassifiable responses or because there were too few of them. Omissions from the breakdowns, where indicated, are as follows:

    Age: 6 (women)

    Social class: 8 (employees)

    Industry (SIC 1980):   26 (employees)

    Accommodation: 8

    Marital status: 4

    Trade union membership: 13 (employees)

    Age of completing full-time education: 6

    Party identification: 22 (identifying with the Communist Party National Front, Scottish National Party, or Plaid Cymru)

    Self-rated racial prejudice: 13

    0   =   Included in the 'state only' base are 90 respondents where information on type of schooling was not available for all household members.

2.   Percentages based on fewer than 50 respondents are bracketed in the tables.

3.   Owing to the effects of rounding weighted data, the weighted bases shown
      in the tables may not always add to 1,719.

4.   Respondents who answered 'don't know' are omitted from Tables 2.7, 2.8,
      2.9, 4.1, 4.2, 4.7, 5.9, 6.9, 6.10, 6.13.
      Respondents not answering the question are omitted from Tables 2.8, 2.9,
      4.1, 4.2, 4.7, 5.9, 6.9, 6.10, 6.13.

Appendix III
The questionnaires

The two questionnaires (interview and self-completion) are reproduced on the following pages. We have removed the punching codes and inserted instead the percentage distribution of answers to each question.

Figures do not necessarily add up to 100% because of rounding, or for one or more of the following reasons.

(i)   We have not included 'not answered' figures here, which are usually very small. They are, of course, included in the tables and on the tape.

(ii) Some sub-questions are filtered, that is they are asked of only a proportion of respondents. In these cases the percentages add up (approximately) to the proportions who were asked them. Where, however, a series of questions is filtered (for instance in Section 2 of the interview questionnaire), we have inserted the base figure at the beginning of the series and percentaged throughout on that base.

(iii) At a few questions, respondents were invited to give more than one answer. In these cases, the percentages usually add to well over 100%.

(iv) The self-completion questionnaire was not completed by 6% of respondents. Instead of re-percentaging the answers, the proportions there add up (approximately) to 94%, minus any non-response to particular questions (which is usually small). The tables and tape contain the full distributions.

scpr

SOCIAL AND COMMUNITY PLANNING RESEARCH

Head Office: 35 Northampton Square London EC1V 0AX. Tel: 01-750 1866
Northern Field Office: Charazel House Gainford Darlington Co. Durham DL2 3EG. Tel: 0325 730 888

P.705

March 1983

SOCIAL ATTITUDES SURVEY

SECTION ONE

Serial No.

Interview started at:
(24 hour clock)

N = 1761

		Col./ Code	Skip to
1.a) Do you normally read any daily morning newspaper at least 3 times a week?	Yes	% 77	b)
	No	23	Q.2

IF YES

b) Which one do you normally read?
IF MORE THAN ONE ASK: Which one do you read most frequently?

ONE CODE ONLY

	Code
(Scottish) Daily Express	8
Daily Mail	10
Daily Mirror/Record	18
Daily Star	4
The Sun	17
Daily Telegraph	6
Financial Times	*
The Guardian	3
The Times	1
Morning Star	—
Other Scottish/Welsh/regional or local daily morning paper	6
Other answer	3

			Skip to
2.a) Generally speaking, do you think of yourself as a supporter of any one political party?	Yes	% 46	b)
	No	54	c)

IF YES, ASK b). IF NO ASK c)

b) Which one? RECORD ANSWER BELOW AND GO TO Q.3.

			Skip to
c) Do you think of yourself as a little closer to one political party than to the others?	Yes	% 25	d)
	No	29	e)

IF YES, ASK d). IF NO, ASK e)

d) Which one? RECORD ANSWER AND GO TO Q.3

IF NO AT a) and c)

e) If there were a general election tomorrow which political party do you think you would be most likely to support?   ONE CODE ONLY

	(b) %	(d) %	(e) %
Conservative	24	9	5
Labour	17	11	5
Liberal			
SDP/Social Democrat	5	5	5
(Alliance)			
Scottish Nationalist			
Plaid Cymru			1
Other Party			*
NONE			8
Don't Know			2

		Col./Code	Skip to

ASK ALL

SHOW CARD 1

3. Which of the four statements on this card comes closest to the way you vote in a general election?

	Code
	%
I vote for a Party, regardless of the candidate	58
I vote for a Party, only if I approve of the candidate	24
I vote for a candidate, regardless of his or her Party	5
I do not generally vote at all	12
Other answer	1

4.a) How likely do you think you are to vote in the next General Election (READ OUT) ...

	Code	Skip to
	%	
...very likely,	70	b)
quite likely,	15	b)
not very likely,	7	Q.5
or not at all likely?	9	Q.5

IF VERY OR QUITE LIKELY

b) Suppose in the next General Election the Party or candidate you prefer has no chance of winning in your constituency, do you think you would (READ OUT) ...

	Code
	%
... still vote for that Party or candidate,	74
vote for another Party or candidate,	5
or not bother to vote at all?	3
Don't know	2

5. There are some people whose views are considered extreme by the majority.

a) Consider people who wish to overthrow the system of government in Britain by revolution. Do you think such people should be allowed to (READ OUT) ... RECORD IN COLUMN a)

		(a)	(b)
		%	%
(i)··hold public meetings to express their views?	Yes	57	56
	No	42	41
	Don't Know	1	2
(ii) teach in schools?	Yes	25	31
	No	72	66
	Don't Know	2	2
(iii)teach in colleges or universities?	Yes	37	41
	No	60	56
	Don't Know	3	2
(iv) Publish books expressing their views?	Yes	74	71
	No	24	27
	Don't Know	1	2

b) Now consider people who say that all blacks and Asians should be forced to leave Britain. Do you think such people should be allowed to ... (REPEAT (i) to (iv) ABOVE AND RECORD IN COL. b)

		Col./ Code	Sk. to

6. Which do you think is generally
better for Britain ...

	%
... to have a government formed by one political party,	47
or for two or more parties to get together to form a government?	49
Don't Know	4

SHOW CARD 2.

7. When an MP is considering a national issue, whose views
do you think he or she should most take into account?
Choose a phrase from the card.

	%
The views of the Party as expressed by the Conferences	16
The views of the local Party	8
ONE CODE ONLY The views of his or her constituents	57
The views of fellow MPs in the same Party	8
His or her own views	7
Other answer	1
Don't Know	2

SHOW CARD 3.

8.a) Still thinking of MPs, which of the personal qualities on this card
would you say are important for an MP to have?   You may choose more
than one, or none, or suggest others. RECORD in Col. a).

b) And which would you say are important for a
local councillor to have? RECORD in Col. b).

	a) MP	b) Local Cllr
	%	%
MORE THAN ONE CODE MAY BE RINGED IN EACH COL. To be well educated	50	31
To know what being poor means	27	17
To have business experience	22	19
To have trade union experience	14	8
To have been brought up in the area he or she represents	48	76
To be loyal to the Party he or she represents	42	21
To be independent minded	37	29
NONE OF THESE QUALITIES	1	1
(SPECIFY) _____ OTHER MP _____ qualities	3	
(SPECIFY) _____ OTHER LOCAL CLLR _____ qualities		3

9.a) Do you think that local councils ought to be controlled
by central government more, less or about the same
amount as now?

b) And do you think that British industry
ought to be controlled by central government more, less or about the same
as now?

c) On the whole would you like to see
more or less state ownership of
industry, or about the same amount
as now?

	More	Less	Same	Don't know
a) Control councils	%13	34	45	8
b) Control industry	%11	43	38	8
c) State ownership	%11	49	33	7

		Col./ Code	Skip to
10.a)	Has there ever been an occasion when a law was being considered by Parliament which you thought was really unjust and harmful? Yes / No	% 31 69	b) c)

IF YES, SHOW CARD 4.

b) Did you do any of the things on this card? Any others?
RECORD IN COL b) BELOW, THEN ASK c) & d) MORE THAN ONE CODE MAY BE
ASK ALL, SHOW CARD 4.   RINGED

c) Suppose a law was now being considered by Parliament which you thought was really unjust and harmful, which, if any, of the things on this card do you think you would do? Any others? RECORD IN COL c) BELOW THEN ASK d). MORE THAN ONE CODE MAY BE RINGED

d) Which one of the things on the card do you think would be the most effective in influencing a government to change its mind? ONE CODE ONLY IN COL d)

	b) Ever done	c) Would do	d) Most effec- tive
	%	%	%
Contact my MP	3	46	34
Speak to influential person	1	10	4
Contact a government department	1	7	5
Contact radio, TV or newspaper	1	14	23
Sign a petition	9	54	11
Raise the issue in an organisation I already belong to	2	9	2
Go on a protest or demonstration	2	8	5
Form a group of like minded people	1	6	4
NONE OF THESE	19	14	9
			1

11.a)	In general would you say that people should obey the law without exception, or are there exceptional occasions on which people should follow their con- sciences even if it means breaking the law?		
	Obey law without exception	% 53	
	Follow conscience on occasions	46	
b)	Are there any circumstances in which you might break a law to which you were very strongly opposed? Yes No Don't know	% 30 61 8	

		Col./ Code	Skip to
12.a)	Do you think that the House of Lords should remain as it is or is some change needed?	%	
	Remain as is	57	Q.13
	Change needed	34	b)
	IF CHANGE NEEDED Don't know	8	
b)	Do you think the House of Lords should be (READ OUT) ...	%	
	.... replaced by a different body,	10	Q.13
	abolished and replaced by nothing,	8	Q.13
	or should there be some other kind of change?	16	c)
	IF OTHER KIND OF CHANGE		
	c) Do you have a particular change in mind?		
	RECORD, BUT DO NOT PROBE		

_____
_____
_____

13.	How about the monarchy or the Royal Family in Britain. How important or unimportant do you think it is for Britain to continue to have a monarchy (READ OUT) ...	%
	... very important,	65
	quite important,	21
	not very important,	8
	not at all important,	3
	or do you think the monarchy should be abolished?	3

14. Now a few questions about Britain's relationships with other countries.

a) Do you think Britain should continue to be a member of the EEC - the Common Market - or should it withdraw?

b) And do you think Britain should continue to be a member of NATO - the North Atlantic Treaty Organisation - or should it withdraw?

	a) EEC	b) NATO
	%	%
Continue	53	79
Withdraw	42	13
Don't know	5	8

	Col./ Code	Skip to

SHOW CARD 5.

15. For each of the countries I read out, please use the card to show how important or unimportant you think it is for Britain to have close links with that country. First, how important is it for Britain to have close links with (READ OUT AND RECORD FOR EACH COUNTRY IN TURN) ...

	Very important	Quite important	Not very important	Not at all important	Don't know
... China?	% 22	43	25	6	5
South Africa?	% 13	32	36	13	6
Russia?	% 29	35	17	16	3
Brazil?	% 7	29	42	13	9
USA?	% 66	28	3	1	1
Nigeria?	% 9	31	39	12	9
Saudi Arabia?	% 32	44	14	5	5

16.a) Do you think the long term policy for Northern Ireland should be for it (READ OUT) ...

	%
... to remain part of the United Kingdom,	28
or to reunify with the rest of Ireland?	58
Other answer	8
Don't know	6

b) Some people think that government policy towards Northern Ireland should include a complete withdrawal of British Troops. Would you personally support or oppose such a policy? Strongly or a little?

	%
Support strongly	38
Support a little	21
Oppose strongly	22
Oppose a little	13
Other answer	3
Don't know	4

17.a) Do you think that the siting of American nuclear missiles in Britain makes Britain a safer or a less safe place to live? RECORD IN COL. a).

b) And do you think that having our own independent nuclear missiles makes Britain a safer or a less safe place to live? RECORD IN COL. b).

	a) American nuclear missiles	b) Own nuclear missiles
	%	%
Safer	38	60
Less safe	48	28
Don't know	12	9

SHOW CARD 6.

c) Which, if either, of these two statements comes closest to your own opinion on British nuclear policy?

	%
Britain should rid itself of nuclear weapons while persuading others to do the same	19
Britain should keep its nuclear weapons until we persuade others to reduce theirs	77
Neither of these	3

		Col./ Code	Skip to

SECTION TWO

Now I would like to ask you about two of
Britain's economic problems - inflation
and unemployment.

18. First inflation: In a year from now, do you expect
     prices generally (READ OUT) ...

19. Second, unemployment: In a year from now, do you expect
     unemployment (READ OUT) ...

	Q.18 PRICES	Q.19 UNEMPLOYMENT
	%	%
... to have gone up by a lot,	24	31
to have gone up by a little,	56	37
to have stayed the same,	12	17
to have gone down by a little,	5	12
or to have gone down by a lot?	1	1
Don't know	2	2

20. If the government had to choose between
     keeping down inflation or keeping down
     unemployment, to which do you think it
     should give highest priority?

	%
Keeping down inflation	27
Keeping down unemployment	69
Other answer	2
Don't know	2

21. Looking ahead over the next year, do you
     think Britain's general industrial performance
     will (READ OUT) ...

	%
... improve a lot,	5
improve a little,	39
stay much the same,	34
decline a little,	13
or decline a lot?	4
Don't know	5

22.a) I am going to read out a number of statements about the possible causes of Britain's economic difficulties. For each one that I read out can you tell me first whether you think it is true or false. READ OUT (i) - (x) AND RECORD ANSWERS IN GRID

SHOW CARD 7

FOR EACH STATEMENT coded 'TRUE' in Col. a), ASK b)

b) How important a factor do you think it has been in causing Britain's economic difficulties? Please choose a phrase from this card.

			(a)		(b)				(a)
			True	False	Very impor- tant	Quite impor- tant	Not very impor- tant	Not at all impor- tant	Don't Know
i.	People are not working hard enough	%	62	37	% 36	24	2	-	1
ii.	Employers are not investing enough	%	65	27	% 34	29	2	-	7
iii.	There has been a decline in world trade	%	84	10	% 50	31	3	-	4
iv.	Wages are too high	%	32	64	% 14	16	2	-	2
v.	Energy costs are too high for industry	%	83	11	% 48	32	3	-	5
vi.	Government spending has been too high	%	47	45	% 23	21	3	-	5
vii.	British industry is badly managed	%	67	26	% 39	25	3	-	5
viii.	British workers are reluctant to accept new ways of working	%	75	22	% 37	33	5	-	2
ix.	The government has not done enough to create jobs	%	70	26	% 45	22	3	-	3
x.	The best school and college leavers don't seek jobs in manufacturing industry	%	55	34	% 19	26	9	1	8

Col./ Code   Skip to

				Col./ Code	Skip to
23.	Here are a number of policies which might help Britain's economic problems. As I read them out will you tell me whether you would support such a policy or oppose it? READ OUT ITEMS (i)-(ix)AND CODE IN GRID.				

	SUPPORT	OPPOSE	DON'T KNOW
Control of <u>wages</u> by legislation %	48	48	3
Control of <u>prices</u> by legislation %	70	27	2
Reducing the level of Government spending on health and education %	13	85	1
Introducing import controls %	72	24	4
Increasing Government subsidies for private industry %	64	31	5
Devaluation of the pound %	16	71	12·
Reducing Government spending on defence %	44	53	3
Government incentives to encourage job sharing or splitting %	61	35	4
Government to set up construction projects to create more jobs %	89	9	2

24.a).	It is said that many people manage to avoid paying their full income tax. Do you think that they should <u>not</u> be allowed to get away with it - or do you think good luck to them if they can get away with it?		
		Should not be allowed	%
			74	b)
		Good luck if they can get away with it	26	Q.25

IF 'SHOULD NOT BE ALLOWED'

b) If you knew of somebody who wasn't paying their full income tax, would you be inclined to report him or her?

		%
	Yes	10
	No	62
	Other answer	2

		Col./ Code	Skip to

25. Thinking of income levels generally in Britain today would you say that the gap between those with high incomes and those with low incomes is (READ OUT) ...

	Col./Code	Skip to
	%	
... too large,	72	
about right,	22	
or too small?	3	
Don't know	2	

SHOW CARD 8

26. Generally how would you describe levels of taxation in Britain today?

a) Firstly for those with high incomes? Please choose a phrase from this card. <u>RECORD ANSWER IN GRID BELOW</u>.

b) Next for those with middle incomes? Please choose a phrase from this card. <u>RECORD ANSWER IN GRID BELOW</u>.

c) And lastly for those with low incomes? Please choose a phrase from this card. <u>RECORD ANSWER IN GRID BELOW</u>.

		a) HIGH	b) MIDDLE	c) LOW
		%	%	%
Taxes are:	Much too high	9	8	35
	Too high	20	36	44
	About right	36	50	16
	Too low	27	4	2
	Much too low	5	*	1
	Don't know	2	2	1

27a) Among which group would you place yourself (READ OUT) ...

	%	
... high income,	3	
middle income,	47	
or low income?	50	

b) How well would you say you are managing on your income these days (READ OUT) ...

	%	
... very well,	9	
quite well,	58	
not very well,	23	
or not at all well?	9	

	%	
23 OR OVER	91	c)
UNDER 23	9	Q.28

INTERVIEWER: <u>CHECK RESPONDENTS AGE</u>.

IF 23 OR OVER

c) Compared with five years ago would you say you were (READ OUT) ...

	%	
... better off financially,	29	
about the same,	25	
or worse off financially?	36	

		Col./Code	Skip to

SHOW CARD 9.

28. Which of these descriptions applies to what you were doing last week, that is the seven days ending last Sunday?   PROBE: Any others?
RECORD BELOW IN COL A.   IF TWO OR MORE CATEGORIES IN COL A, CODE HIGHEST ON LIST AS ECONOMIC POSITION IN COL B

IF ONE CODE ONLY CODED IN COL A, TRANSFER TO COL B AS ECONOMIC POSITION

	COL A	COL B ECONOMIC POSITION	Skip to
	%	%	
In full time education at school or college (not paid for by employer)	2	2	Q.43
In paid work of any sort for at least 10 hours in the week	50	50	Q.29
Away from a paid job because of holiday, temporary illness, etc	3	3	
Waiting to take up a job already accepted	*	*	Q.42
Seeking work	7	7	Q.44
Prevented by temporary sickness or injury from seeking work	1	1	Q.42
Permanently sick or disabled	2	2	Q.50
Wholly retired from work	16	15	Q.46
Looking after the home	32	20	Q.47
Doing something else	1	*	Q.50

FOLLOW SKIP INSTRUCTIONS ABOVE TO GO TO APPROPRIATE QUESTIONS

IF IN PAID WORK OR AWAY TEMPORARILY (CODE 02 or 03) ABOVE

		%	
29.	In your (main) job are you (READ OUT) ... ... an employee,	47	Q.30
	or self-employed?	6	Q.39

ALL EMPLOYEES (CODE 1): ASK Q's 30-38. — N = 817

		%	
30.	In this (main) job, do you normally work (READ OUT) ... ... full time (30 hrs +),	82	
	or part time (10-29 hrs)?	18	

31.a) How would you describe the wages or salary you are paid for the job you do - on the low side, reasonable, or on the high side?   IF 'On the low side': Very low or a bit low?

	%
Very low	13
A bit low	28
Reasonable	54
On the high side	5
Other answer (SPECIFY) _____	*

SHOW CARD 10.

b) Thinking of the highest and the lowest paid people at your place of work, how would you describe the gap between their pay, as far as you know? Please choose a phrase from this card.

	%
Much too big a gap	18
Too big	22
About right	45
Too small	4
Much too small a gap	1
Don't know	10

		Col./Code	Skip to
32.a)	If you stay in this job would you expect your wages or salary over the coming year to (READ OUT) ...	%	
	...rise by <u>more</u> than the cost of living,	15	
	by the <u>same</u> as the cost of living,	46	
	by <u>less</u> than the cost of living,	27	
	or <u>not</u> to rise at all?	9	
	Will not stay in job	2	
	Don't know	2	
b)	Over the coming year do you expect your workplace will be (READ OUT) ...	%	
	... increasing its number of employees,	16	
	reducing its number of employees,	29	
	or will the number of employees stay about the same?	54	
	Other answer	1	
	Don't know	1	
c)	How about your own job? How likely or unlikely is it that you will leave this employer over the next year (READ OUT) ...	%	
	...very likely,	9	d)
	quite likely,	10	d)
	not very likely,	26	Q.33
	or not at all likely?	55	Q.33

IF VERY OR QUITE LIKELY

SHOW CARD 11.

		Col./Code	Skip to
d)	Why do you think you will leave? Please choose a phrase from this card or tell me what other reason there is. <u>MORE THAN ONE CODE MAY BE RINGED</u>	%	
	Firm will close down	2	
	I will be declared redundant	4	
	I will reach normal retirement age	2	
	My contract of employment will expire	1	
	I will take early retirement	1	
	I will decide to leave and work for another employer	7	
	I will decide to leave and work for myself, as self-employed	1	
	Other answer	3	

		Col./ Code	Skip to

33.a) Suppose you were made redundant or your firm closed down, would you start looking for another job, would you wait for several months or longer before you started looking, or would you decide not to look for another job?

	Col./Code	Skip to
	%	
Start looking	84	b)
Wait several months or longer	6	Q.34
Decide not to look	9	Q.34
Don't know	1	Q.34

IF START LOOKING

b) How long do you think it would take you to find an acceptable replacement job?

MONTHS

(MEDIAN) | 0 | 3 | Don't know 8%

IF 3 MONTHS OR MORE ASK c) TO e); OTHERS GO TO Q.34.

	%
c) How willing do you think you would be in these circumstances to retrain for a different job (READ OUT) ... ... very willing,	23
quite willing,	11
or not very willing?	5
Would find job in less than 3 months or don't know how long,	44

	%
d) And how willing do you think you would be to move to a different area to find an acceptable job (READ OUT) ... ... very willing,	6
quite willing,	10
or not very willing?	23
Would find job in less than 3 months or don't know how long?	44

	%
e) And how willing do you think you would be in these circumstances to take what you now consider to be an unacceptable job (READ OUT)... ... very willing,	7
quite willing,	15
or not very willing?	17
Would find job in less than 3 months or don't know how long,	44

		Col./Code	Skip to
34. Have you in the past year done any regular paid work outside your main job?		%	
	Yes	6	
	No	94	

		Col./Code	Skip to
35.a) During the last five years (that is since March 1978) have you been unemployed and seeking work for any period?		%	
	Yes	18	b)
	No	82	Q.36

IF YES

b) For how many months in total during the last five years?

MONTHS

(MEDIAN) | 0 | 6 |

		Col./Code	Skip to
36.a)	For any period during the last five years have you worked as a self employed person as your main job?	%	
	Yes	3	b)
	No	97	c)

IF YES, ASK b). IF NO, ASK c)

b) In total, for how many months during the last five years have you been ıf-employed?

                                                    MONTHS
                            (MEDIAN) | 1 | 8 | Q.37

                            NOW SKIP TO Q.37.

IF NO at a)

c) How seriously in the last five years have you considered working as a self-employed person (READ OUT) ...

	Col./Code	Skip to
	%	
... very seriously,	5	d) & e)
quite seriously,	12	d) & e)
not very seriously,	12	Q.37
or not at all seriously?	69	Q.37

IF VERY OR QUITE SERIOUSLY, ASK d) & e)

d) What were the main reasons you did not become self-employed?

	%
Cost/lack of money/capital	10
Risk	3
Recession/economic climate	1
Other answer	7

e) How likely or unlikely is it that you will work as a self-employed person as your main job in the next five years (READ OUT) ...

	%
... very likely,	2
quite likely,	6
not very likely,	5
or not at all likely?	2
Don't know	1

		Col./Code	Skip to
37.a)	At your place of work are there unions, staff associations, or groups of unions recognised by the management for negotiating pay and conditions of employment?	%	
	Yes	67	b)
	No	33	Q.38

IF YES

b) On the whole do you think these unions or staff associations do their job well or not?

	%
Yes	39
No	26

		Col./ Code	Skip to

38.a) In general how would you describe relations between management and other employees at your workplace? (READ OUT) ...

	Col./Code
	%
... very good,	37
quite good,	47
not very good,	10
or not at all good?	5

b) And in general would you say your workplace was (READ OUT) ...

	Col./Code	Skip to
	%	
... very well managed,	30	
quite well managed,	50	Q.50
or not well managed?	20	

ALL EMPLOYEES NOW GO TO SECTION 3

ALL SELF-EMPLOYED (CODE 2 AT Q.29 : ASK Q's 39-41 ── N = 109

39.a) In your (main) job do you normally work (READ OUT) ...

	Col./Code
	%
... full time (30 hrs+)	91
or part time (10-29 hrs)?	9

b) During the last 5 years (that is since March 1978) have you been unemployed and seeking work for any period?

	Col./Code	Skip to
	%	
Yes	21	c)
No	79	Q.40

IF YES

c) For how many months in total during the last 5 years?

MONTHS

(MEDIAN) | 0 | 6 |

40.a) Have you, for any period in the last five years, worked as an <u>employee</u> as your main job rather than as self-employed?

	Col./Code	Skip to
	%	
Yes	31	b)
No	69	c)

IF YES, ASK b). IF NO, ASK c)

b) In total for how many months during the last five years have you been an employee?

MONTHS

(MEDIAN) | 2 | 4 |

NOW SKIP TO Q.41.

IF NO AT a)

c) How seriously in the last five years have you considered getting a job as an <u>employee</u> (READ OUT) ...

	Col./Code	Skip to
	%	
...very seriously,	3	d) & e)
quite seriously,	5	d) & e)
not very seriously,	4	Q.41
or not at all seriously?	57	Q.41

IF VERY OR QUITE SERIOUSLY ASK d) AND e)

d) What were the main reasons you did not become an employee?

_____

_____

e) How likely or unlikely is it that you will work as an employee, in your main job, in the next five years (READ OUT) ...

	Col./Code
	%
... very likely,	1
quite likely,	1
not very likely,	2
or not at all likely?	3
Don't know	1

	Col./ Code	Skip to

41.a) Compared with a year ago, would you say your business is doing ...(READ OUT AND RECORD IN COL.a)

b) Compared with five years ago, would you say your business is doing ... (READ OUT AND RECORD IN COL.b)

	(a) 1 YEAR	(b) 5 YEARS	Skip to
	%	%	
... very well,	11	15	
quite well,	25	20	
about the same,	48	24	Q.50
not very well,	7	10	
or not at all well?	5	4	
Business not in existence then	2	24	

ALL SELF EMPLOYED NOW GO TO SECTION 3

ALL 'WAITING TO TAKE UP JOB' OR 'TEMPORARILY PREVENTED FROM SEEKING WORK' (CODES 04 OR 06 AT Q.28): ASK Q.42 — N = 18

42.a) During the last five years (that is since March 1978) have you been unemployed and seeking work for any period?

	Skip to
Yes	b)
No	Q.50

IF YES ASK b); IF NO GO TO Q.50

b) For how many months in total during the last five years?

NOW GO TO SECTION 3 — SKIP TO Q.50

ASK ALL IN FULL TIME EDUCATION (CODE 01 AT Q.28): ASK Q.43 — N = 28

43.a) When you leave full time education, do you think you will start looking for a job, will you wait several months or longer before you start looking, or will you decide not to look for a job?

	Skip to
Start looking	b)
Wait several months or longer	
Decide not to look	Q.50
Don't know	

Other answer (SPECIFY) ______________________

IF START LOOKING ASK b); OTHERS GO TO Q.50

b) How long do you think it will take you to find an acceptable job?

IF 3 MONTHS OR MORE AT b) ASK c); OTHERS GO TO Q.50

c) How willing do you think you would be in these circumstances to take what you now consider to be an unacceptable job (READ OUT) ...

	Skip to
...very willing,	
quite willing,	Q.50
or not very willing?	
Don't know	

ALL IN FULL TIME EDUCATION NOW GO TO SECTION 3

		Col./ Code	Skip to

ALL SEEKING WORK (CODE 05 AT Q.28): ASK Q's 44-45 ⌐ N = 118

44.a) In total how many months in the last five
years have you been unemployed and seeking   MONTHS
work?   (MEDIAN) | 1 | 6 |

b) How long has this present period of unemployment
and seeking work lasted so far?
                                                    MONTHS
                                  (MEDIAN) | 0 | 9 |

c) Are you registered with a Jobcentre as   %
unemployed?   Yes   87
                                                    No   13

d) How confident are you that you will find a   %
job to match your qualifications (READ OUT) ... ...very confident,   5
                                              quite confident,   24
                                          not very confident,   40
                                      or not at all confident?   30

e) Although it may be difficult to judge, how long
from now do you think it will be before you find
an acceptable job?   MONTHS
                                  (MEDIAN) | 0 | 6 | Don't know 30%

IF 3 MONTHS OR MORE, ASK f) to h); OTHERS GO TO Q.45

f) How willing do you think you would be in the   %
circumstances to retrain for a different job   ... very willing,   26
(READ OUT) ...   quite willing,   15
                                          or not very willing?   7
        Would find job in less than 3 months or don't know how long 51

g) How willing would you be to move to a different   %
area to find an acceptable job (READ OUT) ... ... very willing,   14
                                              quite willing,   5
                                          or not very willing?   29
        Would find job in less than 3 months or don't know how long 51

h) And how willing do you think you would be in   %
the circumstances to take what you now consider very willing,   12
to be an unacceptable job (READ OUT) ...   quite willing,   16
                                          or not very willing?   21
        Would find job in less than 3 months or don't know how long 51

45. If you received what you would regard as a   %
reasonable living income while unemployed,   Still prefer job   94
do you think you would still prefer to get   Wouldn't bother   6   Q.50
a job or wouldn't you bother?   Don't know   0

        Other answer (SPECIFY)_____   0
ALL SEEKING WORK NOW GO TO SECTION 3

		Col./ Code	Skip to

ALL WHOLLY RETIRED FROM WORK (CODE 08 AT Q.28): ASK Q.46- N = 272

46.a) (Can I just check) are you over 65 (men)/
60 (women)?

	Yes	% 90	b)
	No	10	d)

IF YES ASK b), c) & d). IF NO GO TO d)

b) On the whole would you say the
present state pension is on the
low side, reasonable, or on the
high side? If 'ON THE LOW SIDE':
Very low or a bit low?

Very low	% 23	
A bit low	41	
Reasonable	25	
On the high side	*	

c) Do you expect your state pension in a year's
time to purchase more than it does now, less,
or about the same?

More	% 5	
Less	45	
About the same	35	
Don't know	4	

d) Do you (or does your husband/wife) receive
a pension from a past employer(s)?

Yes	% 50	Q.50
No	50	

ALL RETIRED NOW GO TO SECTION 3 (GREEN)

ALL LOOKING AFTER HOME (CODE 09 AT Q.28): ASK Qs. 47-49- N = 353

47.a) Have you, during the last five years, ever had a full
or part time job of 10 hours per week or more?

	Yes	% 32	b)
	No	68	Q.48

IF YES

b) How long ago was the last occasion?

NO. OF MONTHS AGO

(MEDIAN) 2 4

c) On this last occasion, did you leave
the job of your own accord or not?

	Yes	% 25	Q.49
	No	7	

		Col./ Code	Skip to
	IF NO at Q.47 a)	%	
48.	a) How seriously in the past five years have you considered getting a <u>full time</u> job? (READ OUT) ...		
	... very seriously,	2	c)
	PROMPT, IF NECESSARY: FULL TIME IS 30 HRS+ quite seriously,	4	c)
	<u>PER WEEK</u> not very seriously,	6	b)
	IF VERY OR QUITE SERIOUSLY, GO TO c). IF NOT VERY OR NOT AT ALL SERIOUSLY ASK b). or not at all seriously?	54	b)
	b) How seriously, in the past five years, have you considered getting a <u>part time</u> job (READ OUT) ...	%	
	... very seriously,	2	c)
	quite seriously,	5	c)
	not very seriously,	8	Q.49
	or not at all seriously?	46	
	IF VERY OR QUITE SERIOUSLY AT a) OR b)		
	c) What are the main reasons you did not get a job?		
	_____		
	_____		
	_____		
	_____		

49.a)	How likely or unlikely is it that you will get a full time job in the <u>next</u> five years? Is it (READ OUT) ...
b)	How likely or unlikely is it that you will get a part time job in the <u>next</u> five years? Is it (READ OUT) ...

	a) FULL TIME	b) PART TIME
	%	%
... very likely,	4	10
quite likely,	6	23
not very likely,	17	11
or not at all likely?	71	52
Don't know	1	3

SECTION THREE

SHOW CARD 12.

50. Here are some items of government spending. Which
of them, if any, would be your highest priority
for extra spending, and which next? Please read
through the whole list before deciding.

ONE CODE ONLY IN EACH COL.

	EXTRA SPENDING	
	1st Priority	2nd Priority
	%	%
Education	24	26
Defence	4	4
Health	37	26
Housing	7	13
Public transport	1	2
Roads	2	3
Police and prisons	3	5
Social security benefits	6	6
Help for industry	16	13
Overseas aid	*	1
NONE OF THESE	*	1
Don't know	1	1

SHOW CARD 13.

51. Thinking now only of the government's spending on
social benefits like those on the card. Which, if
any, of these would be your highest priority for
extra spending, and which next?

ONE CODE ONLY IN EACH COL.

	EXTRA SPENDING	
	1st Priority	2nd Priority
	%	%
Retirement pensions	41	23
Child benefits	8	13
Benefits for the unemployed	18	15
Benefits for disabled people	24	33
Benefits for single parents	8	13
NONE OF THESE	1	1
Don't know	1	1

52. I will read two statements. For each one please say
whether you agree or disagree? Strongly or slightly?

a) Large numbers of people these days
falsely claim benefits.

b) Large numbers of people who are
eligible for benefits these days
fail to claim them.

	a) Falsely claim	b) Fail to claim
	%	%
Agree strongly	40	49
Agree slightly	25	32
Disagree slightly	13	8
Disagree strongly	12	3
Don't know	10	7

		Col./Code	Skip to

53. Opinions differ about the level of benefits for the unemployed. Which of these two statements comes <u>closest</u> to your own opinion. (READ OUT)...

%

... Benefits for the unemployed are <u>too low</u> and cause hardship, 46

OR

Benefits for the unemployed are <u>too high</u> and discourage people from finding jobs? 35

Neither 13

Don't know 6

SHOW CARD 14 .

54. Suppose the government had to choose between the three options on this card. Which do you think it should choose?

%

Reduce taxes and spend less on health, education and social benefits 9

Keep taxes and spending on these services at the same level as now 54

Increase taxes and spend more on health, education and social benefits 32

None 2

Don't know 3

---

55. Turning now to the National Health Service. On the whole, which of these three types of family would you say gets best value from their taxes out of the National Health Service (READ OUT) ...

%

... those with high incomes, 24

those with middle incomes, 14

or those with low incomes? 44

Don't know 16

SHOW CARD 15.

56. All in all, how satisfied or dissatisfied would you say you are with the way in which the National Health Service runs nowadays? Choose a phrase from this card.

%

Very satisfied 11

Quite satisfied 44

Neither satisfied nor dissatisfied 20

Quite dissatisfied 18

Very dissatisfied 7

				Col./ Code	Skip to

SHOW CARD 15 AGAIN

57. From your own experience or from what you have heard,
please say how satisfied or dissatisfied you are with
the way in which each of these parts of the National
Health Service runs nowadays? (READ OUT AND RING ONE CODE FOR EACH).

	Very satis-fied	Quite satis-fied	Neither satis-fied nor dissat-isfied	Quite dissat-isfied	Very dissat-isfied	Don't know
First, local doctors/GPs ?	% 33	47	7	9	3	*
National Health Service dentists ?	% 24	49	15	7	3	2
Health visitors ?	% 14	34	39	4	2	6
District nurses ?	% 22	38	31	1	1	6
Being in hospital as an inpatient ?	% 34	40	17	5	1	2
Attending hospital as an outpatient?	% 21	40	16	15	6	2

58.a) Are you covered by a private health insurance
scheme, that is an insurance scheme that allows
you to get private medical treatment?

	%	
Yes	11	b)
No	89	c)

IF YES

b) Does your employer (or you husband's/wife's
employer) pay the majority of the cost of
membership of this scheme?

	%
Yes	6
No	4
Don't know	*

ASK ALL

c) Do you consider the existence of private health schemes
to be a good thing or a bad thing for the National Health
Service, or don't they make any difference to the NHS?

	%
Good	37
Bad	23
No difference	35
Don't know	5

		Col./ Code	Skip to

59.a) Now thinking of private medical treatment in general. Do you consider the existence of private medical treatment in Britain to be a good thing or a bad thing for the National Health Service, or doesn't it make any difference to the NHS?

	%
Good thing	36
Bad thing	25
No difference	35
Don't know	4

SHOW CARD 16

b) Which of the views on this card do you support? You may choose more than one, or none.
(ONE OR MORE CODES MAY BE RINGED)

	Support
	%
Private medical treatment in Britain should be abolished	10
Private treatment in National Health Service hospitals should be abolished	26
The present arrangements for private medical treatment and the National Health Service are about right	41
Private treatment outside National Health Service hospitals should be encouraged to expand	26
Private medical treatment generally should be encouraged to expand	20
NONE OF THESE	4
Don't know	1

60. It has been suggested that the National Health Service should be available only to those with lower incomes. This would mean that contributions and taxes could be lower and most people would then take out medical insurance or pay for health care. Do you support or oppose this idea?

	%
Support	29
Oppose	64
Don't know	7

SHOW CARD 17.

61. Now, a few questions on housing.
First, in general how satisfied or dissatisfied are you with your own house/flat? Choose a phrase from the card.

	%
Very satisfied	44
Quite satisfied	42
Neither satisfied nor dissatisfied	4
Quite dissatisfied	5
Very dissatisfied	5

		Col./Code	Skip to

62.a) How about the area you live in.   Taking everything into account would you say this area has got better, worse or remained about the same as a place to live during the <u>last two</u> years?   (RECORD IN COL a) BELOW)

And what do you think will happen during the <u>next two</u> years: will this area get better, worse or remain about the same as a place to live?
(RECORD IN COL b)

	a) LAST 2 YEARS %	b) NEXT 2 YEARS %
Better	10	11
Worse	20	16
About the same	66	70
Don't know	3	3

63. Does your household own or rent this accommodation?
PROBE AS NECESSARY TO CLASSIFY

	%	
ONE CODE ONLY Owned/being bought leasehold or freehold	65	Q.65
Rented from <u>organisation</u>: Local authority (inc. GLC)	25	Q.64
New Town Development Corporation	1	
Housing Association	2	
Property company	1	Q.65
Other organisation	1	
Rented from <u>individual</u>: Relative	1	
Employer	1	
Other individual	3	

64.a) IF LOCAL AUTHORITY TENANT (CODE 02) ABOVE

Is it likely or unlikely that you - or the person responsible for paying the rent - will buy this accommodation at some time in the future?
IF LIKELY OR UNLIKELY: Very or quite?

	%
Very likely	1
Quite likely	2
Quite unlikely	1
Very unlikely	19
Not allowed to buy	2
Don't know	*

b) How would you describe the rent for this accommodation? Would you say it was (READ OUT) ...

	%
on the high side,	13
reasonable,	10
or on the low side?	*

65. ASK ALL

Now, a few questions on education.

SHOW CARD 18.

First, which of the groups on this card, if any, would be your highest priority for <u>extra</u> government spending on education, and which next?

ONE CODE ONLY IN EACH COL.

	1st priority %	2nd priority %
Nursery/pre-school children	10	12
Primary school children	16	17
Secondary school children	29	25
Less able children with special needs	32	27
Students at colleges, universities or polytechnics	9	15
NONE OF THESE	1	2
Don't know	2	3

		Col./ Code	Skip to
	SHOW CARD 19.		

66. Here are a number of factors that some people think would improve education in our schools.

a) Which do you think is the most important one for children in <u>primary</u> schools - (aged 5-11 years)? Please look at the whole list before deciding. <u>ONE CODE ONLY</u>

b) And which do you think is the most important one for children in <u>secondary</u> schools - (aged 11-18 years)? <u>ONE CODE ONLY</u>

	a) PRIMARY	b) SECONDARY
	%	%
More resources for books and equipment	15	10
Better buildings	2	1
Better pay for teachers	1	1
More involvement of parents in governing bodies	3	1
More discussion between parents and teachers	9	5
Smaller classes	31	10
More emphasis on preparation for exams	1	7
More emphasis on developing the child's skills and interests	19	13
More training and preparation for jobs	1	27
More emphasis on arts subjects	-	*
More emphasis on mathematics	1	2
More emphasis on English	1	1
Stricter discipline	11	19
NONE OF THESE	*	*
Don't know	2	2

67.a) Generally speaking, what is your opinion about private or independent schools in Britain? Should there be (READ OUT) ...

		%
... more private schools,		11
about the same number as now		67
fewer private schools,		8
or no private schools at all?		11
Other answer		1
Don't know		2

b) If there were <u>fewer</u> private or independent schools in Britain today do you think, on the whole, that state schools would (READ OUT) ...

		%
... benefit,		18
suffer,		18
or would it make no difference?		59
Don't know		4

		Col./ Code	Skip to
68.	On the whole, which of these three types of family would you say gets best value from their taxes out of government spending on education (READ OUT) ...		
		%	
	···those with high incomes,	34	
	those with middle incomes,	23	
	or those with low incomes?	30	
	Don't know	12	
69.	Again in general, how would you compare the overall standards of education in schools today with the standards when you were at school. Would you say that standards today are higher, lower, or about the same? IF HIGHER OR LOWER: A lot or a little?		
		%	
	A lot higher now	22	
	A little higher	17	
	About the same	15	
	A little lower now	19	
	A lot lower	22	
	Not educated here	1	
	Don't know	4	
70.a)	It is now compulsory for state secondary schools to publish their GCE and CSE exam results. How useful do you think this information is for parents of present or future pupils (READ OUT) ...	%	
	... very useful,	32	
	quite useful,	35	
	or not really useful?	24	
	Don't know	9	
	Is there any other information you can think of that secondary schools should make available to parents of present or future pupils?	%	
	Yes	28	c)
	No	72	Q.71.
	IF YES		
	c) What information is this?	%	

Records of childrens behaviour = 7   More contact (Parents/Teacher)= 4

Teacher qualifications   = 2 Extra curriculum course available.= 1

Curriculum/Prospectus   = 3 Extent of job training/careers adv.= 2

Class size/Teacher Pupil ratio = 2   Other information =10

		Col./ Code	Skip to
71.a)	Do you feel that opportunities for young people in Britain to go on to higher education - to a university, college or polytechnic - should be increased or reduced, or are they at about the right level now? IF INCREASED OR REDUCED: A lot or a little?	%	
	Increased a lot	22	
	Increased a little	22	
	About right	49	
	Reduced a little	4	
	Reduced a lot	1	
	Don't know	2	
b)	When British students go to university or college they generally get grants from the local authority. Do you think they should get grants as now, or loans which would have to be paid back when they start working?	%	
	Grants	57	
	Loans	38	
	Don't know	4	

		Col./ Code	Skip to
	SECTION FOUR		

In this section I would like first to ask you some questions about crime?

			Col./ Code	Skip to
72.a)	Do you ever worry about the possibility that you or anyone else who lives with you might be the victim of crime?		%	
		Yes	69	b)
		No	31	c)

IF YES

			Col./ Code
b)	Is this (READ OUT) ...		%
		... a big worry,	19
		a bit of a worry,	28
		or an occasional doubt?	22

ASK ALL

			Col./ Code
c)	How safe do you feel walking alone in this area after dark (READ OUT) ...		%
		... very safe,	25
		fairly safe,	38
		a bit unsafe,	22
		or very unsafe?	14

73.a) How common is it for people's homes to be burgled in this area - very common, fairly common or not very common?
RECORD ANSWER IN COL. a)

b) How common is deliberate damage done by vandals in this area - very common, fairly common or not very common?
RECORD ANSWER IN COL. b)

c) How common in this area is it for people to be attacked and to have things stolen from them in the street - very common, fairly common or not very common?
RECORD IN COL. c)

	(a) BURGLARY	(b) VANDALISM	(c) STREET ATTACKS/ THEFTS
	%	%	%
Very common	16	17	4
Fairly common	28	25	10
Not very common	53	58	84
Don't know	1	-	1

			Col./Code	Skip to
74.a)	During the past two years have you ever reported a crime or accident to the police or gone to them for help or advice?		%	
		Yes	35	b)
		No	65	c)
	IF YES ASK b)& c). IF NO GO TO c).		%	
	b) On those occasions how helpful have you found them in the way they dealt with you (READ OUT)...	... very helpful,	17	
		fairly helpful,	10	
		fairly unhelpful,	3	
		or very unhelpful	3	
		Varied	1	
	ASK ALL		%	
c)	During the past two years have you ever been stopped or asked questions by the police about an offence which they thought had been committed?	Yes	17	d)
		No	83	Q. 75
	IF YES		%	
	d) On those occasions how polite have you found them when they approached you (READ OUT) ...	... very polite,	9	
		fairly polite,	4	
		fairly impolite,	2	
		or very impolite?	2	
		Varied	*	
75.a)	ASK ALL During the past two years have you ever been really annoyed about the way a police officer behaved towards you (or someone you know) or about the way the police handled a matter in which you were involved?		%	
		Yes	18	
		No	82	
b)	During the last two years have you ever been really pleased about the way a police officer behaved towards you (or someone you know) or about the way the police handled a matter in which you were involved?		%	
		Yes	29	
		No	70	
	SHOW CARD 20.		%	
c)	In general, how satisfied or dissatisfied are you with the way the police in Britain do their job? Choose a phrase from the card.	Very satisfied	30	
		Quite satisfied	49	
		Neither satisfied nor dissatisfied	9	
		Not very satisfied	10	
		Not at all satisfied	2	

		Col./Code	Skip to

Now moving on to the subject of social class in Britain.

76.a) To what extent do you think people are aware of social class differences in Britain today:(READ OUT) ... Very aware,

	Col./Code
	%
Very aware,	29
quite aware,	43
not very aware,	20
or not at all aware?	3
Don't know	4
Other answer	*

b) To what extent do you think a person's social class affects his or her opportunities in Britain today:(READ OUT) ...

	%
... A great deal,	25
quite a lot,	45
not very much,	25
or not at all?	3
Other answer	*
Don't know	2

c) Do you think social class is more or less important now in affecting a person's opportunities than it was 10 years ago, or has there been no real change?

	%
More important now	22
Less important now	30
No change	46
Don't know	*

d) Do you think that in 10 years time social class will be more or less important than it is now in affecting a person's opportunities, or will there be no real change?

	%
More important in 10 years time	16
Less important in 10 years time	32
No change	49
Don't know	2

SHOW CARD 21.

77.a) Most people see themselves as belonging to a particular social class. Please look at this card and tell me which social class you would say you belong to?   RECORD ANSWER IN COL a)

b) And which social class would you say your parents belonged to when you started at primary school? RECORD ANSWER IN COL b)

	a) NOW	b) AGED 5
	%	%
Upper middle	1	2
Middle	24	16
Upper working	23	12
Working	46	58
Poor	3	9
Don't know	3	2

		Col./Code	Skip to
		%	

78.a) Do you think there is such a thing as
real poverty in Britain today?

Yes	55	
No	44	

SHOW CARD 22.

b) There are different views about what real poverty is nowadays. Please look at this card and tell me which of the statements, if either, comes closest to your own view?

%

Poverty in Britain today is mainly about the shortage of absolute necessities such as food and clothing	26
People in Britain today have enough to eat and wear; the main hardship is in not being able to keep up with the living standards that most people have	67
Neither of these	4

79.a) Do you regard yourself as belonging to any particular religion? IF YES: Which? IF 'Christian' PROBE FOR DENOMINATION.

ONE CODE ONLY

b) Thinking back to the period when you were about 16, would you have described yourself as belonging to a particular religion then? Which? ONE CODE ONLY

a) (SPECIFY) _____
b) (SPECIFY) _____

a) (SPECIFY) _____
b) (SPECIFY) _____

	(a) NOW	(b) PREVIOUSLY
	%	%
No religion	31	25
Christian - no denomination	3	2
Roman Catholic	10	11
Church of England/Anglican	40	43
United Reform Church(URC) /Congregational	1	2
Baptist	1	2
Methodist	4	6
Presbyterian/Church of Scotland	5	6
Other Christian	2	
Other Christian		2
Hindu	*	*
Jew	1	1
Muslim	1	1
Sikh	*	*
Buddhist	-	-
Other non-Christian	*	
Other non-Christian		*

IF RELIGION ENTERED AT a) ASK c). OTHERS SKIP TO Q.80.

c) Apart from such special occasions as weddings, funerals and baptisms, how often nowadays do you attend services or meetings connected with your religion?

%

Once a week or more	13
Less often but at least once in two weeks	3
Less often but at least once a month	6
Less often but at least twice a year	10
Less often but at least once a year	6
Less often	6
Never or practically never	24
Varies	1

ASK ALL

Now I would like to ask you some questions about racial prejudice in Britain.

80.a) First, thinking of <u>Asians</u> - that is people originally from India and Pakistan - who now live in Britain. Do you think there is a lot of prejudice against them in Britain nowadays, a little or hardly any? <u>RECORD IN COL a)</u>

b) And black people   - that is West Indians and Africans - who now live in Britain. Do you think there is a lot of prejudice agains them in Britain nowadays, a little, or hardly any? <u>RECORD IN COL b)</u>

	a) Asians %	b) Blacks %
A lot	54	50
A little	37	40
Hardly any	6	7
Don't know	3	3

c) Do you think there is generally more racial prejudice in Britain now than there was five years ago less, or about the same amount?

	%
More now	45
Less now	16
About the same	36
Other answer (SPECIFY) _____	2

d) Do you think there will be more, less or about the same amount of racial prejudice in Britain in five years time compared with now?

	%
more in 5 years	42
Less	17
About the same	36
Other answer (SPECIFY)_____	.3

e) How would you describe yourself: (READ OUT) ...

	%	
... as very prejudiced against people of other races,	4	f)
a little prejudiced,	31	f)
or not prejudiced at all?	64	".81
Other answer (SPECIFY) _____	*	Q.81

IF 'VERY' OR 'A LITTLE' PREJUDICED

f) Against any race in particular? PROBE AND RECORD. IF 'BLACK' OR 'COLOURED' MENTIONED, PROBE FOR WHETHER WEST INDIAN, ASIAN, GENERAL, ETC. _____

_____

_____

ASK ALL

81.a) On the whole, do you think people of Asian origin in Britain are not given jobs these days <u>because</u> of their race (READ OUT)...

	%
... a lot,	20
a little,	40
or hardly at all?	31
Don't know	8

b) And on the whole, do you think people of West Indian origin in Britain are not given jobs these days <u>because</u> of their race (READ OUT) ...

	%
... a lot,	25
a little,	40
or hardly at all?	27
Don't know	8

Col./ Code

			Col./ Code	Skip to
82.a)	There is a law in Britain against racial discrimination, that is against giving unfair preference to a particular race in housing, jobs and so on. Do you generally support or oppose the idea of a law for this purpose?	Support	% 69	
		Oppose	28	
b)	Do you think, on the whole, that Britain gives too little or too much help to Asians and West Indians who have settled in this country, or are present arrangements about right?	Don't know	2	
			%.	
		Too little	7	
		Present arrangements right	55	
		Too much	32	
		Other answer	*	
		Don't know	4	

INTERVIEWER   ASK VERSION B FOR ALTERNATE
RESPONDENTS.   RING CODE
FOR WHICH VERSION USED.

VERSION A	N = 920
VERSION B	N = 809

VERSION A

83.a) Do you think most white people in Britain would mind or not mind if a suitably qualified person of <u>Asian</u> origin were appointed as their boss? IF 'WOULD MIND':   A lot or a little?   <u>RECORD in COL. a)</u>

b) And you personally? Would you mind or not mind?
IF 'WOULD MIND': A lot or a little?   <u>RECORD IN COL b)</u>

c) Do you think that <u>most</u> white people in Britain would mind or not mind   if one of their close relatives were to marry a person of <u>Asian</u> origin? IF 'WOULD MIND': A lot or a little? <u>RECORD IN COL c)</u>

d) And you personally? Would you mind or not mind?
IF 'WOULD MIND': A lot or a little?   <u>RECORD IN COL d) THEN
GO TO Q. 84.</u>

VERSION B

83.a) Do you think most white people in Britain would mind or not mind if a suitably qualified person of <u>black or West Indian</u> origin were appointed as their boss? IF 'WOULD MIND'<u>:</u> A lot or a little? <u>RECORD IN COL a)</u>

b) And you personally? Would you mind or not mind?
IF 'WOULD MIND':   A lot or a little? <u>RECORD IN COL b)</u>

c) Do you think that <u>most</u> white people in Britain would mind or not mind   if one of their close relatives were to marry a person of <u>black or West Indian origin</u>? IF 'WOULD MIND' : A lot or a little? <u>RECORD IN COL c)</u>

d) And you personally? Would you mind or not mind? IF WOULD MIND:
A lot or a little?   <u>RECORD IN COL d)</u>

	BOSS				MARRIAGE			
	a) Most people		b) Self		c) Most people		d) Self	
	% Asian	% Black	% Asian	% Black	% Asian	% Black	% Asian	% Black
Mind a lot	23	25	11	9	42	49	31	33
Mind a little	30	29	8	12	35	30	20	24
Not mind	43	42	79	79	20	18	47	41
Other anwser (SPEC-IFY)	2	2	1	1	3	2	1	2

				Col./ Code	Skip to

ASK ALL

84. Now I would like to ask you about the obligations that people who have been married or have lived together have towards each other if they separate.

a) Consider a married couple aged about 35, both working at the time of the divorce. They have children at primary school, who remain with the wife.

i) In your opinion, should the man make maintenance payments to support the children?

	%
Yes	92
No	4
Other answer	1
Don't know	1

ii) In your opinion, should the man make maintenance payments to support the wife?

	%
Yes	26
No	64
Other answer	2
Don't know	1

b) Consider another couple also aged 35, both working at the time of the divorce. They have been married for 10 years but have no children.

i) In your opinion, should the man make maintenance payments to support the wife?

	%
Yes	10
No	86
Other answer	1

c) Finally, consider another couple aged 35, both working. They are unmarried and have no children. They separate after living together for 10 years.

i) In your opinion, should the man make maintenance payments to support the woman?

	%
Yes	4
No	93
Other answer	*

85. Do you think that divorce in Britain should be (READ OUT) ...

	%
... easier to obtain than it is now,	11
more difficult,	31
or should things remain as they are?	55
Don't know	3

86. There is a law in Britain against sex discrimination, that is against giving unfair preference to men - or to women - in jobs, housing and so on. Do you generally support or oppose the idea of a law for this purpose?

	%
Support	76
Oppose	22
Don't know	2

		Col./ Code	Skip to
87.	Can I just check your own marital status ...	%	
	A. Married (legally) and living with husband/wife	68	Q.88
	Separated/divorced	5	
	Widowed	10	B*
	Never married	16	
	*ASK B IF APPROPRIATE		
	B. IF SEPARATED, DIVORCED, WIDOWED OR NEVER MARRIED	%	
	Living as married: Yes	2	
	No	26	

IF MARRIED OR LIVING AS MARRIED ASK VERSION A
OTHERWISE ASK VERSION B

VERSION A	INTERVIEWER CODE WHICH VERSION USED: VERSION A	1
		VERSION B	2

88. I would like to ask about how you and your
(husband/wife/partner) generally share some family
jobs. Who <u>does</u> the household shopping -
mainly the man, mainly the woman or
is the task shared equally?
RECORD ANSWER IN GRID BELOW AND CONTINUE WITH ii) - viii)

VERSION B

88. I would like your opinion on how you think some
family jobs should generally be shared. For example,
who <u>should</u> do the household shopping - mainly the
man, mainly the woman or should the task be shared equally?

RECORD ANSWER IN GRID BELOW AND CONTINUE WITH ii) - viii)

ONE CODE FOR EACH ITEM	MAINLY MAN	MAINLY WOMAN	SHARED EQUALLY
i)	Household shopping %	4	46	49
ii)	Make(s) the evening meal %	3	70	26
iii)	Do(es) the evening dishes %	15	34	49
iv)	Do(es) the household cleaning %	3	64	33
v)	Do(es) the washing and ironing %	1	84	14
vi)	Repair(s) the household equipment %	81	5	13
vii)	Organise(s) the household money and payment of bills %	28	32	39
viii)	Decide(s) what colour to decorate the living room %	4	43	52

		(a)	(b)	(c)	(d)
		BEFORE MARRIAGE	HUSBAND EXTRA MARITAL	WIFE EXTRA MARITAL	SAME SEX
		%	%	%	%
Always wrong		16	58	59	50
Mostly wrong		11	25	25	12
Sometimes wrong		17	11	10	8
Rarely wrong		8	1	1	4
Not wrong at all		42	2	1	17
Depends/varies		4	3	2	8

89. Now I would like to ask you some questions about sexual relationships.

SHOW CARD 23.

a) If a man and a woman have sexual relations before marriage what would your general opinion be? Please choose a phrase from this card. RECORD IN COL. a)

b) What about a married _man_ having sexual relations with a woman other than his wife? Please choose a phrase from this card. RECORD IN COL. b)

c) What about a married _woman_ having sexual relations with a man other than her husband? Please choose a phrase from this card. RECORD IN COL. c)

d) What about sexual relations between two adults of the same sex? Please choose a phrase from this card. RECORD IN COL. d)

90.a) Finally in this section, I would like you to tell me whether, in your opinion, it is acceptable for a homosexual person (READ OUT) ... ONE CODE FOR EACH

	Yes	No	Other answer (SPECIFY)
... to be a teacher in a school %	41	53	4
to be a teacher in a college or university %	48	48	2
to hold a responsible position in public life %	53	42	2

b) And do you think homosexual couples should be allowed to adopt a baby under the same conditions as other couples?

	%
Yes	8
No	87
Other answer	1
	2

SECTION FIVE

Finally, a few details about you and your household.

PERSON NO.	Respondent	1	2	3	4	5	6	7	8	9
	%									
91. Sex: Male	46									
Female	54									
b) Age last birthday:										
c) Relationship to respondent:										
Husband/wife										
Son/daughter										
Parent/parent-in-law										
Other relative										
Not related										
d) HOUSEHOLD MEMBERS WITH LEGAL RESPONSIBILITY FOR ACCOMMODATION (INC. JOINT AND SHARED) Sole / Shared	Sole % 34 / Shared 40									

SHOW CARD 24.

ASK ONLY OF RESPONDENT & HUSBAND/WIFE, AND EACH OF RESPONDENT'S SONS/ DAUGHTERS IN HOUSEHOLD

	%									
92. Which of these types of school have you (has he/she) ever attended?										
PRIMARY: State or LA	88									
Private	6									
Voluntary/maintained	7									
SECONDARY: State or LA	84									
Private	8									
Voluntary/maintained	5									

	Col./ Code	Skip to
RESPONDENT ONLY		
93. AGE OF COMPLETING FULL TIME EDUCATION:	%	
15 or under / 16	78	
17 / 18	11	
19 or over	9	
Still at school / Still at college, polytechnic, or university	2	
Other answer	–	

		Col./ Code	Skip to
9^	INTERVIEWER: CODE FROM OBSERVATION		
	ETHNIC GROUP:	%	
	Indian (inc. E. African), Pakistani, Bangladeshi	1	
	Black, African, W. Indian	1	
	White/European	95	
	Other non-white	2	

REFER TO ECONOMIC POSITION OF RESPONDENT (Q. 28) PAGE 11

95.   IF IN PAID WORK (CODE 02 or 03) → ASK a) to d) ABOUT PRESENT MAIN JOB
IF WAITING TO TAKE UP JOB OFFERED (CODE 04) → ASK a) to d)
                                    ABOUT FUTURE JOB
IF SEEKING WORK (CODE 04 or 05) OR RETIRED (CODE 08) → ASK a) to d)
                                     ABOUT LAST JOB

OTHERS GO TO Q. 96

a) What is(was) your job? PROBE AS NECESSARY:

What is the name or title of the job? _____

What kind of work do you do most of the time? IF RELEVANT: What
materials/machinery do you use? _____

_____

b) Do you supervise or are you responsible for the
work of any other people? IF YES: How many?

                     No   A

                    Yes   B

              WRITE IN NO: ☐☐☐☐

c) What does your employer do or make at the place where you usually
work (IF SELF EMPLOYED: What do you do or make ...)? _____

_____

d) Including yourself, how many people are employed at the
place where you usually work (from)? Is it (READ OUT)...

                       ... under 25, A

              OR 25 or more? B

96.a) Are you now a member of a trade union or staff association?

b) Have you ever been a member of a trade union or staff association?

	a) NOW %	b) EVER %
Yes	27	56
No	73	40

c) Have you ever (READ OUT) ... RING ONE CODE FOR EACH

	Yes	No
... attended a union or staff association meeting?	38%	17%
voted in a union or staff association election or meeting?	35	20
put forward a proposal or motion at a union or staff association meeting?	13	41
gone on strike?	19	36
stood in a picket line?	7	48
served as a local official or shop steward?	7	48

ECONOMIC POSITION AND OCCUPATION OF OTHER HOUSEHOLD MEMBER

INTERVIEWER: REFER TO HOUSEHOLD COMPOSITION GRID (Q.91), PAGE 36

IF RESPONDENT HAS NO LEGAL RESPONSIBILITY FOR ACCOMMODATION
ASK Q.97 AND Q.98 ABOUT:

	%
Oldest male with legal responsibility	23
or, if none: Husband of oldest female with legal responsibility	-
or, if none: Oldest female with legal responsibility	4

IF RESPONDENT HAS SOLE LEGAL RESPONSIBILITY FOR ACCOMMODATION:
ASK Q.97 AND Q.98 ABOUT:

Respondent's husband or wife,	14
or, if none: SKIP TO Q.99.	18

IF RESPONDENT HAS SHARED LEGAL RESPONSIBILITY FOR ACCOMMODATION:
ASK Q.97 AND Q.98 ABOUT:

Oldest male who shares legal responsibility,	22
or, if none: Husband of oldest female who shares legal responsibility,	*
or, if none: Oldest female who shares legal responsibility.	19

INTERVIEWER: IF Qs. 97/98 TO BE ASKED, ENTER PERSON NO. FROM H/H GRID. [ ]

SHOW CARD 25.

97. Which of these descriptions applies to what ___ (REFER TO HOUSEHOLD MEMBER) was doing last week, that is the seven days ending last Sunday? Any others? RECORD BELOW IN COLUMN A. IF TWO OR MORE CATEGORIES IN COLUMN A, CODE HIGHEST ON LIST AS ECONOMIC POSITION IN COLUMN B

IF ONE CODE ONLY CODED IN COLUMN A, TRANSFER TO COLUMN B AS ECONOMIC POSITION

	COL A	COL B ECONOMIC POSITION	Skip to
	%	%	
In full time education at school or college (not paid for by employer)	1	1	Q.99
In paid work of any sort for at least 10 hours in the week	55	55	
Away from a paid job because of holiday, temporary illness, etc	2	2	
Waiting to take up a job already accepted	*	*	Q.98
Seeking work	4	4	
Prevented by temporary sickness or injury from seeking work	*	*	
Permanently sick or disabled	2	2	Q.99
Wholly retired from work	14	14	Q.98
Looking after the home	28	20	Q.99
Doing something else	*	*	Q.99

IF IN PAID WORK (CODE 02 OR 03) ASK Q.98 ABOUT <u>PRESENT</u> JOB OF _____ (REFER
TO HOUSEHOLD MEMBER).
IF WAITING TO TAKE UP JOB OFFERED (CODE 04) ASK Q.98 ABOUT <u>FUTURE</u> JOB OF _____.

IF SEEKING WORK (CODE 05 OR 06) OR RETIRED (CODE 08) ASK Q.98 ABOUT <u>LAST</u> JOB.
OTHERS GO TO Q.99.

98.a) What (is/was) his/her job?
PROBE AS NECESSARY:
What is the name or title of the job? _____

What kind of work does (s)he do most of the time? <u>IF RELEVANT</u>: What
materials/machinery are used? _____

_____

_____

What qualifications or training are needed for that job? _____

_____

b) Does (s)he supervise or is (s)he responsible for the
work of any other people? <u>IF YES</u>: How many?   No   A

                                                         Yes   B

                                    WRITE IN NO: [ ][ ][ ][ ]

c) What does his/her employer do or make at the place where (s)he usually
works (IF SELF EMPLOYED: What does (s)he do or make ...)? _____

_____

_____

d) Including this person, how many people are employed at the
place where (s)he usually works (from)? Is it (READ OUT) ...

                                    ... under 25   A

                                    OR 25 or more?   B

<u>ASK ALL</u>

SHOW CARD 26.   N = 926

99.a) Which of the letters on this **card represents** the gross <u>income</u>
from all sources of your household?
ONE CODE IN COLUMN a)

		%	%↓
		a)	b)
Less than £2,000		6	9
£2,000 - £2,999		9	10
£3,000 - £3,999		10	10
£4,000 - £4,999		7	11
£5,000 - £5,999		8	12
£6,000 - £6,999		8	9
£7,000 - £7,999		5	10
£8,000 - £9,999		10	10
£10,000 - £11,999		8	6
£12,000 - £14,999		8	3
£15,000+		10	4
Refused		12	7

<u>IF IN PAID WORK</u>

<u>ASK b). OTHERS GO TO Q.100.</u>

b) Which of the letters on this card
represents your <u>own</u> gross <u>earnings</u>,
before deduction of income tax
and national insurance?
ONE CODE IN COLUMN b)

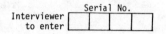

Head Office: 35 Northampton Square London EC1V 0AX. Tel: 01-250 1866
Northern Field Office: Charazel House Gainford Darlington Co. Durham DL2 3EG.

SOCIAL AND   COMMUNITY PLANNING RESEARCH

SELF COMPLETION QUESTIONNAIRE

SOCIAL ATTITUDES SURVEY

March 1983   P.705

Interviewer
to enter

Serial No.

To the selected respondent

We hope very much that you will agree to participate in this important study - the
first in what is planned as an annual series of surveys to be published each summer.
The study consists of this self-completion questionnaire and an interview.

Completing the questionnaire

The questions inside cover a wide range of subjects, but each one can be answered
simply by placing a tick (✓) in one or more of the boxes provided. No special
knowledge is required: we are confident that everyone will be able to offer an
opinion on all questions. And we want the views of *all* people, not just those with
strong opinions or particular viewpoints. The questionnaire should not take up much
of your time and we hope you will find it interesting and enjoyable. It should be
completed by the person selected by the interviewer at your address, and you may be
assured that participation is completely confidential and anonymous.

Returning the questionnaire

Your interviewer will arrange with you the most convenient way of returning the
questionnaire. If he or she has arranged to call back for it, please complete
it and keep it safely until then. If not, please complete it and post it back
in the stamped, addressed envelope *as soon as you possibly can*.

*Social and Community Planning Research is an independent social research institute,
registered as a charitable trust. Its projects are funded by government departments,
local authorities, universities and foundations to provide information on social
issues in Britain. SCPR interviewers carry out around 50,000 interviews per year.
This study has been funded by the Nuffield Foundation and the Social Science Research
Council. Contact us if you require further information.*

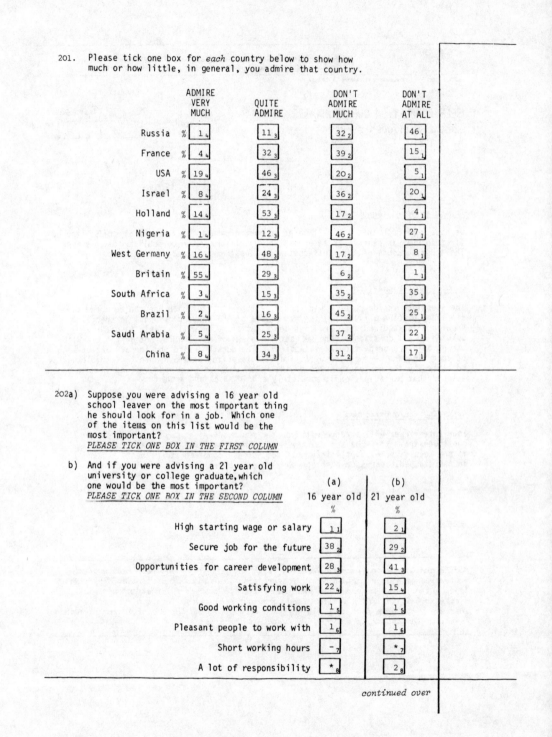

201.   Please tick one box for *each* country below to show how
        much or how little, in general, you admire that country.

	ADMIRE VERY MUCH	QUITE ADMIRE	DON'T ADMIRE MUCH	DON'T ADMIRE AT ALL
Russia %	1 ₄	11 ₃	32 ₂	46 ₁
France %	4 ₄	32 ₃	39 ₂	15 ₁
USA %	19 ₄	46 ₃	20 ₂	5 ₁
Israel %	8 ₄	24 ₃	36 ₂	20 ₁
Holland %	14 ₄	53 ₃	17 ₂	4 ₁
Nigeria %	1 ₄	12 ₃	46 ₂	27 ₁
West Germany %	16 ₄	48 ₃	17 ₂	8 ₁
Britain %	55 ₄	29 ₃	6 ₂	1 ₁
South Africa %	3 ₄	15 ₃	35 ₂	35 ₁
Brazil %	2 ₄	16 ₃	45 ₂	25 ₁
Saudi Arabia %	5 ₄	25 ₃	37 ₂	22 ₁
China %	8 ₄	34 ₃	31 ₂	17 ₁

202a)   Suppose you were advising a 16 year old
        school leaver on the most important thing
        he should look for in a job. Which one
        of the items on this list would be the
        most important?
        PLEASE TICK ONE BOX IN THE FIRST COLUMN

b)   And if you were advising a 21 year old
        university or college graduate, which
        one would be the most important?
        PLEASE TICK ONE BOX IN THE SECOND COLUMN

	(a) 16 year old %	(b) 21 year old %
High starting wage or salary	1 ₁	2 ₁
Secure job for the future	38 ₂	29 ₂
Opportunities for career development	28 ₃	41 ₃
Satisfying work	22 ₄	15 ₄
Good working conditions	1 ₅	1 ₅
Pleasant people to work with	1 ₆	1 ₆
Short working hours	- ₇	* ₇
A lot of responsibility	* ₈	2 ₈

continued over

203 a) Now consider a man aged 35 who smokes 20 cigarettes a day, drinks
        4 pints of beer a day, is about 2 stone overweight, and takes almost
        no exercise. If you were advising him on the most useful action he
        should take to improve his health, which of the four actions below
        would you choose? And which next?
        PLEASE TICK ONE BOX IN EACH OF THE FIRST TWO COLUMNS

   b)   Now, if we were asking about a woman of the same age, what would
        your answer be?
        PLEASE TICK ONE BOX IN EACH OF THE NEXT TWO COLUMNS

	(a) MAN		(b) WOMAN	
	MOST USEFUL	NEXT MOST USEFUL	MOST USEFUL	NEXT MOST USEFUL
	%	%	%	%
Reduce smoking	41 1	20 1	41 1	19 1
Reduce alcohol	11 2	19 2	12 2	18 2
Lose weight	21 3	25 3	25 3	28 3
Take more exercise	17 4	25 4	11 4	23 4

204 Here are a number of circumstances in which a woman might
     consider an abortion. Please say whether or not you think
     the law should allow an abortion in each case.
     PLEASE TICK ONE BOX ON EACH LINE

Should abortion be allowed by law?

	Yes	No
The woman decides on her own she does not wish to have the child %	35 1	52 2
The couple agree they do not wish to have the child %	43 1	42 2
The woman is not married and does not wish to marry the man %	42 1	44 2
The couple cannot afford any more children %	44 1	41 2
There is a strong chance of a defect in the baby %	77 1	10 2
The woman's health is seriously endangered by the pregnancy %	82 1	6 2
The woman became pregnant as a result of rape %	80 1	7 2

205a) Suppose a person has a painful incurable disease. Do you think
that doctors should be allowed by law to end the patient's life
if the patient requests it?
PLEASE TICK ONE BOX

%

Yes 72_1

No 21_2

b) And if a person is not incurably sick but simply tired of
living, should doctors be allowed by law to end that
person's life if he or she requests it?
PLEASE TICK ONE BOX

%

Yes 12_1

No 81_2

206. Are you in favour of or against the death penalty for ...

PLEASE TICK ONE BOX ON EACH LINE

	IN FAVOUR	AGAINST
... murder in the course of a terrorist act %	70_1	20_2
... murder of a policeman %	66_1	22_2
... other murders %	59_1	31_2

207. Listed below are some of Britain's institutions. From what you
know or have heard about each one, can you say whether, on the
whole, you think it is well run or not well run?

PLEASE TICK ONE BOX FOR EACH INSTITUTION

	WELL RUN	NOT WELL RUN
The National Health Service %	49_1	42_2
The press %	49_1	40_2
Local government %	33_1	56_2
The civil service %	40_1	48_2
Manufacturing industry %	40_1	47_2
Nationalised industries %	20_1	69_2
Banks %	85_1	5_2
The trade unions %	27_1	62_2
The BBC %	67_1	22_2
Independent TV and radio %	69_1	20_2
The police %	72_1	18_2
Prisons %	46_1	41_2

continued over

208. How serious an effect on our environment do
you think each of these things has?
PLEASE TICK ONE BOX ON EACH LINE

	VERY SERIOUS	QUITE SERIOUS	NOT VERY SERIOUS	NOT AT ALL SERIOUS
Noise from aircraft %	7	21 $_3$	48 $_2$	16 $_1$
Lead from petrol %	45	34 $_3$	11 $_2$	2 $_1$
Industrial waste in the rivers and sea %	58	27 $_3$	5 $_2$	1 $_1$
Waste from nuclear electricity stations %	59	19 $_3$	10 $_2$	4 $_1$
Industrial fumes in the air %	38	40 $_3$	12 $_2$	2 $_1$
Noise and dirt from traffic %	21	40 $_3$	27 $_2$	4 $_1$

209 a) Which one of these three possible solutions
to Britain's electricity needs would you
favour most?
PLEASE TICK
ONE BOX

	%
We should make do with the power stations we have already	30 $_1$
We should build more coal-fuelled power stations	44 $_2$
We should build more nuclear power stations	17 $_3$

b) As far as nuclear power stations are concerned,
which of these statements comes closest to
your own feelings?
PLEASE TICK
ONE BOX

	%
They create very serious risks for the future	33 $_1$
They create quite serious risks for the future	26 $_2$
They create only slight risks for the future	25 $_3$
They create hardly any risks for the future	8 $_4$

210. Here is a list of predictions about problems that Britain might face.
For each one, please say how likely or unlikely you think it is to
come true *in Britain within the next ten years.*

PLEASE TICK ONE BOX FOR
EACH PREDICTION

	VERY LIKELY	QUITE LIKELY	NOT VERY LIKELY	NOT AT ALL LIKELY
Acts of political terrorism in Britain will be common events %	15 $_4$	38 $_3$	33 $_2$	6 $_1$
Riots and civil disturbance in our cities will be common events %	15 $_4$	41 $_3$	31 $_2$	5 $_1$
There will be a world war involving Britain and Europe %	6 $_4$	17 $_3$	45 $_2$	23 $_1$
There will be a serious accident at a British nuclear power station %	10 $_4$	32 $_3$	40 $_2$	9 $_1$
The police in our cities will find it impossible to protect our personal safety on the streets %	17 $_4$	33 $_3$	35 $_2$	8 $_1$
The government in Britain will be overthrown by revolution %	2 $_4$	5 $_3$	31 $_2$	54 $_1$

211. Which of these statements comes closest to your
      views on the availability of pornographic
      magazines and films?
      PLEASE TICK ONE BOX   %

                                 They should be banned altogether | 31 |₁

          They should be available in special adult shops but not displayed
                                                    to the public | 48 |₂

              They should be available in special adult shops with
                                      public display permitted | 6 |₃

          They should be available in any shop for sale to adults only | 6 |₄

          They should be available in any shop for sale to anyone | 1 |₅

212 a) How much influence would you say the trade unions
       have on the lives of people in Britain these days?   %
       PLEASE TICK ONE BOX
                                       A great deal of influence | 29 |₁

                                       Quite a bit of influence | 38 |₂

                                              Some influence | 22 |₃

                                          Not much influence | 4 |₄
    b) Do you think they have too much
       influence, about the right amount,
       or too little influence?   %
       PLEASE TICK ONE BOX   Too much influence | 55 |₁

                                     About the right amount | 32 |₂

                                          Too little influence | 5 |₃

213 a) Central government provides financial support to housing
       in two main ways. First, by means of allowances to low
       income tenants; second by means of tax relief to people
       with mortgages. On the whole, which of these three types
       of family would you say benefits *most* from central   %
       government support for housing?
       PLEASE TICK ONE BOX   Families with high incomes | 30 |₁

                                     Families with middle incomes | 25 |₂

                                        Families with low incomes | 36 |₃
    b) Which of these three views comes
       closest to your own on the sale of council
       houses and flats to tenants?
       PLEASE TICK ONE BOX   %

          Council tenants *should not* be allowed to buy their houses or
                                                           flats | 10 |₁

              Council tenants *should* be allowed to buy but *only* in areas
                                          with no housing shortage | 29 |₂

              Council tenants *should generally* be allowed to buy their
                                              houses or flats | 54 |₃

    c) Which of the following statements do you think are   TRUE   FALSE
       generally true and which false?
       PLEASE TICK ONE BOX   Council tenants pay low rents % | 23 |₁ | 65 |₂
       ON EACH LINE
                                   Councils give a poor standard of % | 56 |₁ | 33 |₂
                                         repairs and maintenance

          Council estates are generally pleasant places to live % | 36 |₁ | 52 |₂

                                                                  continued over

214 a) The government helps to support the arts
in Britain. On the whole would you like
to see...   %

PLEASE TICK ONE BOX   ... more government support for the arts | 17 1 |

or less government support for the arts | 13 2 |

or about the same amount as now | 55 3 |

b) Which of the items below do   or none at all | 7 4 |
you think should have the highest
priority in government support
for the arts, and which next?

	HIGHEST PRIORITY	2ND HIGHEST PRIORITY
PLEASE TICK ONE BOX IN EACH COLUMN	%	%
National institutions, such as the Royal Opera House, Royal Shakespeare Company, National Theatre	18 1	12 1
Arts events in the regions	10 2	11 2
Museums and art galleries	22 3	16 3
Arts events in schools	14 4	13 4
Promising individual writers, artists and composers	8 5	12 5
Rock and pop concerts for young people	3 6	3 6
Arts events for ethnic minorities	0 7	2 7
Non-professional/amateur arts events	6 8	9 8
Not answered	13	16

215a) Britain controls the numbers of people from abroad that are allowed to
settle in this country. Please say, for *each* of the groups below,
whether you think Britain should allow more settlement, less settlement,
or about the same amount as now.

PLEASE TICK ONE BOX
ON EACH LINE

	MORE SETTLEMENT	LESS SETTLEMENT	ABOUT THE SAME AS NOW
Australians and New Zealanders %	15 1	26 2	52 3
Indians and Pakistanis %	2 1	67 2	24 3
People from common market countries %	6 1	42 2	44 3
West Indians %	2 1	62 2	27 3

b) Now thinking about the families (husbands, wives, children, parents)
of people who have *already* settled in Britain, would you say in
general that Britain should ...   *PLEASE TICK ONE BOX*
(%)

... be stricter in controlling the settlement of close relatives | 53 1 |

or less strict in controlling the settlement of close relatives | 8 2 |

or keep the controls about the same as now | 32 3 |

216. There has been a lot of debate among teachers about how British schools should cater for children whose parents come from other countries and cultures. Do you think in general that schools with many such children should...

PLEASE TICK ONE BOX ON EACH LINE

	YES	NO
...Provide them with special classes in English if they require them %	77₁	14₂
Provide them with separate religious instruction if their parents request it %	32₁	56₂
Allow those for whom it is important to wear their traditional dress at school %	43₁	46₂
Allow them to study their mother tongue in school hours %	16₁	73₂
Teach them about the history of their parents' country of origin and its culture %	40₁	48₂
Teach all children about the history and culture of these countries %	74₁	16₂

217. Finally, please tick one box for each statement below to show how much you agree or disagree with it.

	AGREE STRONGLY	JUST AGREE	NEITHER AGREE NOR DISAGREE	JUST DISAGREE	DISAGREE STRONGLY
More women should enter politics %	25₅	27₄	33₃	4₂	4₁
Parents with unhappy marriages should stay together for the sake of their children %	10₅	16₄	18₃	23₂	26₁
It is wrong for mothers of small children to go out to work %	25₅	17₄	19₃	18₂	13₁
Women generally handle positions of responsibility better than men do %	9₅	14₄	45₃	16₂	9₁
A wife should avoid earning more than her husband does %	6₅	8₄	21₃	22₂	35₁
Children nowadays get too little discipline from their parents %	51₅	23₄	9₃	7₂	3₁
Children have an obligation to look after their parents when they are old %	18₅	21₄	21₃	18₂	15₁
It should be the woman who decides how many children a couple has %	14₅	13₄	23₃	19₂	23₁
Children are essential for a happy marriage %	17₅	11₄	23₃	18₂	23₁

continued over

217. continued.

	AGREE STRONGLY	JUST AGREE	NEITHER AGREE NOR DISAGREE	JUST DISAGREE	DISAGREE STRONGLY
Women should always have their babies in a hospital or nursing home %	27 5	21 4	22 3	16 2	7 1
Contraceptive advice and supplies should be available to all young people whatever their age %	20 5	24 4	12 3	17 2	21 1
Smoking cannabis (marijuana) should be legalised %	6 5	6 4	9 3	14 2	58 1
It is acceptable to use animals for testing and improving cosmetics %	3 5	8 4	10 3	17 2	55 1
It is acceptable to use animals for testing medicines if it could save human lives %	29 5	39 4	9 3	8 2	8 1
Fox hunting should be banned by law %	31 5	12 4	25 3	13 2	11 1
Social workers should put the child's interests first even if it means taking a child away from its natural parents %	30 5	31 4	17 3	10 2	5 1
Social workers have too much power to interfere with people's lives %	19 5	25 4	30 3	13 2	5 1
The welfare state makes people nowadays less willing to look after themselves %	22 5	27 4	20 3	16 2	9 1
People receiving social security are made to feel like second class citizens %	21 5	25 4	19 3	17 2	10 1
The welfare state encourages people to stop helping each other %	13 5	22 4	26 3	22 2	9 1
People rely too much on doctors instead of taking more responsibility for their own health %	19 5	33 4	18 3	17 2	7 1
Older people should be encouraged to retire earlier to reduce unemployment %	34 5	32 4	12 3	10 2	5 1
Employers give too few opportunities to older people when recruiting staff %	25 5	33 4	22 3	9 2	3 1

Subject index

Microfiche tables

Over two hundred key tables from the survey have been reproduced on a micro-fiche (which is contained in a pocket at the back of the hardback edition of this book). Copies of the microfiche can also be ordered directly from Gower at a cost per copy of £3.00 including postage and packing. Apply to Jeane Bennett at Gower House, Croft Road, Aldershot, Hampshire. The key and index to the microfiche tables are shown below. For further details, consult the questionnaires in Appendix III.

Key to analysis breaks

A 301 – age within sex
A 302 – region/type of district
A 304 – Social Class of respondent
A 305 – Standard Industrial Classification (1980) of respondent's employment
A 306 – annual gross household income
A 307 – economic position of respondent (last week)
A 308 – religion of respondent
A 309 – accommodation of respondent's household
A 310 – marital status of respondent
A 311 – household type
A 313 – membership of trade union
A 314 – age of completing full-time education
A 315 – types of school attended by respondent
A 316 – legal responsibility of respondent for accommodation
A 317 – party identification
A 318 – self-assigned social class

Index to microfiche

Q64A	X	A302	Q72C	X	A301	Q84B	X	A301
Q64A	X	A304	Q72C	X	A302	Q84B	X	A310
Q64A	X	A306	Q73A	X	A301	Q84C	X	A301
Q63B	X	A302	Q73B	X	A301	Q84C	X	A310
Q64B	X	A304	Q73C	X	A301	Q85	X	A301
Q64B	X	A306	Q74AB	X	A301	Q85	X	A308
Q65A	X	Q65B	Q74CD	X	A301	Q86	X	A301
Q67A	X	A306	Q75A	X	A301	Q212A	X	A301
Q67B	X	A306	Q75B	X	A301	Q212A	X	A305
Q68	X	A301	Q75C	X	A301	Q212A	X	A313
Q68	X	A304	Q78A	X	A301	Q212B	X	A301
Q68	X	A306	Q78A	X	A302	Q212B	X	A305
Q68	X	A314	Q78B	X	A301	Q212B	X	A313
Q68	X	A315	Q78B	X	A302	Q214A	X	A301
Q70A	X	A301	Q79A	X	A301	Q214A	X	A302
Q70A	X	A304	Q79C	X	A301	Q214A	X	A317
Q70A	X	A317	Q84A1	X	A301	Q214B	X	A301
Q72AB	X	A301	Q84A1	X	A310	Q214B	X	A302
Q72AB	X	A302	Q84A2	X	A301	Q214B	X	A317
			Q84A2	X	A310			

DATE DUE

11. 06. '85	
DEC 1 5 1985	
12 19 '86	